Parenting Beyond Belief

On Raising Ethical, Caring Kids
Without Religion

Edited by Dale McGowan

Foreword by Michael Shermer

D0390877

American Management Association

New York ◆ Atlanta ◆ Brussels ◆ Chicago ◆ Mexico City ◆ San Francisco
Shanghai ◆ Tokyo ◆ Toronto ◆ Washington, D.C.

This publication is designed to provide accurate and authoritative information in regard to the subject matter covered. It is sold with the understanding that the publisher is not engaged in rendering legal, accounting, or other professional service. If legal advice or other expert assistance is required, the services of a competent professional person should be sought.

Poems by Yip Harburg appearing on pages 113, 146, 160, 177, 183, and 230 are © The Yip Harburg Foundation and are used with permission.

For information regarding the following material used with permission, please see the page on which each one begins: "Good and Bad Reasons for Believing" by Richard Dawkins, page 13; "I'd Rather Play Outside" by Anne Nicol Gaylor, page 24; "To Easter Bunny or Not to Easter Bunny?" by Noell Hyman, page 90; "Oh Karma, Dharma, Pudding and Pie" by Philip Appleman, page 134; "The End, As We Know It" by Noell Hyman, page 161; "Thoughts on Raising a Curious, Creative, Freethinking Child" by Robert E. Kay, page 186; "Does God Exist?" by Stephen Law, page 198; and "The Idea That Changed the World" by Kristan Lawson, page 230.

Library of Congress Cataloging-in-Publication Data

Parenting beyond belief : on raising ethical, caring kids without religion / edited by Dale McGowan.
     p. cm.
   Includes bibliographical references and index.
   ISBN-10: 0-8144-7426-8 (pbk.)
   ISBN-13: 978-0-8144-7426-6 (pbk.)
   1. Parenting—Religious aspects. 2. Religious education of children. 3. Free thought. I. McGowan, Dale.

BL2777.R4P37 2007
649'.7—dc22

                                        2006038883

Printing number
10   9   8   7   6   5   4   3   2   1

Contents

Contents

Foreword
A License to Secular Parenthood

In the 1989 Ron Howard film *Parenthood*, the Keanu Reeves' character, Tod Higgins, a wild-eyed young man trying to find his way in life after being raised by a single mom, bemoans to his future mother-in-law that you need a license to drive, have a dog, or even to fish—but they'll let anyone be a father.

The "they" here is presumably the government, which has, despite its intrusion into just about every other aspect of our lives, thankfully stayed out of the parenting business. Nevertheless, the observation is a cogent one because when you become a parent there are no required courses on how to do it. I became a parent the same way just about everyone else has: by stumbling into it without any planning whatsoever. I hadn't given it much thought until it happened. But when it did, I learned how to parent the same way as everyone else: on the job in real time. Fifteen years later I'm still learning.

I wish I could have had a book like *Parenting Beyond Belief* when I was starting out on this endless (and endlessly fulfilling) journey. It is choc-a-block full of advice, tips, suggestions, recommendations, anecdotes, and moving (and often funny) stories from a remarkably diverse range of authors who make you laugh and cry at the same time. This is the first book that I know of on parenting without religion. It is almost a given in our society that kids should be raised with religion, because if they aren't, they will grow up to be juvenile delinquents, right? Wrong. Wronger than wrong. Not even wrong. The assumption is so bigoted and breathtakingly inane that it doesn't deserve a debunking, but it gets one nonetheless in this volume, from nonbelievers of all stripes, who show how and why raising children without religion is not only a loving and ethical approach to parenthood, it is an honorable one.

My wife and I are raising our daughter, Devin, without religion. There was no conscious decision to do so, no formal plan. We don't believe in God and so the subject just never comes up. Since I am a social scientist, I am well aware of the powerful influence parents can have on the religious, political, and social attitudes of their children, so if I took any proactive steps in the parenting of my daughter in this regard, it was not to be proactive in influencing her too strongly in any one direction. As I told her in a letter that I gave her on the occasion of her transitioning from middle school to high school:

> Our beliefs about people, society, politics, economics, religion, and every-thing else are shaped by our parents and family, friends and peers, teachers and mentors, books and newspapers, television and the Internet, and culture at large. It is impossible for any of us to hold beliefs of any kind that are not significantly influenced by all these different sources. Up until about the age you are now—early teens—your beliefs have been primarily shaped by your parents. And since I am in the business of researching and writing about beliefs, as well as expressing them in public forums, I fear that my own rather strongly held beliefs may have had an undue influence on you; that is, my hope is that whatever it is you decide to believe about whatever subject, you have thought through carefully each of those beliefs and at least tried to make sure that they are your beliefs and not those of your parents. It matters less to me what your specific beliefs are than that you have carefully arrived at your beliefs through reason and evidence and thoughtful reflection.

We all do the best we can as parents, which was the central message of *Parenthood,* as evidenced in the scene where Steve Martin's character, Gil Buckman, has a nightmare in which his son has grown up maladjusted and is now holed up in a college bell tower shooting students because his father messed him up by making him play second base. Gil's plaintive plea—that he did the best he could—might be said by any parent. Here I am reminded of Robin Williams' riff on parenting, in which he recalls two dreams: in one, his son proclaims "I'd like to thank the Nobel Academy for this great honor," and in the other his son says "ya want fries with that?"

Nobel Prize or supersize fries—either way (or anything in between) I shall always love Devin and attempt to teach her the fundamental principles of a moral life. These principles are important whether there is a god or not, but especially if not. If this is all there is, and if there is no one out there keeping score, then parenthood is elevated to transcendency.

Michael Shermer

Michael Shermer is the Publisher of *Skeptic* magazine (www.skeptic.com), a monthly columnist for *Scientific American,* and the author of *Why People Believe Weird Things, How We Believe, The Science of Good and Evil,* and *Why Darwin Matters.*

Preface

The good life is one inspired by love and guided by knowledge.

Bertrand Russell

I remember clearly the first vegetarian I ever knew, a friend from college named Kari. She had given up what I considered one of the great joys of life. Kari could look forward to no seared orange duck, no filet mignon in mustard-caper sauce, no southern fried chicken, for the rest of her days. I just didn't get it. This stuff is *delicious*, after all. *Maybe she just hasn't had a really good steak,* I reasoned to myself. That had to be it.

One day I interrupted her morning carrot break in mid-crunch to ask Kari what on earth she could possibly be thinking.

She assured me she'd had a good steak—quite a few, in fact. And pork chops had been a favorite since childhood. She loved the taste of meat. But she had looked into the issues around the consumption of meat—far more deeply than I *ever* had—deciding at last that the negatives clearly outweighed the positives. Eating meat is incredibly unhealthy, she said, not just marginally so, and involves unspeakable cruelty to our fellow creatures. She didn't want to be a part of that, so she stopped eating meat.

We lost touch after college, but if Kari has kids, I'll bet she has raised them according to those values, since she would want the best for them. But knowing her, I'm also sure she'd want them to come to vegetarianism as their own life stance only if they reasoned it out and adopted it as their own value—not because she forced it on them. They would know their mother's strong feelings and the reasons behind them, then decide for themselves once they were old enough if it was right for them.

I have a lot of respect for that kind of parenting.

Now I'm raising kids of my own, trying hard to give them the best of my experience and values. I'm not a vegetarian, though I've considered that a character flaw of mine ever since Kari. But there's another area about which I've developed some heartfelt opinions: religious belief and practice.

Just as Kari had plenty of good steaks, I had a lot of positive experience with religious people and institutions. I've known many wonderful religious people and have found much that is compelling and comforting in religious teachings.

I developed a particular interest in "the big questions" at the age of 13 when my dad died. My grief was tempered by a consuming curiosity about death, from which tumbled a thousand questions about life. I began a serious engagement with religious questions, attending churches in nine denominations, reading the scriptures of my own culture and others, asking questions of ministers, priests, theologians, and lay believers, and reading carefully the arguments for and against religious belief—coming at last to the strong conclusion that religious claims are human-created fictions.

Religious friends are often baffled. This stuff is *delicious,* they say. Afterlife rewards, unconditional love, ultimate meaning . . . I agreed—they are yummy. But I'd come to the further conviction that religious belief, for all its benefits and consolations, also does real harm to us, individually and collectively. The negatives far outweighed the positives for me, so despite all its comforts and consolations, I set religion aside.

I'm not indifferent to theological questions, any more than Kari's vegetarianism meant she was indifferent to questions of diet and animal welfare. I am *fascinated* by religious questions, as are most secularists, and take them very seriously. Kari's position resulted from the seriousness of her interest; she believed vegetarianism was the *right* choice, even believed that I too should adopt it, though she wasn't about to force it on me or anyone else. That's why I'll bet even her kids would ultimately have a choice.

The same is true of my parenting regarding religion: I really *do* believe I've made the best moral and intellectual choice in setting religion aside. I think the negatives of religious belief outweigh the positives, but I would never want to see someone forced to believe as I do. That includes my children. They deserve an honest chance to work things out for themselves. The process, not a given outcome, is the thing.

Which brings us at last to our topic.

Parenting Beyond Belief is a book for loving and thoughtful parents who wish to raise their children without religion. Not that this is the only "right" way to parent; it would be just as silly to imply that one cannot raise good, intelligent, moral, and loving children in a religious home as to imply the opposite. There are scores of books on religious parenting. Now there's one for the rest of us.

Religion has much to offer parents: an established community, a predefined set of values, a common lexicon and symbology, rites of passage, a means of engendering wonder, comforting answers to the big questions, and consoling explanations to ease experiences of hardship and loss. But for most secularists, these benefits come at too high a price. Many feel that intellectual integrity is compromised, the word "values" too often turned on its head, an us-versus-them mentality too often reinforced. Religious answers are found unconvincing yet are held unquestionable. And so, in seeking the best for our children, we try to chart a path around the church—and end up doing so without a compass.

Parenting Beyond Belief demonstrates the many ways in which the undeniable benefits of religion can be had without the detriments. Just as vegetarians must find other sources of certain vitamins, minerals, and proteins, secular parents must find other ways to articulate values, celebrate rites of passage, find consolation, and make meaning. Fortunately, just as the vegetarians have beans, fortified grains, and soy milk to supply what they need, secular parents have *Parenting Beyond Belief.*

So welcome, then, to a parenting book for theological vegetarians.

Approach and Focus

This is not a comprehensive parenting book. It'll be of little help in addressing diaper rash, aggression, or tattling. It is intended as a resource of opinions, insights, and experiences related to a single issue—raising children without religion—and the many issues that relate directly to it.

You may also note a relative lack of prescriptive instruction. Although our contributors include MDs, PhDs, and even two Reverend Doctors, there's little attempt to dictate authoritative answers. Our writers suggest, inform, challenge, and encourage without ever claiming there's only one right way. (Unlike a childcare guide I can see on my shelf right now, with the subtitle *The Complete and Authoritative Guide.* Holy Moses!) And a good thing, too—secularists are a famously freethinking bunch. It's the attribute that ended us up secularists, after all—that desire to consider all points of view and make up our own minds.

This is also not a book of arguments against religious belief, nor one intended to convince readers to raise their children secularly. This book is intended to support and encourage those who, having already decided to raise their children without religion, are in search of that support and encouragement.

There are many outstanding resources for adults wishing to consider the arguments in support of and in opposition to religious belief itself. And that's important work: Intellectual and ethical maturity can be measured in part by a person's willingness to engage in constant reflection on what he or she holds to be true and good. Parents in particular must be able to articulate the foundations of their own values and beliefs at a moment's notice—and what better describes the appearance and disappearance of opportunities in parenting than "a moment's notice"? Ungrounded, unexamined beliefs, whether secular or sacred, are the most inflexible, the least open to reconsideration and revision. In order to raise children whose convictions are grounded in reflection and an openness to change, we must model the same.

You may encounter some new terminology, including labels for the various categories of disbelief and ideas from philosophy. Each such word is defined in a glossary at the end of the book.

Parenting is already among the toughest of jobs. Living secularly in a religious world is among the most difficult social choices. When these challenges are combined, and a parent wishes to raise children without religious influences, the difficulties are compounded. But despite the difficulties, a large and growing number of parents are rising to the task. In 1990, 8 percent of respondents to a *USA Today* poll identified themselves as nonreligious. By 2002 that sector had grown to 14.1 percent.[1] The U.S. Census of the year 2000 counted 37.3 million households in the United States with school-age children. These numbers yield a conservative estimate of 7 million individual nonreligious parents in the United States today. Another of the purposes of this book is the clear establishment of that simple fact. It's easy to assume that every parent on your block, everyone cheering in the stands at the soccer game or walking the aisles of the supermarket, is a churchgoing believer. It's the assumed default in our culture. But it isn't true. All you need is to realize that *they are making the same assumption about you.* You are not remotely alone.

A good illustration of the presence of closeted disbelief is brought home to me whenever I attend book club discussions of a novel of mine. The main character is a secular humanist and the themes center on belief and disbelief, so discussion always turns to the beliefs of the club members. At some point, someone will say something like, "You know what? I never had the name for it before, but I guess I'm a secular humanist, too." A ripple of surprise goes around the group—not judgment, not condemnation, just genuine wonder as the members realize how much we all assume incorrectly about those we think we know well. "Me too," someone else will say, followed usually by a third and fourth. Twenty, 30, even 50 percent of a given group always turns out to be nonbelievers, *all of whom had assumed they were alone in their disbelief.* There is real elation in overturning false assumptions, accompanied by a deep enrichment of relationships after this diversity of belief is unpacked.

The same is true among secular parents: We are present, but not remotely accounted for. The proliferation of secular parenting discussion forums and freethought family organizations attests to the growing interest and need for a book that brings the many issues around secular parenting into focus. Such a book can also help to counter the stigma and ignorance surrounding religious disbelief by simply illustrating what is already going on quietly all around us: the raising of healthy, happy, ethical children in the absence of religious ideology.

It was during my tenure as editor of the Family Issues page of the Atheist Alliance website that I first became aware of the scarcity of resources for secular parents. A brief flirt with the idea of writing a book myself was fortunately cast aside in favor of the current format: a collection of essays by many writers, each bringing a different perspective and set of experiences to the task. In the pages that follow, you will read Dr. Jean Mercer on moral development; comedian Julia Sweeney on her uncertain and often hilarious grapplings with the religious influences swirling around her adopted daughter; Richard Dawkins' open letter to his daughter; illusionist and debunker Penn Jillette on being a new secular father; Dr. Gareth Matthews on talking to children about evil; Donald B. Ardell on secular meaning and purpose; legendary bluegrass musician Pete Wernick on the "mixed marriage"; Tom Flynn and yours truly facing off on the Santa Claus question; excerpts from the writings of Mark Twain, Bertrand Russell, and Margaret Knight; and essays by over twenty other physicians, educators, authors, psychologists, and everyday secular parents, plus recommended resources for further investigation of this boundless topic.

One thread runs throughout this book: Encourage a child to think well, then trust her to do so. Removing religion by no means guarantees kids will think independently and well. Consider religion itself: Kids growing up in a secular home are at the same risk of making uninformed decisions about religion as are those in deeply religious homes. In order to really think for themselves about religion, kids must learn as much as possible about religion as a human cultural expression while being kept free of the sickening idea that they will be rewarded in heaven or punished in hell based on what they decide—a bit of intellectual terrorism we should never inflict on our kids, nor on each other. They must also learn what has been said and thought in *opposition* to religious ideas. If my kids think independently and well, then end up coming to conclusions different from my own—well, I'd have to consider the possibility that *I've* gotten it all wrong, then. Either way, in order to own and be nourished by their convictions, kids must ultimately come to them independently. Part of our wonderfully complex job as parents is to facilitate that process without controlling it.

As editor, I've encouraged these outstanding authors to retain their individual styles and approaches, even to articulate contrasting opinions on a given question, confident that you as a secular parent can handle the variety and would want nothing less. This is "big tent secularism," offering many different, even contradictory perspectives on living without religion. What other book would include two ministers and Penn Jillette? The authors' approaches are at turns soberly academic, hilariously off-the-cuff, inspiring, irreverent, angry, joyful, confident, confused, revealing, and empowering. Skip around, dip and dive, and be sure to challenge your natural inclinations. If the reverends make you feel most comfortable, you should read Dawkins, Tanquist, Barker, and Jillette—there's an incredible amount of insight there. And if the religious impulse seems like a completely alien thing to you, read Gibbons, Matthews, and Nelson for an equal dose of wisdom. There are countless ways to be a nonbeliever and no need to fit everyone into a single skin.

Note also that all editorial material—chapter introductions, book reviews, preface, and my own essays—represents just one perspective on these questions.

It happens to be the most brilliant and accurate perspective, but it is only one, and my fellow contributors should not be assumed to agree with everything that surrounds their own contributions.

I hope you find this a worthwhile contribution to the bookshelf for those of us taking on the wonderful and humbling task of raising the next generation of people inspired by love and guided by knowledge.

Dale McGowan, Ph.D.

Endnotes

1. Cathy Grossman, "*Charting the unchurched in America,*" *USA Today* 3/7/02: www.usatoday.com/life/dcovthu.htm

For Becca, Erin, Delaney, and Connor, my raisins

Acknowledgments

Many people have contributed time, talent, and advice to this unique project.

I began by seeking the guidance of some of the giants of freethought, including Jan Loeb Eisler, Dan Barker, Annie Laurie Gaylor, Bobbie Kirkhart, and Margaret Downey. I am grateful for their advice and encouragement, which included help in generating the extraordinary final list of contributors.

Nearly every writer I invited to contribute agreed to do so, always with great enthusiasm, and showed endless patience through the long editorial process. I could not have had a more intelligent and generous group of colleagues for this complex task.

Many thanks to the classiest agent in the business, Dr. Uwe Stender of the TriadaUS Literary Agency, for calmly and expertly guiding the book to a publisher.

Special thanks as well to Christina Parisi of Amacom Books for seeing the value in such a book, for shepherding the manuscript through the publishing process, and for going the extra mile during that process to enhance her understanding of parenting issues by giving birth.

I am grateful to Paula Wagener Lutz, John Pellegrini, and Becca McGowan for input and advice that significantly improved the manuscript prior to publication.

My deepest thanks go to the four people who made this book possible by making me a father: Becca, my wife and dearest friend, and Erin, Delaney, and Connor, our three cool and amazing kids.

Personal Reflections

Introduction

The first and most important task of *Parenting Beyond Belief* is to let secular families know they are not alone—that millions of other families are wrestling with the same challenges and asking the same questions. This chapter includes personal reflections by freethinking parents and children, as well as adults recalling when they *were* children, all grappling with familiar issues and offering hard-won advice to parents raising kids without religion.

A second task—as noted in the Preface—is to raise high the big tent of disbelief. Just as there is no one "right way" to raise children, there are many different ways to be a nonbeliever. This chapter is framed in a perfect pair of bookends to illustrate the range of approaches to secular parenting. If Penn Jillette is a bull in a china shop, Julia Sweeney is the one running around catching plates and saying *Oh, jeez*. Their approaches are different, but the wattage of wisdom and insight in these two essays could light up the Vegas strip. Norm Allen continues with tales of growing up in a Baptist home where his mother nonetheless encouraged her children to think hard and well—even questioning the existence of God.

Oxford biologist Richard Dawkins shares a heartfelt letter to his 10-year-old daughter Juliet about his own intellectual values. And just as readers of a certain perspective might be unnerved by the presence of ministers in these pages, so may some others find Dawkins' approach disrespectful to religious belief. There is a good reason for this: He does not respect religious belief. Not one bit.

This raises an important question, one that makes for excellent dinner table conversation. Is it okay to disrespect someone's beliefs? Notice that the subject is *beliefs*, not *believers*—we can presumably agree that people themselves deserve respect. But can we allow disrespect—not just disagreement, but *disrespect*—for opinions?

If the word "respect" is to retain any meaning whatsoever, then respect must not be granted to all opinions automatically. I might disagree with an opinion but still respect it, if I feel it was arrived at by legitimate means. I have several Libertarian friends, for example, who think all taxes are coercive and should be eliminated. I, on the other hand, think reasonable taxes are an excellent means to accomplishing good collective ends. Though I disagree strongly with my friends, I respect their opinion, since they back it up with reasoned arguments.

I also have some friends who believe their actions are dictated by the constellations. When asked their reasons for this belief, they offer anecdotes, selective observations, and special pleading. I love and respect these friends personally, but it would be silly to say I respect their beliefs in astrology, since I do not respect the reasoning behind them. I don't often browbeat these friends about it, since their beliefs do not greatly impact the world, but I withhold my respect for those beliefs.

Because he thinks religion *does* greatly and negatively impact the world, Richard Dawkins' disrespect for religion leads him to passionate and strident denunciation of what he sees as a real and present danger. After the attacks of September 11, he wrote, "My last vestige of 'hands off religion' respect disappeared in the smoke and choking dust of September 11, 2001, followed by the 'National Day of Prayer.'"[1] While it is perfectly acceptable for readers to disagree with such an opinion or with the way it is expressed, this impassioned and well-informed voice should no more be excluded from the conversation than those thoughtful religious nontheists at the other end of our big tent.

Secular kids themselves are well represented by Emily Rosa, who describes an upbringing that kept her "itching for the truth" and a fourth-grade science experiment that briefly catapulted her into the national spotlight. She also offers some serious advice to secular parents to *relax, play, laugh, lighten up*—so as not to raise a grim generation of obsessive debunkers.

Like Emily Rosa, Anne Nicol Gaylor grew up in a freethought home. Anne describes her family's interactions with religious neighbors and friends in "I'd

Rather Play Outside." We also hear the great twentieth-century philosopher and peace advocate Bertrand Russell describe his upbringing, which—despite his deceased father's explicit instructions to the contrary—took place under Christian guardianship. The effort to instill religion in the boy failed to take, producing instead one of the most articulate and persuasive voices of disbelief in modern times. And Dan Barker rounds out the chapter with a fascinating dual perspective: First, as an evangelical minister, Dan raised four children in a Christian home, then he lost his faith, divorced, remarried, and is now raising a daughter in a home actively devoted to freethought.

Readers may reasonably wonder why these personal essays—indeed most of essays in the book—refer almost exclusively to Christianity when speaking of "religion." This reflects only the cultural context of the authors and of the expected readership for this book. Since most of the readers and writers will have grown up in a Christian-influenced culture, it is natural that discussions of religion are most often framed in terms of that local manifestation of religious belief. There is also a tendency to address Catholicism more often than other denominations. This stems from two facts: that Catholicism is the oldest and most visibly dogmatic of the Christian denominations and that more nonbelievers, interestingly, were formerly Catholics than anything else. Again, the context with which a writer has the most experience will naturally figure more prominently in his or her work.

Though each of these stories is unique, common threads run throughout these essays, including courage, honesty, and optimism. There are many good ways to raise children, with or without religion. These examples are not models to follow but invitations to find your own way—and assurances that you will.

Navigating Around the Dinner Table

Julia Sweeney

I LOVED BEING CATHOLIC. Well, most of the time. I mean, I didn't like it when people didn't answer my questions or take my sporadic natural skepticism seriously. But other than that, I felt lucky. I mean, being Catholic was cool to me. I felt sorry for the people I met who weren't. Which were hardly any people. Because everyone I knew was Catholic. And they *belonged.* Not just to parishes and schools, but to this great big club called Catholic. And there were rituals we all knew and outfits we wore—school uniforms. And the priests wore all black except when they were saying a Mass, when they wore a *cape!* I mean, come on, it rocked. Plus there were all the other medieval-like things associated with being Catholic. You knelt in obedience and submission, but to me this was not humiliating—it was like you lived in a castle! And incense was strewn through the Church on occasion, and that too seemed mystical and otherworldly. And then there was the fact that everybody I knew knew everybody else and where they went to school and where their parents went to school. It was a close-knit, safe feeling.

But then I grew up, opened my eyes, and realized I didn't think there was any supernatural reason for doing all these things. I didn't think there was any good evidence for a God at all, let alone one who cared who showed up at church. And I moved away from Spokane to Los Angeles, a place where Catholicism didn't knit the community in the way that I had experienced. Even when I did go to a Catholic Church in L.A., my mind has this pesky habit of actually *listening* to the words being said at Mass. I would inevitably leave angry, or bemused and distant like an anthropologist, but certainly not connected. Eventually I stopped going and just got used to describing myself as an atheist. Then I got *proud* of saying I was an atheist. And during this time, I adopted a little girl from China.

It didn't dawn on me right away that I wasn't raising her with any religion. I mean religion to me meant those old ritualistic ceremonies that we went to when we visited my home town. And it was still a little fun to go—I mean, my dad or my brother would hold my daughter and she wriggled like the other 2- and 3-year-olds. But then a couple of things happened that changed everything.

The first thing was that my dad died.

Wow. Just saying that shows you I had changed. I didn't say he "passed away," because he didn't pass away. He died. My daughter was 4½ at the time and very close to my father. He was the guy she made Father's Day cards for on Father's Day, the man who she liked to have hold her. My dad used to take naps next to my daughter on the bed and I remember seeing them in there— my father with his oxygen machine and my daughter curled up next to him— and it was all so dreamy and loving and cute. And so, it was a big deal when he died. And my daughter had questions.

When she asked "What happens after we die?" I said, "To be honest, darling—we decompose." And she wanted to know what that meant. A bird had died in our backyard and so we watched how it disappeared a little bit every day. When I tell this story to people, they look at me horrified. Like I was forcing some horrifying truth onto a little kid too small to understand it. But actually, she got it just fine, possibly because I didn't *only* say that. I said two more things. "When you die, your body decomposes," I said. "It breaks down into all these teeny parts you can't even see—like dirt or air even. And then those particles become part of something else." And my daughter said, "Like what?" And I said, "Well, like a flower or air or grass or dirt or even another person." And she said, "Well, I want to be another person!" And I said, "Yes, I understand. But even if some of your molecules became part of another person, it wouldn't be you. Because You are You and when You are gone, there will never ever be another You in this world. You are so special and unique that this world will only ever make one of You. With You they broke the mold, so that's it! Only You. Right here, right now."

And she seemed to kind of get that. In fact, it made her feel special.

And then I told her a second thing: that her grandfather did live on after he died, inside of the people who were remembering him. And in the ways he influenced those people, even when they weren't thinking of him. Like, how Grandpa just *loved* orange sherbet. Now, because of that, we eat orange sherbet too and we remember him when we do it. Or even things that we might not think about him while we do, like when we watch some basketball on TV. We might do that because of Grandpa who loved to watch basketball on TV. Because of him, we are different. In probably thousands or even millions of ways. And that difference is what makes him live after he dies.

And she really got that.

Only one problem: Her friends at school were asking her if her grandfather was up in heaven. And she was thrown, because to say "no" sounded bad and to say "yes" wasn't what I had told her. One day we were walking home from the park with one of her friends, and the friend said, "Did you see your grandfather's spirit fly up to heaven when he died?" And my daughter looked at me and said, "Did it?" And I said, "No, we don't believe in things like that." And my daughter parroted me, "Yeah, we don't believe in that." And for a second she looked confident repeating me, and then her face crinkled up and she frowned and directed her eyes downward.

> " I was seized with compassion for my little girl and how she will be navigating herself in a world where she will be a little bit different. I didn't have this burden. I was told what everyone else was told. "

Suddenly I was seized with compassion for my little girl and how she will be navigating herself in a world where she will be a little bit different. I didn't have this burden. I was told what everyone else was told. Grandpas died and went to heaven. You would see them later when you died. Vague memories arose of my own childhood images of heaven, of a long dining table with a gold tablecloth and a feast. It was easier for me, in that way, than it will be for her.

But while I was having all these thoughts, my daughter and her friend had nonchalantly moved on to talking about their American Girl dolls. No biggy. But that moment, I think, is when all of the "what we believe" discussions began. And it made me uncomfortable. My daughter would often start conversations with me by saying, "So, we believe that . . ." And frankly I hated the whole word "believe" and I also hated that she was just taking what I said as absolute truth, because in the perfect world of my head, she wouldn't be indoctrinated with *anything*. She would come up with her own answers, and she would never say things like, "We believe" or "We don't believe." But then I got more seasoned as a mother and realized that basically that's what we do all the time as parents, no matter what we "believe." Our job is to socialize our kids, and they have evolved to look to us for answers. Not providing those answers is wrong.

I got a little more comfortable saying things about what we "believe." Like, we believe it is good to take the garbage out. Honestly, it seems silly now that I write it. But that's how I got comfortable with that word. We believe in treating people nicely. We believe you shouldn't tell people lies. We believe that you should do your homework. *That* kind of believe.

Finally, I would say things like, "Lots of people believe that after someone dies, they live on. But I think that is just their way of not feeling as sad as they might about whoever they loved who died. I think that when people die, they die. And we should feel really sad and also feel happy that the flower of that person ever got to live at all." And even though many of my friends thought this was too big of a concept for a 4- or 5-year-old, after explaining it several times, I do think she got it.

That didn't mean, of course, that other people, like my mother, weren't also telling her what *they* believed about my dad's death. When we visited my mother, she and my daughter would make cookies and I would hear my mother going on and on about how Grandpa was in heaven and we were going to see him again and he was there with Mike, my brother who passed away. And later, when my daughter asked about this discrepancy, I just said, "We believe different things." And amazingly, Mulan got that just fine—even though it sort of made me mad. Because what story is going to seem better? The one where someone decomposes, or the one where he's at a big dinner table in the sky with other people who died? Decomposition does not stand a chance against the dinner table. But for me and Mulan, those discrepancies or different stories didn't become as traumatic as I thought they would.

A few months after this, Mulan started kindergarten at our local public school. And as part of her day at school, she said the "Pledge of Allegiance." She proudly repeated it to me, and the "under God" part made me flinch. "You don't have to say 'under God' you know," I said—and her eyes widened with fear. "What do you mean?" I said, "You can just keep your mouth closed during that part. I don't believe in God. These people in the government allowed that to get stuck in there much later. I wouldn't say it if I were you."

A few days later she came home and said, "I have to say it. Because it's nice, it's being nice to say it. You have to be nice and so you say it." I don't think I have ever heard a more heartbreaking sentence from my child. I am probably more sensitive to this, for many more reasons than religion. I have tried to stop doing things automatically because they are "nice" for years and years because I find myself drowning in doing a million things for people because it's "nice." On the other hand, it's expedient to pressure children to conform. It makes sense. It encourages community and all the behaviors that we are trying to instill in them. I understood her dilemma.

Fortunately a friend of mine suggested a solution. "How about telling her to say, 'under laws' instead of 'under God?'" Brilliant! I told my daughter the idea. She looked at me like I was from Mars. It was her first, truly, "I've-got-an-insane-mother" look. But now when she comes home from school, as the year has worn on, she'll tell me. Today I said, "under God." Another day she will report that she said, "under laws." And I figure she will find her own rhythm.

Recently I was in Spokane with Mulan on Memorial Day. The whole family was making their way up to Holy Cross Cemetery, where many members of our family are buried. Even though this is a Catholic cemetery, and icons litter the lawns, I love it there. I am all for burial in a plot with your family. I find it extremely comforting. I have picnicked there on days when it wasn't Memorial Day. In fact, everyone in our family does this. It's a destination for us. And I love it.

Well, we were heading towards the cemetery and my daughter was in an ornery, crappy, poopy mood. She didn't want to go. My mother, who was driving, made the mistake of saying, "God wants us to go." She was mostly trying to be funny. But my daughter yelled out, "I don't believe in God! I only believe in things that you have evidence for and there is NO EVIDENCE FOR GOD!" The way she said it was petulant and snotty. I was so angry with her. But in that instant, even though I had to reprimand her for her "tone" and demeanor and even though she started a tantrumy cry and begged for a cheese stick and began kicking her legs and I wanted to throttle her for it—in spite of all of this, I knew instantly that ultimately she would be okay. She had spirit and gumption and she could say something that was unpopular (at least in that car at that moment.) And more than not believing in God, that seemed like the best influence I could ever have on her.

Thinking My Way to Adulthood

Norm R. Allen, Jr.

CHILDREN ARE NATURALLY curious about religion, and I was no different. I was reared by Baptist parents in a place and time where theism was the norm. People who went to church were held in high regard by the community, while those who did not were frowned upon. Such is still the case throughout much of the world.

But I had an advantage over many children of religious parents: In our home there were no taboos. We were encouraged to always ask questions and to demand logical answers to those questions. If the answers to the questions seemed illogical, we were taught to be skeptical.

The issue of religion was no different. We were allowed—even encouraged—to question the supposed existence of God.

One day I asked my mother how we could be sure that we were worshipping the One True God. She said that we could never be sure and that we could only continue to ask questions and try to grow in knowledge and wisdom. I then asked her what would happen if I decided to change religions one day. She said that that would be fine and that she would still love me. Then I asked her what would happen if I decided not to believe in God at all. She said that as long as I came by my decision honestly, that would be fine, too.

> " I asked my mother what would happen if I decided not to believe in God at all. She said that as long as I came by my decision honestly, that would be fine. What profound gifts my mother gave me in those simple assurances. "

What profound gifts my mother gave me in those simple assurances: an invitation to think for myself, coupled with the promise of unconditional love.

And the gifts kept coming. My parents never tried to choose my heroes and heroines for me. I would pick them myself, and regardless of whether my parents approved, they would buy me literature so that I could learn more about them. They trusted me to learn about them on my own.

Despite growing up in a Baptist home, I was obviously raised differently from children in fundamentalist families. Fundamentalists are taught to value those who agree with them more highly than those who differ from them, which leads to bigotry. Moreover, they value unquestioning obedience to God more highly than openness to new ideas. They value what they believe to be revealed Truth over the difficult search for many truths.

I was also fortunate in the particular Baptist Sunday school I attended during my teen years. My Sunday school teacher was like a philosophy of religion teacher, posing difficult questions and allowing us to do the same. We were even permitted to question the existence of God. All religionists are not closed-minded, just as all freethinkers are not open-minded on all issues. What is of the utmost importance is exposing children to critical thinking as opposed to mindless indoctrination.

> 66 All religionists are not closed-minded, just as all freethinkers are not open-minded. 99

Most children are not as fortunate in their early encounters with the church. Most are essentially brainwashed into religion almost as soon as they begin to speak. Many of them are taught to believe everything they learn about God. Questioning the existence of God is deemed not only inappropriate but downright sinful, even blasphemous. By the time many children reach adolescence, the religious conditioning is complete, and in many cases, irreversible.

Parents who decide to send their children to church at an early age should find a church that values critical thinking. It might be a Unitarian Universalist congregation. In rare cases it might even be a Catholic church—the Jesuits have been renowned for their willingness to explore ideas.

Parents should also be aware of the teachings of any house of worship their children might attend. Some churches are homophobic and sexist. Some are opposed to interracial marriages. Some teach that only members of their religion will make it to heaven and that everyone else will go to Hell. Parents must understand that no religious text is perfect and that religious teachings can cause their children—and society—immeasurable harm.

Just as it is important to sharpen the critical thinking skills of children, it is also important that they not be victimized by inhumane teachings. Even though I grew up in a relatively relaxed environment, I was constantly fearful of going to Hell. This is a tremendous—and totally unnecessary—psychological burden for children to

> 66 People who have the courage to doubt the existence of God are also likely to engage in critical thinking in other areas of life. 99

have to bear. I strongly feel this is tantamount to child abuse, and no loving parent should encourage his or her children to embrace such an unconscionable belief.

People who have the courage to doubt the existence of God are also likely to engage in critical thinking in other areas of life. I was a child of the 1960s. There were competing schools of thought on many issues. Among Black intellectuals, some were advocates of integration and passive resistance. Others were advocating self-defense, violent revolution, and separatism. There were highly intelligent people on both sides of the debate. It was not simply a matter of trying to determine which side had the smartest people, but of trying to decide which side was closest to the truth. This is when I began to greatly sharpen my critical thinking skills.

As I grew older, I learned that much of the teaching of history is politically motivated. Furthermore, the roles of Blacks, women, and other groups were routinely ignored or downplayed. I discovered that what you learn outside the classroom is often more important than what you learn inside it. If we do not have the chief hand in our own education, we are apt to fail miserably in life. This is one of the most important lessons in critical thinking that we must impart to children.

Throughout much of my life I have enjoyed solitude and have not depended upon peer support for my beliefs and ideals. But such is not the case with most children. They need reinforcement and support. It is extremely difficult for them to be alone in their beliefs. When most of the children around them belong to a religion other than theirs, they are likely to feel alienated. They are likely to ask their parents why their beliefs differ from those of the majority.

In these cases, it is best to try to give children the opportunity to be around other children who share their beliefs. This does not mean that they should embrace a form of tribalism. It simply means that they probably need a sense of shared community. With the growth of the Internet, it has become easier than ever to find like-minded people and groups for the good of one's children, so this valuable source should not go neglected.

There will certainly be painful experiences in the lives of all children. These experiences will provide great opportunities for the development of critical thinking skills. The most painful experience of my childhood occurred when my dog died. My mother told me that our beloved pet was in Heaven. That was somewhat comforting, but it did not agree with what I had learned in church. Our Sunday school teachers always taught us that only human beings could make it to Heaven or Hell. Though I could not put it into words at the time, I understood that Heaven was a concept rooted in wishful thinking and the desire for immortality. This was a major step on my personal journey toward freethought.

It is only natural for parents to want to protect their children from ugly truths. But children are stronger than many adults believe. Rather than shield them with popular and deeply cherished illusions, parents should help their children to answer the difficult questions they will invariably have.

Critical thinking could make children more willing to stand up for their rights and the rights of others. Indeed, some of the most important movements in history began because people questioned authority. Abolitionists asked why slavery had to be considered as part of the natural order. The leaders of the civil rights movement asked why segregation had to be the order of the day. (Incidentally, many children participated in that movement.) Women and gays demanded their rights, as did many other groups. Where there is no critical thinking, there is no progress. If the children are our future, then critical thinking must be their guide.

Finally, positive thinking should accompany critical thinking. Critical thinking should be used to increase our level of happiness. Most of us would prefer that our children be happy critical thinkers rather than ingenious nihilists. Teach them to be positive and to enjoy life. Then when they become adults, let them lead the way.

Good and Bad Reasons for Believing

Richard Dawkins

DEAR JULIET,

Now that you are ten, I want to write to you about something that is important to me. Have you ever wondered how we know the things that we know? How do we know, for instance, that the stars, which look like tiny pinpricks in the sky, are really huge balls of fire like the sun and are very far away? And how do we know that Earth is a smaller ball whirling round one of those stars, the sun?

The answer to these questions is "evidence." Sometimes evidence means actually seeing (or hearing, feeling, smelling . . .) that something is true. Astronauts have traveled far enough from earth to see with their own eyes that it is round. Sometimes our eyes need help. The "evening star" looks like a bright twinkle in the sky, but with a telescope, you can see that it is a beautiful ball—the planet we call Venus. Something that you learn by direct seeing (or hearing or feeling . . .) is called an observation.

Often, evidence isn't just an observation on its own, but observation always lies at the back of it. If there's been a murder, often nobody (except the murderer and the victim!) actually observed it. But detectives can gather together lots or other observations which may all point toward a particular suspect. If a person's fingerprints match those found on a dagger, this is evidence that he touched it. It doesn't prove that he did the murder, but it can help when it's joined up with lots of other evidence. Sometimes a detective can think about a whole lot of observations and suddenly realize that they fall into place and make sense if so-and-so did the murder.

Scientists—the specialists in discovering what is true about the world and the universe—often work like detectives. They make a guess (called a hypothesis) about what might be true. They then say to themselves: *If* that were really true, we ought to see so-and-so. This is called a prediction. For example, if the world is really round, we can predict that a traveler, going on and on in the same direction, should eventually find himself back where he started. When a doctor says that you have the measles, he doesn't take one look at you and *see* measles. His first look gives him a *hypothesis* that you *may* have measles. Then he says to himself: If she has measles, I ought to see . . . Then he runs through the list of predictions and tests them with his eyes (have you got spots?); hands (is your forehead hot?); and ears (does your chest wheeze in a measly way?). Only then does he make his decision and say, "I diagnose that the child has measles." Sometimes doctors need to do other tests like blood tests or X-rays, which help their eyes, hands, and ears to make observations.

The way scientists use evidence to learn about the world is much cleverer and more complicated than I can say in a short letter. But now I want to move on from evidence, which is a good reason for believing something, and warn you against three bad reasons for believing anything. They are called "tradition," "authority," and "revelation."

First, tradition. A few months ago, I went on television to have a discussion with about fifty children. These children were invited because they had been brought up in lots of different religions. Some had been brought up as Christians, others as Jews, Muslims, Hindus, or Sikhs. The man with the microphone went from child to child, asking them what they believed. What they said shows up exactly what I mean by "tradition." Their beliefs turned out to have no connection with evidence. They just trotted out the beliefs of their parents and grandparents, which, in turn, were not based upon evidence either. They said things like: "We Hindus believe so and so"; "We Muslims believe such and such"; "We Christians believe something else." Of course, since they all believed different things, they couldn't all be right. The man with the microphone seemed to think this quite right and proper, and he didn't even try to get them to argue out their differences with each other. But that isn't the point I want to make for the moment. I simply want to ask where their beliefs came from. They came from tradition. Tradition means beliefs handed down from grandparent to parent to child, and so on. Or from books handed down through the centuries. Traditional beliefs often start from almost nothing; perhaps somebody just makes them up

> " Traditional beliefs often start from almost nothing. . . . But after they've been handed down over some centuries, the mere fact that they are so old makes them seem special. People believe things simply because people have believed the same thing over the centuries. "

originally, like the stories about Thor and Zeus. But after they've been handed down over some centuries, the mere fact that they are so old makes them seem special. People believe things simply because people have believed the same thing over the centuries. That's tradition.

The trouble with tradition is that, no matter how long ago a story was made up, it is still exactly as true or untrue as the original story was. If you make up a story that isn't true, handing it down over a number of centuries doesn't make it any truer!

Most people in England have been baptized into the Church of England, but this is only one of the branches of the Christian religion. There are other branches such as Russian Orthodox, the Roman Catholic, and the Methodist churches. They all believe different things. The Jewish religion and the Muslim religion are a bit more different still, and there are different kinds of Jews and of Muslims. People who believe even slightly different things from each other go to war over their disagreements. So you might think that they must have some pretty good reasons—evidence—for believing what they believe. But actually, their different beliefs are entirely due to different traditions.

Let's talk about one particular tradition. Roman Catholics believe that Mary, the mother of Jesus, was so special that she didn't die but was lifted bodily in to Heaven. Other Christian traditions disagree, saying that Mary did die like anybody else. These other religions don't talk about her much and, unlike Roman Catholics, they don't call her the "Queen of Heaven." The tradition that Mary's body was lifted into Heaven is not an old one. The bible says nothing on how she died; in fact, the poor woman is scarcely mentioned in the Bible at all. The belief that her body was lifted into Heaven wasn't invented until about six centuries after Jesus' time. At first, it was just made up, in the same way as any story like "Snow White" was made up. But, over the centuries, it grew into a tradition and people started to take it seriously simply *because* the story had been handed down over so many generations. The older the tradition became, the more people took it seriously. It finally was written down as an official Roman Catholic belief only very recently, in 1950, when I was the age you are now. But the story was no more true in 1950 than it was when it was first invented six hundred years after Mary's death.

I'll come back to tradition at the end of my letter, and look at it in another way. But first, I must deal with the two other bad reasons for believing in anything: authority and revelation. Authority, as a reason for believing something, means believing in it because you are told to believe it by somebody important. In the Roman Catholic Church, the pope is the most important person, and people believe he must be right just because he is the pope. In one branch of the Muslim religion, the important people are the old men with beards called ayatollahs. Lots of Muslims in this country [the UK] are prepared to commit murder, purely because the ayatollahs in a faraway country tell them to.

When I say that it was only in 1950 that Roman Catholics were finally told that they had to believe that Mary's body shot off to Heaven, what I mean is that in 1950, the pope told people that they had to believe it. That was it. The pope said it was true, so it had to be true! Now, probably some of the things that that pope said in his life were true and some were not true. There is no good reason why, just because he was the pope, you should believe everything he said any more than you believe everything that other people say. The present pope[2] has ordered his followers not to limit the number of babies they have. If people follow this authority as slavishly as he would wish, the results could be terrible famines, diseases, and wars, caused by overcrowding.

Of course, even in science, sometimes we haven't seen the evidence ourselves and we have to take somebody else's word for it. I haven't, with my own eyes, seen the evidence that light travels at a speed of 186,000 miles per second. Instead, I believe books that tell me the speed of light. This looks like "authority." But actually, it is much better than authority, because the people who wrote the books have seen the evidence and anyone is free to look carefully at the evidence whenever they want. That is very comforting. But not even the priests claim that there is any evidence for their story about Mary's body zooming off to Heaven.

The third kind of bad reason for believing anything is called "revelation." If you had asked the pope in 1950 how he knew that Mary's body disappeared into Heaven, he would probably have said that it had been "revealed" to him. He shut himself in his room and prayed for guidance. He thought and thought, all by himself, and he became more and more sure inside himself. When religious people just have a feeling inside themselves that something must be true, even though there is no evidence that it is true, they call their feeling "revelation." It isn't only popes who claim to have revelations. Lots of religious people do. It is one of their main reasons for believing the things that they do believe. But is it a good reason?

Suppose I told you that your dog was dead. You'd be very upset, and you'd probably say, "Are you sure? How do you know? How did it happen?" Now suppose I answered: "I don't actually know that Pepe is dead. I have no evidence. I just have a funny feeling deep inside me that he is dead." You'd be pretty cross with me for scaring you, because you'd know that an inside "feeling" on its own is not a good reason for believing that a whippet is dead. You need evidence. We all have inside feelings from time to time, sometimes they turn out to be right and sometimes they don't. Anyway, different people have opposite feelings, so how are we to decide whose feeling is right? The only way to be sure that a dog is dead is to see him dead, or hear that his heart has stopped; or be told by somebody who has seen or heard some real evidence that he is dead.

> " People sometimes say that you must believe in feelings deep inside, otherwise, you'd never be confident of things like "My wife loves me." But this is a bad argument. There can be plenty of evidence that somebody loves you . . . outside things to back up the inside feeling. "

People sometimes say that you must believe in feelings deep inside, otherwise, you'd never be confident of things like "My wife loves me." But this is a bad argument. There can be plenty of evidence that somebody loves you. All through the day when you are with somebody who loves you, you see and hear lots of little tidbits of evidence, and they all add up. It isn't a purely inside feeling, like the feeling that priests call revelation. There are outside things to back up the inside feeling: looks in the eye, tender notes in the voice, little favors and kindnesses; this is all real evidence.

Sometimes people have a strong inside feeling that somebody loves them when it is not based upon any evidence, and then they are likely to be completely wrong. There are people with a strong inside feeling that a famous film star loves them, when really the film star hasn't even met them. People like that are ill in their minds. Inside feelings must be backed up by evidence, otherwise you just can't trust them.

Inside feelings are valuable in science, too, but only for giving you ideas that you later test by looking for evidence. A scientist can have a "hunch" about an idea that just "feels" right. In itself, this is not a good reason for believing something. But it can be a good reason for spending some time doing a particular experiment, or looking in a particular way for evidence. Scientists use inside feelings all the time to get ideas. But they are not worth anything until they are supported by evidence.

I promised that I'd come back to tradition, and look at it in another way. I want to try to explain why tradition is so important to us. All animals are built (by the process called evolution) to survive in the normal place in which their kind live. Lions are built to be good at surviving on the plains of Africa. Crayfish are built to be good at surviving in fresh water, while lobsters are built to be good at surviving in the salt sea. People are animals, too, and we are built to be good at surviving in a world full of—other people. Most of us don't hunt for our own food like lions or lobsters; we buy it from other people who have bought it from yet other people. We "swim" through a "sea of people." Just as a fish needs gills to survive in water, people need brains that make them able to deal with other people. Just as the sea is full of salt water, the sea of people is full of difficult things to learn. Like language.

You speak English, but your friend Ann-Kathrin speaks German. You each speak the language that fits you to "swim about" in your own separate "people sea." Language is passed down by tradition. There is no other way. In England, Pepe is a dog. In Germany he is *ein Hund*. Neither of these words is more correct, or more true than the other. Both are simply handed down. In order to be good at "swimming about in their people sea," children have to learn the language of their own country, and lots of other things about their own people; and this means that they have to absorb, like blotting paper, an enormous amount of traditional information. (Remember that traditional information just means things that are handed down from grandparents to parents to children.) The child's brain has to be a sucker for traditional information. And the child can't be expected to sort out good and useful traditional information, like the words of a language, from bad or silly traditional information, like believing in witches and devils and ever-living virgins.

It's a pity, but it can't help being the case, that because children have to be suckers for traditional information, they are likely to believe anything the grown-ups tell them, whether true or false, right or wrong. Lots of what the grown-ups tell them is true and based on evidence, or at least sensible. But if some of it is false, silly, or even wicked, there is nothing to stop the children believing that, too. Now, when the children grow up, what do they do? Well, of course, they tell it to the next generation of children. So, once something gets itself strongly believed—even if it is completely untrue and there never was any reason to believe it in the first place—it can go on forever.

> " Once something gets itself strongly believed—even if it is completely untrue and there never was any reason to believe it in the first place—it can go on forever. "

Could this be what has happened with religions? Belief that there is a god or gods, belief in Heaven, belief that Mary never died, belief that Jesus never had a human father, belief that prayers are answered, belief that wine turns into blood—not one of these beliefs is backed up by any good evidence. Yet millions of people believe them. Perhaps this is because they were told to believe them when they were young enough to believe anything.

Millions of other people believe quite different things, because they were told different things when they were children. Muslim children are told different things from Christian children, and both grow up utterly convinced that they are right and the others are wrong. Even within Christians, Roman Catholics believe different things from Church of England people or Episcopalians, Shakers or Quakers, Mormons or Holy Rollers, and are all utterly convinced that they are right and the others are wrong. They believe different things for exactly the same kind of reason as you speak English and Ann-Kathrin speaks German. Both languages are, in their own country, the right language to speak. But it can't be true that different religions are right in their own countries, because different religions claim that opposite things are true. Mary can't be alive in Catholic Southern Ireland but dead in Protestant Northern Ireland.

What can we do about all this? It is not easy for you to do anything, because you are only ten. But you could try this. Next time somebody tells you something that sounds important, think to yourself: "Is this the kind of thing that people probably know because of evidence? Or is it the kind of thing that people only believe because of tradition, authority, or revelation?" And, next time somebody tells you that something is true, why not say to them: "What kind of evidence is there for that?" And if they can't give you a good answer, I hope you'll think very carefully before you believe a word they say.

Your loving Daddy

Growing Up Godless:
How I Survived Amateur
Secular Parenting

Emily Rosa

IN 1987, I WAS BORN a seven-pound godless heathen, content with enjoying and exploring the world around me. My mother was delighted with my natural state.

Mom determined that, as much as possible, I would grow up without the intrusion of religion—or atheism. She, and later my stepfather, believed that when I reached a certain level of maturity and experience, I could decide such matters for myself.

Mom set out early to teach me the things she values: honesty, fairness, freedom, the fun of exploration and looking for evidence, and the notion that hard work pays off.

Things progressed well through my wee toddler years when Mom had control over things. She allowed me the time and the opportunity for exhaustive study of my environment. So when I became determined to break into neighbors' cars with an old key, she followed after me down the street as I tried the locks to my heart's content. Once she stood by as I asked every shopper in the grocery store whether they had a penis or vagina.

The first intrusions of religion came in preschool. My mother won't lie, so when the Santa Claus myth came up, she told me right off that he was make-believe, and that she could be his helper *(wink, wink)* if I wanted. One year I really wanted to enjoy the fantasy, so I ordered my mom, "Don't tell me about Santa being make-believe." I still knew the score and didn't have the let-down that my friends did later.

The truly hardest time was learning about death. I had seen the animated movie *Land Before Time,* in which the beloved mother dinosaur dies, though her spirit occasionally appears to give advice to her son. The thought of losing my own mom was devastating, and I even started to contemplate my own death. Teachers at preschool noticed my depression. They kindly advised my mom to comfort me with hope of an afterlife. She couldn't honestly do that, yet felt at a loss for how to comfort me, except to be with me as much as possible during that difficult time. Since then, death has probably been more on my mind than it has with most kids, and it may account for my abiding interest in forensic sciences and my appreciation for how precious life is.

When my first science fair loomed in the fourth grade, I chose to do a boring color separation experiment with M&Ms but lost interest when I realized I couldn't eat the candy. My attention wandered to a videotape showing nurses claiming to heal people by waving their hands over them. These nurses were practicing "Therapeutic Touch" (TT), which they explained was an ancient religious practice called "laying on of hands," but with a lot of extra Eastern mystical ideas. Among these was the idea that a "human energy field," or HEF, exists around every person, and that TT practitioners touch and manipulate it with their hands. The HEF felt spongy, they said, like warm Jello, and even "tactile as taffy."

Given these religious aspects, some adults might not have questioned TT any further. But with my upbringing, I was itching for the truth. Could those nurses really feel something invisible with their hands?

I asked mom if I could test TT for the science fair, and she replied, "Sure, if you can figure out a way to test it." With a little thought, I had my testable hypothesis: If these nurses can feel a real HEF, then they should be able to feel it when they aren't looking.

The cardboard display boards used at the fair gave me the idea of how I could shield the nurses' vision. The nurses would put their hands through holes in the cardboard; I randomly put my hand near one of theirs and asked them which of their hands felt my HEF.

I tested some very nice TT practitioners who couldn't detect the presence of an HEF any better than guessing (with 48 percent correct answers). Everyone who entered the science fair got a blue ribbon, but I also got my answer.

My experiment was repeated for the TV program, *Scientific American Frontiers,* and the combined results (only 44 percent right) were statistically significant and published in *JAMA* (*Journal of the American Medical Association*). It became a sort of Emperor's New Clothes event that the media jumped on. James Randi gave me his "Skeptic of the Year Award," and *Skeptic* magazine, recognizing the potential of kid experimenters, launched *Jr. Skeptic.* I also had a great time at the Ig Nobel Awards[3] as a presenter that year.

TT practitioners came up with silly explanations for why they didn't pass my test—the air conditioning blew away my HEF, for example—and continue the practice religiously. But to date, none has ever refuted my experiment with another one.

My hometown didn't take much note of my experiment, so I could go back to being a regular kid. Kids mostly just want to play with their friends, and religion isn't that big a deal—though it is, unfortunately, to parents. I could ask a friend, "Do you think God really exists?" and only get a shrug in return. But I soon learned that if I asked that within a parent's earshot, I could be banished from their home, and even be labeled a weirdo. I can remember some neighborhood boys throwing rocks at me and calling me "satanic." (I asked mom why they called me "Titanic.")

> Kids mostly just want to play with their friends, and religion isn't that big a deal—though it is, unfortunately, to parents. I could ask a friend, "Do you think God really exists?" and only get a shrug in return. But I soon learned that if I asked that within a parent's earshot, I could be banished from their home, and even be labeled a weirdo.

Circumstances made me learn ways to appear an acceptable playmate. If asked what church I attended, I would answer truthfully, "Well, my mom and stepdad don't go to church, and my dad and stepmom are Catholic. I haven't decided yet." This put me in the damned-yet-savable category. While that made me a target for conversion, I thought it an acceptable trade-off for having someone to play with.

Having parents who take on creationism or the Pledge of Allegiance also put a strain on my social life. Though my folks would ask my approval before acting, I couldn't always predict what I was in for. Some kids reflected their parents' attitudes and shunned me. Fortunately for me, I had a few really good friends who would still sit with me at lunchtime.

My parents put their foot down when it came to "youth group." I'd been invited by friends to attend this gathering of teens for Christian rock, food, and Bible lessons. My parents relented when they learned it was also a place for me to meet atheist teenagers who had been sent there by their parents to be brought back into the fold.

Atheist philosophy was easier to sort out than the value of being an atheist. I found many atheists—well, *unpleasant*. While I have met some remarkable atheists who are actively involved in making the world more civilized, I am frequently disappointed by atheists who gather only to indulge in rude jokes and angry religion-bashing. Give me the company of happy-go-lucky religionists any day.

My best advice to secular parents is to try not to raise grim, cynical, god-obsessed atheist children. Along with the usual secular values (such as appropriate tolerance/intolerance, morality, critical thinking, appreciation for reason and science), don't forget to impart social graces, playfulness, and humor. Those go far in our short existences.

And as for my parents' naïve plan to keep me from religion until I became an adult—frankly, it didn't work. I suggest instead that children be given lots of information about all sorts of religious concepts. Satisfy their natural curiosity. Trust them to sort out the real from the unreal.

> Along with the usual secular values (such as appropriate tolerance/intolerance, morality, critical thinking, appreciation for reason and science), don't forget to impart social graces, playfulness, and humor. Those go far in our short existences.

Excerpt from the Autobiography of Bertrand Russell

My father was a Freethinker, but died when I was only 3 years old. Wishing me to be brought up without superstition, he appointed two Freethinkers as my guardians. The Courts, however, set aside his will, and had me educated in the Christian faith. . . . If he had directed that I should be educated as a Christadelphian or a Muggletonian, or a Seventh Day Adventist, the Courts would not have dreamed of objecting. A parent has a right to ordain that any imaginable superstition shall be instilled into his children after his death, but has not the right to say that they shall be kept free from superstition if possible. . . .

I was taken on alternate Sundays to the (Episcopalian) Parish Church at Petersham and to the Presbyterian Church at Richmond, while at home I was taught the doctrines of Unitarianism. . . . At [age 15] I began a systematic investigation of the supposed rational arguments in favor of fundamental Christian beliefs. I spent endless hours in meditation upon this subject. I thought that if I ceased to believe in God, freedom, and immortality, I should be very unhappy. I found, however, that the reasons given in favor of these dogmas were very unconvincing. . . .

Throughout the long period of religious doubt I had been rendered very unhappy by the gradual loss of belief, but when the process was completed I found to my surprise that I was quite glad to be done with the whole subject.

I'd Rather Play Outside

Anne Nicol Gaylor

I GREW UP IN A freethought home, so it was very easy for me not to indoctrinate our children in anything approaching a religion. My own family's attitude toward religion was "laissez-faire," and it was natural for me to carry on. Religion was something other people did. I think a large number of people attend church for purely social reasons, and if families find their society elsewhere, the *raison d'etre* for churchgoing just doesn't exist.

When our children were little, a neighbor who was into Christianity once asked to take our oldest child to Sunday School. It was a Congregationalist church, not a nightmare-inducing sect, so I readily agreed.

When they returned, I asked the neighbor how Andy had liked it. A bit ruefully, with a smile, he replied, "He said he'd rather play outside."

My husband's family was religious, and when they visited in Madison or when our children visited them, we were very careful to allow the children, without comment, to accompany their grandparents to church. A couple of times I dropped the children off at a church service or function. Their reaction was somewhat like our own: Other things seemed more useful and interesting.

Until recently, public schools in Wisconsin, for the most part, were neutral in matters of religion, so freethinking children did not have the problems in school that so many report today. Wisconsin had a State Supreme Court decision in 1890 against bible reading in the public schools, the result of a suit brought by Catholic parents in Edgerton. The legal precedent this decision set served several generations of Wisconsin students very well.

When religion is introduced in the classroom, students who are different from the majority are singled out for criticism or ostracism. They are made to feel like outsiders in their own school.

Whether a family is freethought or of a religious bent, it serves us all well to protect Thomas Jefferson's wall of separation between church and state. In-

---

First appeared in *Lead Us Not Into Penn Station,* © 1983 by Anne Nicol Gaylor. Used with permission of the Freedom From Religion Foundation.

troducing religion into the public schools tears down that wall; it builds walls between children.

To keep church and state forever separate is a goal worth fighting for; it was crucial to the founding and perpetuation of our government. Maintaining that wall is essential for the happiness and well-being of public school-children who may hold minority views.

My Father's House

Dan Barker

When I was a child I thought of childish things:
Eternal life in paradise with angel wings,
A father up in heaven who would hover over me,
And tell me what to think, tell me what to be;
But now that I have grown,
It's time to use my own good mind.

I'm outa here! Let me outa here!
I found my own place—
I've left my father's house behind.

A normal Dad is really glad to realize
His little child has now become, before his eyes,
An independent person who can stand on steady feet,
An equal human being with character complete.
But God is not that way—
He orders me to stay his child.

For God so loved the world he gave his only son—
A sacrifice to pay the price for everyone—
And if you believe that this deserves a Fatherhood Award,
You can move in with the guy, and he will be your Lord.
But listen to this song:
Forever is a long, long time!

lyrics from *My Father's House* © 2004 by Dan Barker

My mother-in-law, Anne Gaylor (founder of the Freedom From Religion Foundation), claims that you can't raise children. Children raise themselves. We parents are simply facilitators. If we are the natural parents, we bequeath some of our genetics, for better or worse. We give them a home, an environment in which to feel safe and grow, access to education, resources, healthcare, love, and friendship. Then we let nature take its course. It's not as though, if we failed to do some critical task, the kids would never grow up, never find a way through life. Anne's four children grew up just fine; I married one of them.

I'm not an expert on child raising. I don't think anyone really is. My only claim to credibility is that I do have five children. Having children of your own does make you a kind of expert, though that is probably because much of our learning comes through our mistakes. Kids should not be forced into a strait-jacket of parental expectations. I think parents who obsess about how to raise their children may actually do more harm than good. This is the children's world too, and they are finding their way just like we did. Thinking back on how I was raised, I am surprised to remember that I never once thought of myself as "the son of my parents." Yes, of course, I had a Mom and a Dad, and they were great parents, good examples, and I was proud of them and love them dearly, but I never considered it was my "purpose" in life to be an extension of *their* lives. I never saw myself as "little Norman Barker," put on this earth to make him look good. What child has ever thought that way? (The dedication to my book *Losing Faith in Faith: From Preacher to Atheist* is "To Norman Barker, my only father." If we do need a father figure, it may as well be a real person. My dad is someone who has truly earned my respect.)

I think most freethinking parents have similar feelings. We don't want to force our kids into any mold, unless reason and kindness are molds—well, no, reason and kindness are open-ended, not constricting. What we truly want is the satisfaction of seeing our children become mature, self-reliant human beings, at any age, thinking for themselves, free and happy. Parents who want anything else are obsessed with control and not free and happy themselves.

My first four children were the product of a Christian marriage, from the time when I was a minister. They are all great human beings—generous, thoughtful, caring. The three girls are now raising children of their own and doing a wonderful job. My son is still single, a chef and a guitar player. Even though we took them to church as children and tried to instill "Christian" values, they ended up thinking for themselves. In this case, the religion didn't seem to do too much damage. My Christian wife and I divorced, mainly for religious reasons,[4] and this clearly had an impact on the four kids, as all divorces do. However, I think we were lucky. My former wife and I decided that we would never place the children in a position where they were forced to choose between parents. My love and support for the kids has always been unconditional, and they know it. I repeatedly told them that they are free to think their own thoughts. They don't have to agree with me. They don't have to be atheists or agnostics in order to earn my respect. Consequently, at least two of them now have views that I would call "freethinking," and the other two, although perhaps nominally religious, are quite liberal and open in their beliefs, which also counts as "freethinking" where the rubber meets the road in their daily lives. I don't think any of them goes to church, not regularly, although one was attending a Unitarian fellowship for a while. To my former wife's credit—she later remarried a Baptist minister and remains a conservative believer—her love for the kids has not been tempered by the fact that we all don't agree.

I married Annie Laurie Gaylor in 1987. She is a third-generation freethinker and editor of *Freethought Today*. She and I are now co-presidents of the Freedom From Religion Foundation. Our daughter Sabrina, a fourth-generation freethinker, is currently in high school. She has been raised with a complete lack of religion. She went to a friend's bat-mitzvah some years ago, but beyond that has never been to a church or worship service other than the occasional Unitarian fellowship where Annie Laurie or I have spoken or performed. Most Unitarians are freethinkers, and our "service" was nonreligious.

When Sabrina was little, she had a vivid imagination, like most children. (She still does!) We all had a lot of fun pretending, playing games with imaginary creatures and friends. That is a healthy part of learning and growing. Rather than tell Sabrina that the Tooth Fairy and Santa Claus were lies, we told her that we were *pretending* they were real, just like characters in a book or cartoon. She never had to go through the process of unlearning Santa or the Easter Bunny. We figured that this would allow her to have the fun of childhood imagination, not deprived of anything that her friends might have, yet not having to deal with the thought that her parents had deceived her. She "got it" from the very beginning.

When Sabrina was about 3 or 4, I reminded her that we were just pretending and wanted to confirm that she truly grasped the concept of imagination. I guess I was a little worried that she might think we were expecting her to actually believe the stories, but she didn't. She was quite clear and sensible. "I know it's just pretend, Dad. But it's fun."

So I asked her, "How do you know the difference between what is pretend and what is real?"

"It's easy," she said immediately. "Things that are pretend can do things that you can't do."

Wow. She pretty much summed up naturalistic philosophy in those few words. "Things that you can't do" was her way of saying "things that can't be done." We never explicitly taught her this world view. We had not been taking her to "Atheist Sunday School" in order to indoctrinate her as a materialist. We were not making her memorize "agnostic scriptures" or sing "naturalistic hymns." She was simply a normal child in an environment that allows for individual thinking, and left on her own was quite capable of making natural distinctions. Imagination is an amazing thing. It can be a fount of creativity, or, if taken seriously, a source of immense confusion. Just think what the world would be like if the Apostle Paul or Muhammad or Joseph Smith had been cautioned not to take his imagination literally.

> " Imagination is an amazing thing. It can be a fount of creativity, or, if taken seriously, a source of immense confusion. Just think what the world would be like if the Apostle Paul or Muhammad or Joseph Smith had been cautioned not to take his imagination literally. "

Of course, over the years, Sabrina has heard Annie Laurie and me talking about freethought and state/church separation. She has come to some of the meetings of the Freedom From Religion Foundation and listened to many of the speeches. So perhaps this amounts to a kind of "freethought education," though it is all voluntary.

I should be careful when I say that Sabrina is being raised as a "fourth-generation freethinker." That is technically not correct. She is a freethinker, and we are a freethinking family, but a person's identity is not tied to his or her family. Sabrina knows that she is free to choose otherwise. She knows that she has the liberty to become a Buddhist, Catholic, Mormon, or Pentecostal. She also knows that if she made such a decision, we would be disappointed and that we would be equally free to argue with her about it. However, we all agree that her choices are not mandated by her parents' disappointment. In any event, there seems to be little danger that someone like Sabrina, having grown up in a freethinking environment, would be attracted to dogmatism.

In his book *The God Delusion*, Richard Dawkins denounces those who identify children by the religion of their parents. There is no such thing as a Christian child or a Muslim child or an atheist child, he insists. We should call them children from a Christian or Muslim or atheist family. To call someone a "Catholic child" is to claim that the views of parents can be forced into the minds of children. Children might indeed grow up to adopt the views of their parents, as so often happens with religious indoctrination—and we have to wonder how truly "free" such a choice is—but the children, as children, are not free to responsibly choose their own lifetime religious identity.

> If you teach a generation of children that they are sinful creatures by nature, that left on their own they are morally corrupt, deserving of eternal torment in Hell, that they are not to be trusted to think their own (selfish, evil) thoughts, all of this can become—has become—a self-fulfilling prophecy.

Steven Pinker's great book *The Blank Slate* shows that we come prepackaged with a basic "human nature" that is not as malleable as many religious, political, and philosophical systems imagine. We are who we are, biological organisms in a natural environment, and we get into deep trouble if we try to deny it.

I think the greatest problem with religious systems such as Christianity is their pessimistic view of human nature. If you teach a generation of children that they are sinful creatures by nature, that left on their own they are morally corrupt, deserving of eternal torment in Hell, that they are not to be trusted to think their own (selfish, evil) thoughts, all of this can become—has become—a self-fulfilling prophecy. Whole segments of the population grow up with a negative self-image, thinking they really are rotten, in need of a savior or father figure. They are told they are "bad," so they act like it. Their religion exaggerates and demonizes normal human feelings, turning them into cosmic struggles with evil, creating devils to be fought instead of problems to be solved.

At the 2005 World Religions Conference, I was asked to represent atheism, sitting on the stage with a Buddhist, Muslim, Christian, Jew, Sikh, Hindu, and Native American spiritualist. (I accepted the invitation only after making it clear that atheism is not a religion, and they agreed to include it as a "world philosophy.") The theme of the conference was "salvation," and each of us was asked to summarize our respective positions on that topic. After pointing out that "sin" is a religious concept, hence "salvation" is merely a religious solution to a religious problem—would we respect a doctor who ran around cutting people with a knife in order to sell them a bandage?—I ended with these words: "If salvation is the cure, then atheism is the prevention." Many in the audience laughed at that comment, some who should not have been laughing. They got the point: Much of religious education is an endeavor to solve a non-problem. It is a confusing waste of time.

It is better to tell children that they are okay the way they are. Most secular parents are optimistic about human nature. We do not make our children feel bad for being—well, children. We do our best to affirm the positive potential of our children, and of ourselves. Religious or not, the best parents are the ones who prepare their children for *this* world first.

■ ■ ■ ■ ■ ■

Passing Down the Joy of Not Collecting Stamps

Penn Jillette

SAINT IGNATIUS LOYOLA, the founder of the Jesuit Order, once said "give me the child until he is 7 and I will show you the man." Some web pages say that might really be a Francis Xavier quotation, others say it was "some Jesuit" who said it, and all the careful web pages credit it to "some guy."

Little kids have to trust adults or they die. Trust has to be built in. So while you're teaching them to eat, stay out of traffic, and not drink too much of what's underneath the sink, you can abuse that trust and burn in the evil idea that faith is good. It'll often stick with them longer than not drinking bleach. It seems if someone snuck the idea of faith into you at an early age, you're more likely to do it to your own kids.

If your childhood trust was not abused with faith or if somehow you kicked it in your travels down the road, your work is done. You don't have to worry too much about your kids. You don't ever have to teach Atheism. You don't have to teach an absence of guilt for things they didn't do. As Atheist parents, you just have one more reason to keep your kids away from priests. Tell your kids the truth as you see it and let the marketplace of ideas work as they grow up.

> " Tell your kids the truth as you see it and let the marketplace of ideas work as they grow up. I don't know who said, "Atheism is a religion like not collecting stamps is a hobby," but it's a more important idea than any Jesuit ever came up with. "

I don't know who said, "Atheism is a religion like not collecting stamps is a hobby," maybe it was Francis Xavier, or more likely The Amazing James Randi, but some guy or gal said it, and it's a more important idea than any Jesuit ever came up with. You have to work hard to get kids to believe nonsense. If you're not desperately selling lies, the work is a lot easier.

My kids are really young, they're still babies, they can't even talk yet, but what the hell, we're still a little bit careful what we say. When someone sneezes we say, "That's funny," because it is. We don't have any friends who are into any kind of faith-based hooey, so our kids will just think that "damn it" follows "god" like "Hubbard" (or something) follows "mother." That's cool. That's easy.

I know this is unfashionable in the Atheist community, but truth just needs to be stated, it doesn't have to be hyped. (This is the point where you check again who wrote this chapter. Remember what Bob Dobbs said, "I don't practice what I preach because I'm not the kind of person I'm preaching to.")

There is no god, and that's the simple truth. If every trace of any single religion were wiped out and nothing was passed on, it would never be created exactly that way again. There might be some other nonsense in its place, but not that exact nonsense. If all of science were wiped out, it would still be true and someone would find a way to figure it out again. Without hype, Lot's salt-heap ho would never be thought of again. Without science, the Earth still goes around the sun and someday someone will find a way to prove that again. Science is so important because it's a way to truth, but the truth doesn't depend on it. Reality exists outside of humans, religion does not. The bad guys have to try to get the kids early to keep their jive alive. We good guys should try to get the truth out there, but the stakes just aren't as high for us. Most anyone who is serious about science will lose some faith. Maybe not all their faith, but they'll lose a hunk of it before getting that Nobel Prize. No matter how bad the polls on Americans look, the people that do science for a living aren't being fooled. The polls on belief in evolution make the USA look bad, but maybe Turkey is the only Western country with worse pollsters than the USA, ever think of that?

Evolution is the truth. And with truth comes a lack of panic. I don't lose sleep over creation myths being taught in public schools. Who trusts anything from government schools? "Better to be uneducated than educated by your government." (That quotation is mine.) The bad guys always have to fight for their ideas to be taught. They must cheat. Government force, propaganda, and hype are the tools you desperately need when you're wrong. Truth abides.

Dr. Richard Dawkins had a christian education, but he kicked that way before taking his seat in the Darwin BarcaLounger at Oxford. The bad guys got the Dawk until he was 7. So what? That race has been run, they fought the truth, and the truth won. I went to Sunday school and the reality of the creationist myth stayed as true for me as the certainty that the Greenfield High School football team was going to win the Turkey Day game because we had P. . .E. . .P. . .PEP! PEP! PEP! Jesus christ, doesn't anyone but Paul Simon and me remember it was all crap we learned in high school anyway and all the kids always knew it?

Evolution was true before Darwin. Evolution was true in the sixteenth century when Loyola did or didn't start that quotation. Evolution has been true as long as there has been life on earth, and it always will be true. If you pick your side carefully, you don't have to fight as hard.

All this assumes you're an out-of-the-closet Atheist parent. Truth doesn't live in the closet. You have to make it clear to everyone including your kids that there is no god. If you're not doing that every chance you get, then the other side will win. They'll win only in the short term; we only get to live in the short term. You don't have to fight, but you have to do your part, you have to tell the truth. You have to be honest. You don't have to force schools to say there's no god, but you have to say it. You have to say it all the time. No one can relax in a closet.

Those of us who are out of the closet Atheist parents have all that extra time on Sunday mornings to love our kids. We can use that time to hold them, laugh, and dance around together. Tell your kids there's no god and be done with it. Jesus christ, your kids aren't stupid.

Chapter One Endnotes

1. "Religion's Misguided Missiles," *The Guardian,* September 15, 2001.
2. John Paul II at this writing.
3. The Ig Nobel Awards are a parody of the Nobel Prize. Sponsored by the Annals of Improbable Research, a humorous parody of a scientific journal, the Ig Nobels recognize weird, funny, or otherwise odd scientific (or pseudoscientific) "achievements."
4. Editor's note: See Dan's book *Losing Faith in Faith* to learn more about his "deconversion."

Additional Resources

Many books have included heartfelt personal reflections by those who have found their way out of religious faith and into naturalism. Many of these include stories of childhood and parenthood; all are fascinating reading. Most are intended for adult readers.

- Sweeney, Julia. *My Beautiful Loss of Faith Story.* Coming May 2008, Henry Holt & Co. Following on the heels of her stage show *Letting Go of God,* this is Julia's memoir of her slow transition out of Catholicism into naturalism. Sure to be another thoughtful, hilarious, and moving description of struggles and joys we all experience as nonbelievers.
- Willson, Jane Wynne. *Parenting Without God: Reflections of a Humanist Mother.* Educational Heretics Press, 1998. A marvelous set of personal reflections and remembrances, intelligent and articulate in the inimitable British fashion, recalling Willson's experience as a mother raising children without religion. A world of wisdom in a scant 76 pages.
- Barker, Dan. *Losing Faith in Faith: From Preacher to Atheist.* Freedom From Religion Foundation, 1992. In *Surprised by Joy,* C. S. Lewis described his transition from atheist to Christian. *Losing Faith in Faith* is a thoughtful counterpoint to Lewis' classic, following Dan's personal journey from missionary, touring evangelist, and Christian songwriter to atheist and freethought activist.
- Allen, Norm Jr., ed. *African American Humanism: An Anthology.* Prometheus, 1991. A powerful collection of essays by twenty-one African and African American humanists, including Zora Neale Hurston and W.E.B. DuBois, with biographical sketches. An important attempt to put to rest the myth that all African Americans are Christians.
- VIDEO: *The God Who Wasn't There.* Beyond Belief Media, 2005. Former fundamentalist Brian Flemming takes viewers through his years in a strict Christian school where hell was promised to those who doubted. But he doubted anyway, first terrified and then intrigued by his growing realization that, though the wheel of religion keeps spinning, there's no hamster.

Living with Religion

Introduction

Religion is an understandable response to being human. It's not always a *good* response—sometimes it's counterproductive, and often downright danger-ous—but it is an understandable impulse. Our brains have evolved to seek patterns and find causes. This pattern- and cause-finding is a good thing, something that has served us well for millions of years. And when we don't know the answer, we guess—also a good thing, as long as you stay open to whatever new and better answers might float by.

I loved "religion" growing up and spent countless hours reading about it—though it wasn't the religion of my neighbors and relatives I was soaking up, but the religion of Ancient Greece and Rome, better known now as myths. I found the stories fascinating and recognized them as creative attempts to un-derstand the world. They revealed something not just about being Greek or Roman or ancient, but about being *human*. The ancients marveled at the stars, just as I did, feared death, and wondered why spring came so reliably, year after year, why Africans and Europeans look different, how the world began, how spiders got so good at weaving, why we go to war and fall in love. They didn't reveal much about the world, these myths, but they spoke volumes about hu-manity.

The similarities between cultural myths can be striking. A deity miracu-lously impregnates a mortal woman, who then gives birth to a great leader and deliverer of men. A father, on divine instructions, prepares to sacrifice his only son, and moments later, a ram appears. A little guy defeats a giant with one blow. A divine one miraculously turns a paltry plate of food into a banquet to feed the many. If you were born into Western Civilization after the fourth century, you'll clearly recognize these as stories from the Jewish and Christian scriptures. If you were born before then, however, you'd have recognized them as Greek and Roman myths. They are both.

Cultural legends and myths are among our greatest inheritances from the past. They are real treasures, insights into the human condition, diminished not one whit by the fact that most were once thought true by the great majority of those who heard them. Persian, Greek, Roman, Sumerian, Norse, Celtic, and Egyptian mythologies passed into the category of recognized fiction, while the Abrahamic mythologies are still considered "religions" by many. They too will most likely pass into recognized fiction, whether ten or ten thousand years from now, almost certainly to be replaced by new religions, most of which will borrow mythic archetypes from *their* predecessors . . . and on turns the great karmic wheel.

In the Preface to this book, I said that I had "set religion aside." Actually, that's a bit like saying someone who rides a bike to work has set traffic aside. I'm still in it, still surrounded by it, and I always will be. Religion, for better or worse, is likely to be a permanent part of the human world. Our job as secular parents is not to work toward a religion-free world, but to help our kids learn to happily and peacefully co-exist with religion.

Co-existence does *not* mean silent acceptance of all consequences of religious belief. To the contrary: Silence and inaction in the face of dangerous immorality is itself immoral. We have to engage religious people and institutions in just the way we wish to be engaged ourselves, as co-participants in the world. We should reasonably but loudly protest the intolerance, ignorance, and fear that is born of religion while at the same time reasonably and loudly applauding religious people and institutions whenever charity, tolerance, empathy, honesty, and any of our other shared values are in evidence. An important part of this is recognizing that not all expressions of religion and not all religious people are alike. Be sure to help kids recognize that the loudest, most ignorant, and most intolerant religious adherents—whether raving radical Muslim clerics or raving radical Christian televangelists—do not represent all believers, nor even the majority. Though institutional religion itself is an unfortunate thing, the majority of individual believers are decent and thoughtful people with whom we have more in common than not. Saying that to yourself once in a while, and to your kids, can move the dialogue further forward than just about anything else.

The vision we should encourage in our children is not a world free of religion but one in which *no* idea or action is granted immunity from discussion and critique—including, of course, our own. *That* is the vision of living with religion to which this chapter is devoted.

Some of the authors in this chapter warn against the ill effects of religious evangelism, including the demonization of honest disbelief and the erosion of our religiously nonpartisan public schools (see Stu Tanquist's "Choosing Your Battles" and Ed Buckner's "Secular Schooling"). Others are optimistic about the prospects of cooperation, right down to the sharing of a home and marriage between a believer and a nonbeliever (Wernick, "Parenting in a Secular/Religious Marriage"). We also hear from the first of two Unitarian Universalist ministers in the book, the Reverend Dr. Roberta Nelson. Like all ministers in the fascinating UU denomination (which is majority nontheistic), Dr. Nelson has an enormous amount of personal experience navigating the amorphous middle between religious belief and doubt. While raising children without religious belief is perfectly acceptable, she writes, raising children who are religiously illiterate is not. Here as well is Margaret Downey's moving description of encountering discrimination fueled by ignorance, first as a child in a mixed-race family, then as a mother helping her son withstand the shocking transition from an open and accepting Boy Scout troop to one that demeans, insults, and finally dismisses him for his beliefs.

The Additional Resources section includes several resources for religious literacy. One of the most enlightening and gentle ways to help children accept myth for its insights into humanity while keeping it distinct from fact is to steadily trace the patterns of the complete human mythic tapestry. Buy a good volume of classical myths for kids *and* buy a volume of bible stories for kids. To whet kids' appetites and introduce the pantheon of gods, read a few of the basic myths—Cronos swallowing his children, Zeus defeating the Titans and dividing the tripartite world, Icarus, Phaeton, and so on. Then begin interweaving Christian and Jewish mythologies, matched if you can with their classical parallels. Read the story of Danae and Perseus, in which a god impregnates a woman, who gives birth to a great hero, then read the divine insemination of Mary and birth of Christ story. Read the story of the infant boy who is abandoned in the wilderness to spare him from death, only to be found by a servant of the king who brings him to the palace to be raised as the king's child. It's the story of Moses—and the story of Oedipus. No denigration of the Jewish or Christian stories is necessary; kids will simply see that myth is myth.

Ideally, kids can come to a view of our mythic inheritance, including Judeo-Christian myth, as a creative attempt to understand an incomprehensible world when there were few other means to do so. With the rise of science, our real understanding has dwarfed even our richest mythic creations for pure wonder and awe-inspiration, but the myths remain dazzling, mesmerizing tributes to our collective imagination, to be admired and enjoyed. A child whose exposure to the explosive wonder of science (see Chapter 8) grows in parallel to his or her engagement with myth is unlikely to allow them to mix. Our creative fictions and our marvelous facts are each too precious in their own domains for us to do without either. The more we bring children to a real understanding of religious belief, the greater chance they will have of coming to terms with it, of living with it—and of having believers learn at last to live with and understand them in return.

Parenting in a Secular/Religious Marriage

Pete Wernick, Ph.D.

MY WIFE AND I MET in 1969 at ages 23 and 24. After being raised a Jewish believer, I had been an atheist for about seven years. Joan identified as an "ex-Catholic" and was quite negative about her Catholic upbringing and the Church. Though not an atheist, she supported my penchant for writing and collecting uplifting nontheistic essays. We would improvise little heartfelt rituals and statements. At our wedding five years later, the ceremony we wrote and read to our gathered family and friends was full of heart and free of theism.

About eight more years later, around the time our son came along, Joan began returning to Catholicism. Eventually she embraced it fully, following the example of her parents, whom she came to think of as heroes, having lovingly raised nine children even after her dad was stricken with severe polio.

The schism between our beliefs seriously concerned us both. We recognized many problems in having different worldviews. The threat to our marriage was first and foremost. As both of us believed children strongly benefit from a unified home with clearly agreed policies, the threat to good childraising seemed even more dire. As enthusiastic and idealistic new parents, we felt strongly motivated to make it work.

An atheist and a Catholic in a marriage? It's surely a head-shaker. The "soul connection" we'd had now felt to me more like a triangle. As a sociologist mindful of statistics, I knew well that marriages of religiously mismatched partners are less likely to succeed and generally "not recommended." I had a vague dread that we might have hard collisions of will and a fear that deepening commitments would lead her toward patterns I might find intolerable.[1] Indeed, in our marriage ceremony we acknowledged the threat of growing apart. Distressed, I started seeing a counselor and did a lot of complaining. The counselor settled on the mantra, "What are you going to do?" After weighing the agonizing alternatives, I finally knew I wanted to keep our family together and make it work as well as possible. With that as the goal, there was a lot of hard work to do.

> As a sociologist mindful of statistics, I knew well that marriages of religiously mismatched partners are less likely to succeed and generally "not recommended."

We went to counseling together, where we received training in principles and techniques of fair communication. On subjects as complicated and volatile as religion and childraising, this was a must. We worked on hearing each other out without interrupting, pausing to consider before answering, respectfully acknowledging each others' statements, and especially—one of the best inventions ever—the "I" statement, which replaces accusatory "you" statements. "You're always interrupting," becomes "When you interrupt, I'm frustrated because I need you to hear me."

Addressing our marriage, the first and best exercise was affirming our common ground. We shared a deep love for each other and more than twelve years of good history. We both wanted to live good lives, follow reasonable morals, be kind and thoughtful, and so on. We both wanted to be with and give a lot of love to our son, to see him grow up well in a two-parent household. This powerful motivation helped us stay the course through many painful compromises and disappointments.

> The first and best exercise was affirming our common ground. We shared a deep love for each other and more than twelve years of good history together. We both wanted to live good lives, follow reasonable morals, be kind and thoughtful, and so on. We both wanted to be with and give a lot of love to our son, to see him grow up well in a two-parent household.

We individually inventoried the points of conflict, and with our counselor's help developed fair policies on each.

A useful tool was the palliative "agreeing to disagree," that is, not considering disagreement a problem if it doesn't affect a decision about behavior. Most religious disagreements don't directly affect what we *do*, but concern which abstractions we take as fact or not. I found I could sometimes consider her "outrageous" beliefs something like her having interests, hobbies, or politics that I didn't empathize with. The challenge is greater regarding the different *behaviors* called for by differing religious beliefs (such as praying or attending different services or meetings), but in general these can go on independently, leaving lots of opportunity for common ground.

We well understood the importance of not introducing or stressing disharmony when not necessary. We pledged to avoid picking on each other's beliefs, especially around Will. We agreed that to maintain harmony, anything provocative such as art, symbols, or statements of religious belief would not be displayed in common areas of the house such as the living room, dining room, or our bedroom. No books or movies addressing religious themes or issues. Our two individual rooms were and still are exempted—and indeed, we each festooned our respective spaces with photos of the pope and Mother Theresa, and blunt atheist cartoons. On the rare occasions we initiated conversation on religion, we did it with care, maintaining standards of good decorum as though in public.

It turned out that in raising Will, we agreed on almost everything (other than the obvious). The Golden Rule is really the main rule of good-hearted, decent people, and we had no disagreement on that. We agreed on restricting our son's exposure to violence and sex on TV, both at home and at friends' houses, and found in time that he was free to go his own way regardless of our leanings.

We also understood he would in time develop his own religious orientation but naturally aimed for a fair balance in his exposure to our beliefs during his most formative years. It seemed reasonable for each of us to freely talk about religion from our own view, always in the context of an understood choice of beliefs and with guidelines on how to phrase our beliefs: No proselytizing— that is, attempting to convince. Any comment on a religious subject should include "I believe . . ." not just stating something as though it were true. Note the difference between "God loves you" and "I believe God loves you," for example, or between "There is no god" and "I see no reason to believe in a god." Joan would often take care to add, "You know, Dad feels differently about this." For a beleaguered atheist in a family of fifteen Catholic in-laws and twenty-six Catholic nieces and nephews, Joan's gift of acknowledgment gave me solace.

Our agreement extended to requesting that family members honor our compromise and not upset our hard-won balance by giving religious gifts or talking religious talk to our son.

The fact that my wife's extended family was much larger and nearer than mine caused an unavoidable tilt in the number of Catholic-context occasions we attended as a family, whether weddings, holidays, or even premeal graces at family birthday gatherings. Also unavoidable was the fact that many of these graces were delivered by the impressive Archbishop Stafford, a close family friend.

Naturally, Joan wanted to bring Will to Catholic church at times. I couldn't deny her taking him on Christmas and Easter and a few other Sundays a year. There was no obvious "atheist" church I could bring Will to, but I settled on the local Unitarian church with its nice building and kids' program. I can't say I felt very much like a Unitarian "bringing my son into Unitarianism," but I did find comfort that the beliefs fit me pretty well, and a bit of community was offered. Early in the service, the kids would leave for Religious Education classrooms. Not a big hit for Will, which led me to bring him less often than I might have. Taking him regularly perhaps would have established a routine that he would have accepted more, but with the assumption of parity between Catholic churchgoing and my choice of "services," I felt better about the "neither" choice.

Joan would typically attend Sunday church while Will and I stayed home. We would walk down to creek in the back of our property, my idea of communing with nature. We'd sit and talk, and I'd try to steer the discussion to the wonders of the universe, and the need for people to be good to each other. Sometimes we'd talk a little philosophy, with typical themes being "If there is no God, how did we get here?" and "If there were a good god, why would he let so many good young people get sick and die?" That's about as much as I had to offer him as an alternative to church, sad to say.

I acutely regretted that there was no easy way to provide "a secular infrastructure" for my son. There was no building, no costumed officiant, no history with stories to take the imagination back in time. It bothered me to think that for all the large numbers of atheists nationwide, there was scarcely any networking going on at the local level. Nothing at all kid-oriented. Virtually nothing written for nontheist kids.[2] The more I explored what was available in reading material and local organizations, the more I saw a pretty inert, introverted, mostly older population with little vibrancy and spark.

One December when Will was about 7 or 8, the local humanists had a holiday party and asked me to provide some music. I thought it would be nice to bring my family, as perhaps a counterbalance to the heavy-duty Christmas style of my in-laws. The party was dour and dreary, just not any sort of fun. My wife quietly went out to the car and wept. I received a scrawled note from my son requesting, "Please don't take me to any more humanist parties."

I haven't—and haven't been tempted either. Will passed out of his young formative years with just about no chance of exposure to a secular infrastructure.

In recent years, I have taken great consolation in the words of my friend Joe: "Kids learn from modeling. How you live is more important than what you say your beliefs are." How true! At this point, Joan and I feel we did the best we could in raising Will, now 24. He is a responsible, considerate young adult with a mind of his own and a willingness to work toward good goals.

Looking back, I see that over time we gained confidence that we could maintain our individual identities, and that we could trust our working compromise in how to expose our son to our divergent beliefs.

I came to a strikingly positive, though almost preposterous realization: What we were doing amounted to *a model for world peace!* I figured if we could live together with relatively low friction on this very divisive issue, there was hope for the Israelis and Palestinians.

Sure, this statement sounds ludicrous on the surface. But in fact we had learned to use some primary tools of the still-new discipline of conflict resolution:

- Finding and affirming common ground and a common goal.
- Agreeing to disagree on matters that are opinion only.
- Agreeing not to provoke unnecessarily.
- Developing policies concerning behavior, using compromise, and mediated if necessary by a professional.
- Maintaining parity and evenhandedness as much as possible: If something applies to one, it also applies to the other.
- In time, learning to trust the stability of the resolution, building confidence in it and satisfaction in the hard-won accomplishment of peace.

The science of maintaining individual dignity and balance through understanding and disciplined compromise may well be the science that saves the world.

On Being Religiously Literate

Rev. Dr. Roberta Nelson

TODAY WE ARE FACED with the need to be religiously literate in order to grasp the true significance of the religious dimensions that underlie the news, TV, films, and books and to better understand our co-workers, neighbors, and friends.

Unless our children are isolated and do not ask questions, they are bound to hear "stories" that are confusing, troubling, or raise additional issues. They will have questions: *Who is Jesus, Buddha, Mohammed? What is the Bible; why do so many people think it's so important? Why did Jesus die? What is Passover, or Ramadan? Why doesn't Rachel celebrate Christmas, Halloween, birthdays? What is a savior? Where is heaven? Where will I go when I die? What's this about some people going to hell? Who is this God guy? Why do people say we have to believe in him?*

These are some of the questions and issues that I have helped parents and young people deal with as a Unitarian Universalist minister. Included among these were many secular parents who came to the churches I served because they found it difficult going it alone. They wanted answers and ways of dealing with complex religious issues. They wanted an education for their children and soon realized they needed it for themselves as well.

> Choosing not to affiliate or join a religious community does not shield a parent from religious questions. If you do not provide the answers, someone else will—and you may be distressed by the answers they provide.

Choosing not to affiliate or join a religious community does not shield a parent from these questions—you will still need to be able to answer some or all of them. If you do not provide the answers, someone else will—and you may be distressed by the answers they provide.

I grew up in a Boston neighborhood where there were Catholic, Protestant, unchurched and a few Jewish families. Most of the neighborhood and the school I went to were white, with a small number of blacks. There were differences, but I do not remember hostility or anger toward one another because of our different views or religion. There was almost no division by class or race.

By the time my children were in school the number of unchurched families had grown substantially; there were still Catholic, Protestant, and Jewish families, but there were also children whose families were Muslim and Baha'i. There were more black families and a growing number of Hispanic families, and there was more diversity among the Protestant traditions. There were tensions in the school when differing views were expressed, often between homogenous groups dependent on race and class.

New Hampshire Avenue starts in Washington, DC, and ends a few miles later in Montgomery County, Maryland. In her recent book, *A New Religious America*, Diana Eck describes the religious pluralism evident along or just off this road: a Cambodian Buddhist Temple with its sloping tiled roof, a new copper-domed mosque of the Muslim Community Center between an onion-domed Ukrainian Orthodox Church and a Disciples of Christ Church, a new brick Gujarati Hindu Temple, a Jain Temple, and Hispanic Pentecostal, Vietnamese Catholic, and Korean evangelical congregations along with more traditional English-speaking mainline churches.

Our children are growing up and learning in this environment. As adults, it is our responsibility to adapt to the changes, engage with the issues, and begin to learn along with them about the rich histories, cultures, and religions of the people who are making our neighborhoods, schools, and wider communities a collage of race, color, and creed. Regardless of whether we call ourselves religious, we are our children's first and primary religious educators.

In the UU church I grew up in, I learned about the dignity and worth of all people, the importance of asking questions and searching for answers, ethical decision making, and trust. I also learned that not all questions had concrete answers and that answers could change with time as I gained experience and knowledge.

We were a churched family, but my parents were extremely influential in educating us by example and deed about valuing and appreciating differences, as well as guiding us to realize that not all the decisions and ideas we saw and heard around us needed to be equally valued. There were conversations about the issues of the day especially around religion, politics, and race. We were encouraged to express our views and to listen to the views of others. In reality, my parents were my first religious educators. The church was their community of support for shared ideas and values.

As parents, we are our children's guides and mentors and role models. It is an awesome responsibility. Today we are living in an age of increasing diversity in religion, language, sexuality, gender roles, class, and politics. All of these will raise issues that are polarizing and confusing, and at times frightening to our children and youth, maybe even to ourselves. Therefore we need to have an understanding of this new worldview and its impact on our lives. We cannot take these issues lightly, but we must not be overwhelmed by them. I believe that most parents can be excellent mentors if they take some time to honor their own yearnings, wonderings, and reflections, and then—most importantly—to share them with their children.

We need to ask ourselves how we can counteract the negative images and ideas that are written and portrayed of people who are not like "us."

Like so many things, values are "caught as well as taught." Our values cannot be esoteric or removed; they need to be lived in the everyday and undergirded by our principles. Family life is where those connections are made, where stories are told and remembered, and where a wider perspective is embraced. And just as they will indeed hear answers to religious questions, one way or another, children will indeed learn values, one way or another—if not from us, then inevitably from someone else. We have a choice to assume that responsibility or to simply allow it to happen, with what could be serious consequences.

What most of us hope for are happy, healthy, and ethical children. The world we currently live in makes it almost impossible to have the regular, dependable qualities we long for. However, we need to strive to create an environment that honors who we are. Some of the things that will help us are times to be and do together, time unstructured and flexible, time to be companions on the journey.

This journey will inevitably invite questions—questions that are hard to answer, conflicting ideas, shared feelings and emotion, painful consequences, risk, and compassion.

To be committed to the values that permeate our way of being together, we must learn to listen—really listen, to be flexible and open, and to share what we think and why. We also need to model taking a stand on what we believe and living with the consequences.

We live in a world of ambiguity and incongruity. We strive to be ethical and know that our paths are often strewn with pebbles, rocks, and an occasional boulder. Our ability to maneuver the rocky paths will help young people live with their own questions, issues, and concerns.

Our role is to help our young people to build an ethical framework, enabling them to become responsible adults who are capable of being responsible decision makers, understanding of and connected to those around

Ten Ways to Promote Religious Literacy in Your Family

1. Find books about world religions in public or university libraries—many are available for each developmental level—or explore Beliefnet.com (see Additional Resources at end of chapter).
2. Watch and discuss television series about religions—on the air or on DVD.
3. Take a course in comparative religion at a local community college.
4. Accept an invitation from a neighbor or co-worker to join in a celebration of a special holiday or occasion. This can only happen if you have developed an ongoing relationship (for instance, being invited to a Seder at Passover).
5. Visit a variety of local congregations.
6. Visit and discuss special religious art exhibits.
7. A teen might choose to write a paper on an issue that has religious implications.
8. Share your own interest and ideas with your children about an issue, book, film, etc.
9. The UU Church of the Larger Fellowship (www.clfuu.org) provides excellent materials for people who do not have access to a congregation.
10. UU ministers and religious educators are available to help.

them—including those significantly different from themselves. In a recent *New York Times* article, Thomas Friedman wrote of his daughter's high school graduation from what is considered to be a neighborhood school. "I sat there for two hours listening to each one's name pronounced. I became both fascinated and touched by the stunning diversity—race, religion, ethnicity. . . . As I mingled I found myself surrounded by families in which no one spoke English."

It is in these awakenings that one of our central challenges as parents becomes clear: To raise children in the midst of this "stunning diversity," we must educate for empathy, for a deep understanding of our shared humanity. And because so large a portion of our fellow human beings articulate their own meaning, purpose, and values through their religions, it is essential that our children know as much as possible about those religions: their beliefs and practices, their literatures and traditions, and their meaning to their practitioners. To be fully engaged members of the human society, they must be religiously literate.

An important part of this literacy is the recognition that humans have a "spiritual" dimension, broadly defined—a yearning for meaning and purpose, a connection to the rest of humanity and life on Earth, a sense of existential wonder and mystery. Whether expressed theistically or secularly, it is a part of being fully human. In *Secrets of Strong Families,* John DeFrain and Nick Stennett reported that the primary expres-

> ❝ Because so large a portion of our fellow human beings articulate their own meaning, purpose, and values through their religions, it is essential that our children know as much as possible about those religions. ❞

sion of families' spiritual dimension is not in formal ritual but in everyday life. These families literally practice what they preach. They believe that the challenges and trials of life are bearable and surmountable because of their spiritual resources. They feel they need the spiritual dimension to give lasting meaning to their lives.

Rabbi Abraham Heschel writes, "The place to look for spiritual sustenance is in everyday existence. Even the most simple deeds can be full of wonder." This reflection on wonder allows us to put spirituality in a different context and frees us to acknowledge it in our lives, regardless of our orientation to religious questions. My husband and I led a parent group where we asked the participants to write on the word *spirituality.* Some thought of it as being "fully connected—with nature, other people, and things." Others called it "living a life in a fully conscientious, caring way," "recognizing that we're part of a life force that encompasses all," or "the mysterious, the 'awe-full,' anything that transcends the individual's consciousness"—or simply "experiencing wonder." Thus broadly defined, secular parents can embrace the idea of spirituality and understand religion as one attempt to speak to this human longing.

It is my hope that we will make a covenant with our children to be their companions and guides on a magnificent journey, in which they know the meaning of transcendence, a process of moving over and going beyond real or imagined boundaries—and recognize the myriad ways in which the rest of humanity has done the same.

Choosing Your Battles

Stu Tanquist

BEN FRANKLIN WISELY SAID, "In this world, nothing is certain but death, taxes, and religious zealots." OK, so I added that last part. Were he here today, however, I suspect that Ben would add it himself.

There are many tolerant and respectful religious believers in this world, of course, and to each his or her own. By religious zealots, I mean those who feel a divinely mandated duty to assimilate everyone into their own world view. When their tactics involve imposing their faith on others—especially by telling children that they must believe in a god in order to be good—I get a bit testy. I don't make their children eat my cooking. It only seems fair that my child shouldn't have to swallow their wafers.

Aggressive evangelical movements like the Child Evangelism Fellowship (CEF) specifically target children aged 5 to 12, working to secure "decisions to accept Christ as Lord and Savior." They know that they need to hook children at a young age, before they are old enough to think for themselves.

But it isn't just groups like CEF seeking religious allegiance from our children. There is also a subtler, often well-meaning desire by mainstream religionists to share something that is meaningful to them or to save children from some imagined divine retribution. Well-meaning or not, such evangelism of children nonetheless seeks to cut off the process of independent thought before it begins. It's this aspect of religious indoctrination that is most unacceptable—the idea that doubt is bad, that unquestioning acceptance is good, that there is only one possible right answer, and that someone else has already figured out what that answer is.

> As a secular parent, I feel an obligation to help my child develop effective reasoning skills so she can form her own conclusions in all areas of life. I don't want her to blindly adopt my views.

Our kids can and must be helped to fend off these unacceptable intrusions. As a secular parent, I feel an obligation to help my child develop effective reasoning skills so she can form her own conclusions in all areas of life. I don't want her to blindly adopt my views. My hope is that her conclusions will logically follow from a careful process of critical thinking.

Of course if that were the case, this book would not be necessary.

It's necessary to distinguish between religious *believers* and religious *evangelists*. An *evangelist* is defined as a Christian who actively attempts to convert others to his or her religion. And even in a secular home (unless you raise your kids in a protective bubble), conflict with religious evangelists is inevitable. Such evangelists include teachers who impose religious views on young captive audiences, outside groups who obtain privileged access to our public schools, or our own secular government legislating that children recite a god pledge in school. The attempts are relentless and unlikely to diminish anytime soon. I for one can't *wait* until we are "left behind"!

While some problems cannot be ignored, the challenge lies in determining where to draw the line. Some issues are too trivial to address, and others are simply insurmountable. Some would require a high investment of energy for small gain, while others entail genuine risk. The challenge is determining how to pick your battles.

A Little About Us

As a single secular parent living full-time with my 16-year-old daughter, I feel extremely fortunate. We have a wonderful relationship and truly enjoy each other's company. We also appreciate living in a home that is completely free from religion—except for the occasional door-to-door belief peddler.

Our home life wasn't always this way. At the impassioned request of my now ex-wife, our daughter attended Catholic school from preschool through seventh grade. At the time I was an apathetic nonbeliever. Knowing how important religious education was to my wife and her family, I agreed to pay for several sets of snazzy blue plaid uniforms and years of private school tuition.

Our daughter initially thrived in religious school, though she grew tired of the inherent rigidity and required conformity. By the seventh grade, she was a self-professed nonbeliever, though she achieved the high score in her religion class that year. That was the year she decided enough was enough. Much to her mother's chagrin, she insisted on leaving her classmates for public school. She has never looked back—at least not fondly.

The change created new challenges in our home. Religious teaching in her Catholic school was to be expected, of course, but the promotion of religion in our public school system has been hard for both of us to swallow.

The Issue of Authority

We have two explicit "rules" posted in our home: (1) Always question authority; (2) when in doubt, see rule 1.

These two simple rules—really one, of course—are a source of pride for my daughter and an ongoing wonder for her friends. And yes, these rules apply to my own authority as well. This may seem counterproductive to many parents, especially to those who struggle with disciplinary issues. Quite frankly, it has not been a problem. To the contrary, this simple concept has been a wonderful and positive influence in our home.

I should note that our rules encourage her to *question* my comments, decisions, and rationale, to receive justifications beyond "because I said so." They do not authorize anarchy. Inviting *questioning* is not the same as a complete abdication of responsibility. As her parent and legal guardian, I obviously need to put my foot down from time to time. The point is that my daughter is encouraged to openly and freely challenge my views, without fear of consequence for the challenge. If I am a good parent, my parenting should stand on its own merit, both in terms of her perception and the kind of person she becomes. Conversely, if I blinded myself to criticism, how would I know if I'm a good parent or not? That sounds like a recipe for self-delusion.

Our house rules are a recognition of the error in reasoning called the *argument from authority*. People commit this fallacy when they blindly accept statements made by people in a position of authority. It is important to remember that regardless of expertise, credential, or experience, none of us is infallible. We can all be wrong and so should not be placed above honest question or challenge.

We live in a society that values authority. Political leaders cry treason when U.S. citizens oppose war and its related atrocities. Religious authorities expect us to sit silently and still while they tell us what to believe. In Minnesota, as in many other states, school authorities lead our children in reciting a weekly pledge to god and country—as if we don't have enough unthinking patriotism on this planet. Children who opt out risk being ostracized by teachers and classmates. This potential soon became apparent at my daughter's school.

The "Nonmandatory" Pledge

While attending eighth-grade parent–teacher conferences, we were informed soberly that our daughter was not standing for the Pledge of Allegiance. I was unaware that she had made this choice and glowed with pride. Having children stand and recite a rote pledge to their country is something I would not expect from a free democratic nation—especially when they are further compelled to declare that nation to be "under God." If our country deserves the respect of its citizens, that respect should be earned and freely and individually expressed. If we need to bolster love of country through semi-coerced oaths, something ain't right. I love my dog because she makes me happy. Imagine making up for a lousy dog by reciting a dog pledge: "I pledge allegiance, to my dog. . ."

I asked the teacher why he thought it was important to share this information about our daughter. He began squirming in his seat, then said at last that it really wasn't important—he just thought we would want to know. I retorted that it must be important to him since he felt compelled to bring it up. Again, the same awkward response. He clearly understood that our daughter was within her legal right to abstain, and it was now painfully apparent that I was unsympathetic to his concern. Recognizing that this issue was now a non-issue, I moved on to talk about things that really mattered, like our daughter's academic progress and learning needs.

Classroom Proselytizing

Things really got dicey the following year when my daughter brought home "values assessments" from her health class—a survey intended to measure a student's developing moral and ethical sense, personal assets, and social stress. The survey consisted of a number of statements; each time the student agreed with the statement, she garnered additional points toward a high "values" score. In a cumulative assessment of this type, every "no" counts against the final total—which in the case of this survey would indicate a student whose values need some attention. Perhaps you can see why some of the statements caught my eye:

- I attend weekly religious services.
- I reach out to develop my spirituality.
- I have taught Sunday School class or have otherwise taken an active part in my church.
- I will take my children to church services regularly.
- I believe in a Supreme Being.
- I believe that it is important to support a church by giving time and/or money.
- Each day I try to set aside some time for worship.
- It is important to me that grace be said before meals.

- I believe there is life after death.
- I read the Bible or other religious writings regularly.
- I believe in the power of prayer and meditation.

The assessments were clearly skewed to show that nonreligious students have higher stress, lower values, and worse assets. That was enough to raise my hackles. My first step was important—I spoke with my daughter to see if she had concerns about me pursuing the matter. It quickly became apparent that she too found the statements insulting and wanted to see the matter addressed. I considered scheduling a meeting with the teacher—something I recommend whenever possible before escalating—but this was not the first time I had been made aware of the influence of this particular teacher's religious bias in the classroom. At an orientation earlier in the year, in a presentation reeking of religious language and influence, he had made clear his intention to focus on abstinence to the near total exclusion of birth control education. Given his tendency toward religious proselytizing in the classroom, I was concerned that he might initially recant, then resume his underhanded tactics once my daughter moved on. To prevent this, I turned to the Freedom From Religion Foundation (FFRF) for help.

> 66 My daughter brought home a "values assessment" from her health class that was clearly skewed to show that nonreligious students have higher stress, lower values, and worse assets. That was enough to raise my hackles. 99

As a life member of FFRF, I called co-president Annie Laurie Gaylor to see what she might suggest. She graciously offered to write a letter on our behalf— and boy did she. Annie Laurie wrote a powerful letter to the principal and copied the superintendent. Though initially resistant, the principal eventually replied that the issue had been resolved. Ninth graders at Burnsville High can no longer substitute health class for church.

My daughter was thrilled each time a copied letter arrived from FFRF and proud to have had the courage to do the right thing. She still managed to pull an "A" from the class, but then the teacher didn't have much choice. Her test scores were stellar.

Surviving a Mixed Marriage—or Not

Adherents of competing religions are reasonably close in thought, especially different Christian denominations, so it doesn't seem at first glance that intermarriage should present too many problems. But after seventeen years of marriage to a devout Catholic, I now understand why Catholics seek Catholics, Mormons seek Mormons, and jocks seek cheerleaders. While liberal believers seem capable of navigating a mixed marriage, the deck is clearly stacked against disciples of moderate and especially fundamentalist sects. They generally don't mix with nonbelievers either. In our marriage, I tried to be flexible, and we both compromised. However, on matters relating to religion and our daughter, opportunities offered for compromise were few and far between.

As noted earlier, I entered our marriage as an agnostic who was indifferent to religious belief. I have since come to appreciate the power that religious emotions hold over the human mind. Because religion was so important to my wife, I supported her desire to require that our daughter attend church until she was an adult. We went to church as a family when she was young, but I found that my skeptical mind could only take so much ritual and repetition. I soon learned to savor my Sunday mornings on the deck with a good freethought book and a tasty cigar, a "ritual" I still enjoy.

Though I tried not to intentionally influence our daughter's views on religion, she couldn't help noticing that Dad no longer attended church. Church

Weighing the Options

When considering whether to challenge religious intrusion in our lives, there are many factors to consider:

- Is your child concerned about the consequences?
- Could your child be negatively impacted by the challenge? Might he or she be ostracized at school by teachers or students?
- If successful, how significant would the change be? Would it positively benefit other families and children?
- Could you and your family be negatively impacted?
- What are your chances of success?
- How much time and resources are required?
- Do you risk damaging existing relationships?
- Is this likely to be a short-term or long-term fix?
- Is legal action necessary?
- Are there other parents or organizations that could assist you?
- Are you bored? Do you really need the spice this will add to your life?
- Would it feel rewarding both to you and your child if you succeeded?

had always been a source of conflict in our home. Our daughter rabidly objected to obediently subjecting her rear end to another hour on a hard wooden bench. Her objections gradually became more forceful, to the point where her behavior ruined the otherwise desirable experience for her mother.

I was quietly sympathetic to both sides of the conflict and strived to remain neutral, which is easier said than done. Things eventually snowballed when our daughter started questioning religious doctrine and later announced that she too was a nonbeliever.

I was eventually fired as a husband and found myself living full-time with our daughter. I kept the house, the kid, and the dog. What a sweet deal. I quickly purged the house of crucifixes, ditched the artificial Christmas tree, and sent Santa packing. My daughter loves the freedom and autonomy she now enjoys in our secular home. She was recently accepted as a full-time student at a major university, which she will attend in lieu of her junior and senior high school years. The religious zealots can be found there as well—but she has the reasoning skills to find her own way now, thanks in part to the battles we chose to fight so she had a chance to develop them.

Choose Your Battles Wisely

The battle for your child's mind is real. Many religious enthusiasts—some well-meaning, some certainly not—are working tirelessly to derail our children's ability to think for themselves about the big questions and to substitute the principles of one particular religious view for the plurality and freedom of belief inherent in our nation's founding principles. Their tactics are sophisticated and sometimes bold, sometimes subtle. I have tremendous respect for freethinkers and liberal believers alike who make the effort to oppose assaults on our precious liberties. It is my hope that readers of this book will do their part to protect our freedoms. As with any form of activism, one person can only do so much. As a parent, you have many demands on your time, including attending to the needs of your children—though in some cases, standing up for their right to think for themselves is an important way of attending to their needs. It's important to consider the most appropriate course of action. For minor infractions, try to start small and give individuals the opportunity to make corrections. Consider going directly to a classroom teacher, for example, rather than escalating the issue to the principal or superintendent—though in some situations, as noted, you'll want to start at the top.

In some cases, a personal meeting is likely to be better received and therefore may be more effective than an impersonal email or letter, though the latter offers a written record of exactly what was said. If possible, solicit feedback from others before initiating contact. Bounce ideas off of trusted friends, family, or colleagues. And finally, try to maintain a positive, nonconfrontational tone. Remember that the ultimate goal is to resolve the issue in the interests of your child and other children, not to make the veins in the various adult foreheads stand out. You may find that some folks are willing to make changes if you make the effort to help them understand your concern.

Final Thoughts

Secular parenting can be a wonderful experience, even for those living in intolerant communities. We have the opportunity and responsibility to help our children develop effective reasoning skills, a trait sorely needed on our troubled planet. It is rewarding to know that our children will be empowered to think for themselves as they navigate this credulous world. I find it especially rewarding to know that the respect I feel from my daughter is sincere and not a response to an authoritarian parenting style. I feel comfort knowing that if I were a lousy parent, she'd be the first to let me know. Better to find out now when there is time to make adjustments.

Finally, remember the two rules on authority and consider establishing them as guidelines in your home. They apply equally well to adults.

Teaching Children to Stand on Principle—Even When the Going Gets Tough

Margaret Downey

THERE ARE TIMES WHEN being a good parent is easy and fun—times when everything falls into place, struggles are few and far between, and the way forward is level and well-marked.

But despite our best efforts and intentions, there are also times when the path is not so clear, times when we are forced to make difficult choices as our values collide with the world around us. These collisions are hardest when our children are in the middle. It's often tempting to withdraw and easy to convince ourselves that it is in the best interests of the kids to do so. But when our most deeply felt principles are involved—principles like kindness, courage, honesty, and diversity— withdrawal can easily teach children that principles are only worth standing up for when the going is easy.

> " When our most deeply felt principles are involved— principles like kindness, courage, honesty, and diversity—withdrawal can easily teach children that principles are only worth standing up for when the going is easy. "

I absorbed this lesson in the way that is both hardest and best—by learning it alongside my child. But the evolution of my principles began long before I was a parent.

I was 15 years old when, after a long process of reading, thinking and questioning, I came to identify myself as an Atheist. My first marriage, to a Catholic man, dissolved when we disagreed on such questions as the baptism of our infant daughter. I married again three years later, this time to someone who did not attend church or believe in God. He was kind, honest, reliable, and a terrific father. I was glad to have another child with Tom as my loving husband. Matthew was born when my daughter Holly was 9 years old.

Tom and I had no family pressure to baptize Matt. Tom's parents were not religious, and they never went to church. My mother and many others from my side of the family had given up their religious beliefs by then as well.

Unlike religious parents, we did not require our children to memorize passages from Atheist literature or attend a weekly Atheist meeting. There were no early morning wake-up calls to attend a Freethought sermon. We did not parade our children around like puppets, mimicking what we believed.

Our Sunday mornings began with the smell of a big breakfast. Our traditional Sunday "worship" took place in our kitchen. We worshiped each other and thanked the adult income-makers for providing us all with good food, a roof over our heads, and all the comforts we never took for granted. Sunday breakfast was a time for planning the upcoming week (we all brought our calendars to the table), discussing the events of the past week, distributing allowances, enjoying good food, and a lot of joy in being a family.

Before I knew it, my son was 12, and I was picking him up outside the public school where his Boy Scouts of America (BSA) meeting was held. But something was horribly wrong. The minute he saw me, he burst into tears. I immediately hugged him and asked what had happened to upset him so much.

Choking back the tears, he said, "We have to find a religion, Mom, and we have to pick one before the next troop meeting."

We had moved to Bloomington, Illinois, from Sussex, New Jersey, a few months earlier, and the first thing we did was locate another Boy Scout troop for our son. The New Jersey troop had been so nice, so accepting of me as an Atheist, and so willing to accommodate our belief system. We naïvely anticipated the same open-arms welcome from an Illinois BSA troop. How wrong we were!

> The new Illinois troop leader looked through my son's BSA handbook the evening of Matt's first meeting. He noticed a page where the word God had been crossed off and replaced with the word "good." "What are you," the troop leader demanded, "some kind of *Atheist?!*"

Apparently, the new Illinois troop leader looked through my son's BSA handbook the evening of Matt's first meeting. He noticed a page where the word God had been crossed off and replaced with the word "good."

Many other pages that had been approved by the New Jersey troop leader were now considered invalid. How dare we replace the word "God" with "science," "humanity," and "nature"!

"What are you," the troop leader demanded of my son, "some kind of *Atheist?!*"

My son had never heard that word before and honestly answered that he didn't think we were. On further questioning, the troop leader discovered that we did not go to church and did not read the Bible in our home. He demanded that Matt tell us that if he did not have a religion in two weeks, he was not welcome to return.

The traumatic event led to much discussion in our household. We talked about the importance of honesty and dignity. We discussed other religious beliefs my son knew about from his friends and even looked up a few unfamiliar religions that BSA troop leader said were "acceptable." After all the discussions and research, we turned to our son and asked him, "Well, Matt—do you want to pick a religion now, or do you want wait until you are older?"

He said that he did not believe in any God, and he was thinking that maybe BSA troop just made a mistake. "The New Jersey people loved us, right?"

Yes, I assured him, the New Jersey troop loved us, and I, too, thought that perhaps the Illinois troop was simply misguided. I called the troop leader a few days before the date of the next scheduled meeting to discuss the matter. His first question was, "Well—have you selected a religion?" There was no discussion, no attempt at compromise, no kindness, and no respect for our family's chosen life stance. When I answered that we would not be forced into selecting a religion just to fit in, he hung up on me.

Before I could investigate the problem much further, we moved again, this time to West Chester, Pennsylvania. Our next-door neighbor greeted us on the first day of our arrival dressed in a BSA troop leader uniform, along with his son, dressed in his Cub Scout uniform.

My kind and loving neighbor suggested that we join BSA right away so that Matthew could make new friends and join him and his son in BSA activities. "Great," I said. "Where do we sign up?"

My neighbor told me to simply come to the next meeting. But what if Matt was traumatized again? I could not stand the heartbreak. I decided to submit an application but determine ahead of time if the Pennsylvania troop was more like the New Jersey troop (open and loving) or the Illinois troop (intolerant and mean-spirited). The application itself contained the word "God." We replaced the word with "good" and sent the application to the West Chester BSA office with our membership fee.

Within a few days, the application and check were returned to us along with an official statement from BSA national headquarters: "No boy can grow into the best kind of citizen," it said, "without recognizing an obligation to God."

I was shocked and insulted. Had our time with BSA in New Jersey meant nothing? Apparently so. Then I got angry.

Reading the words that so demeaned us as an Atheist family and questioned our patriotism and our ethical values of honesty, kindness, and courage, I was reminded of what I had witnessed growing up in the 1950s and 1960s in Baton Rouge, Louisiana. My mother was an immigrant from Puerto Rico. Her first daughter, my half-sister Martha, was gentle, beautiful, and dark-skinned—the sweetest little girl anyone would ever want to meet. I saw strangers sneer at her. They did not know her at all. *Why would they show such contempt toward her?* I wondered.

"Martha can't go in there with you," my mother cautioned as I held Martha's hand to enter the bathroom at our local public park.

"Why?" I asked.

"Just because. Now let go of her hand," she insisted.

I saw the hurt and pain in Martha's face as she let go of my hand. From that point on, the message of segregation dawned on me, slowly but traumatically. I began to notice that Martha could not drink from the same water fountain, sit at the front of the bus with me, or swim in the public pool when I took swimming lessons.

When we went to school, Martha was chased home by the rock-throwing children of bigots who screamed racial epithets at her. She ran home almost every day, and I ran with her. One day I heard my mother tell a neighbor that Martha was the housekeeper's child and that she was just taking care of her for a while. Our house helper was an African American woman whom we all loved—but I knew it wasn't true. The lie my mother told was so horrible that I decided right then and there to always be honest—even if it made life a little more difficult. Now, forty years later, my son was being prejudged, stereotyped, and insulted, his potential as a good citizen discounted, not because of the color of his skin but just because of what he was thinking. I could not fight injustices as a child, but I could do so now. I filed a discrimination complaint against the Boy Scouts of America with the Pennsylvania Human Relations Commission.

The year was 1991. It took nine years for the Commission to investigate our complaint.

The wait was horrendous, and our family suffered greatly when the details of the case were publicly disclosed. My husband's job was threatened, I received death threats, and we lived in constant fear that someone would reveal who our son was and where he went to school. BSA disclosed my son's full name to a *Philadelphia Inquirer* journalist—one week prior to his high school graduation. This mean-spirited tactic was used purposely to prevent me from seeking any further action against BSA. The article was unexpected, and so was my son's reaction. I went to his room to tell him how sorry I was that he had been exposed as the protestor against BSA's bigoted membership policy. I thought for sure that he would be upset and angry that on his last week of school he had to face teachers and fellow students who were surely going to turn on him.

Instead, my son hugged me tightly and said, "It's OK, Mom. I'm proud of what we've done and I'm proud of you."

I cried tears that had built up over the years. His hug and his words made the trauma worth it to me, and I began to cry out of pure love and appreciation for my son's understanding and devotion. I wanted so much to protect him, but I also wanted to show that through hard work, conviction, and determination, a social injustice can be corrected. I wanted my activism to be a role model for my children. I wanted them to remember their mother as someone who would not accept second class citizenship, negative stereotyping, and blatant prejudice—against anyone!

We eventually lost our case. In 2001, BSA declared itself a private organization, no longer servicing the public at large, which gave it the right to discriminate against whomever it chose. Today, it is gays and Atheists. Tomorrow it could be Jews, Mexicans, or handicapped children.

BSA has already begun the process of disassociating itself from the Unitarian Church because Unitarians are "too tolerant" of gays and Atheists. Many troops across the nation have been disbanded by BSA national office because they protested against the national membership policy that excludes gays and Atheists from the program. It is sad to see an organization we once loved, respected, and supported turn into just another private hate group. I can only hope that future generations will see the errors of BSA's current leadership and reclaim the organization's mission and purpose to bring back the true meaning of BSA tenets.

When my son wrote his college entrance essay, I knew that I had accomplished my goals. He wrote that his mother was courageous and principled and that he hoped to also tear down negative stereotyping when he entered

Roanoke College in Virginia, a school with a Lutheran affiliation. He was accepted and did well. After receiving a degree in physics, Matt took a job in the United States Air Force, where he is entrusted with top-secret military clearance.

And this is the boy that the Boy Scouts of America said could "...*never grow into the best kind of citizen...*"

I urge all parents, secular and otherwise, to stand proud as role models and to advocate honesty when dealing with difficult problems. Never be a hypocrite in language or action. Core values are those your children will come to see as the true morality. And with them, and your guidance, your children will respect you, and you will respect yourself.

Secular Schooling

Ed Buckner, Ph.D.

> To educate a child perfectly requires profounder thought,
> greater wisdom, than to govern a state.
>
> —William Ellery Channing, 1838

FEW TASKS UNDERTAKEN BY parents and communities are more important than the education of our children. Several key questions arise in any discussion of the nature and purpose of that education—questions that any parent should take seriously, consider with care, and answer. Some of these are of particular interest to secular families:

- Why should secular parents support public schools (or oppose "vouchers")?
- Is moral education possible in the public schools (where it would have to be taught without a religious basis of some kind)? Isn't it in fact impossible to separate religious belief or ideas from education, unless education is taken to mean nothing more than rote learning?

• Why should parents support the separation of church and state within public schools?

This essay explores these issues and offers some suggestions.

Supporting Public Schools

All thoughtful citizens, even those who aren't parents and never expect to become parents, should support public schools. The same goes for parents who want to home school their children or who pay to have them attend private schools, whether religious or secular.

Our society is more interdependent than ever. We all gain by a better-educated population and are all threatened by a less well-educated one. Our whole economy—not just our own jobs or businesses—depends directly on workers having and maintaining complex skills. Our democratic governance will cease to be self-governance if most of us don't understand our own society and its political philosophy. And our culture will be cheapened instead of enriched if we do not have a broadly educated citizenry, a populace able to appreciate all that life and art have to offer.

Only a public school system has any chance of educating nearly everyone, and only such a system can hope to instill a common education, language, historical knowledge, and basic moral values across the population. Public schools deserve universal support for all these reasons. That's why vouchers—grants of tax dollars to individual parents to spend at the private schools of their choice, supposedly as a way to encourage freedom and improve education—are a bad idea. Vouchers encourage, and may even guarantee, socially debilitating segregation. They certainly endanger religious liberty. Our children need to learn firsthand that different isn't worse. All our children can gain greatly by seeing other children cope and succeed, the more so if those other children have a wide range of different abilities, ethnicities, interests, geographical origins, and cultures.

> " Our children need to learn firsthand that different isn't worse. All our children can gain greatly by seeing other children cope and succeed, the more so if those other children have a wide range of different abilities, ethnicities, interests, geographical origins, and cultures. "

A major argument advanced by private school and voucher supporters is that we have, under another very successful program, done exactly what proposed school vouchers would do, without harm to public universities or to church/state separation or liberty. Veterans since World War II have had various public funding, usually known as GI Bill educational benefits, for going to whatever institution of higher learning they wish. And Notre Dame or Bob Jones University can be chosen as easily as State University. But the comparison of vouchers with the veterans' benefits misses a crucial set of differences: Veterans are adults making choices that are optional, including the choice to attend at all. As adults, they are full citizens, entitled to make choices that may not be deemed wise or in the best interests of the society at large. But children are generally unable to decide with any effective power of their own how much to let the beliefs of their parents affect their educational decisions—and parents deciding for their children is not the equivalent of adult veterans deciding for themselves.

An occasional argument advanced by voucher supporters against church/state objections is that education is a local matter, not a matter to be addressed by the federal government or the federal courts. That argument ignores the Fourteenth Amendment (and the bloody Civil War that led to it), which proclaimed in 1868 that the rights of a citizen of the United States cannot be abridged by state or local governments. And many state constitutions explicitly protect religious liberty. The other major basis for supporting public schools and opposing vouchers is, as already noted, that vouchers would encourage destructive segregation in our society. Taking tax dollars out of public schools and sending those dollars to private schools, even nonreligious institutions, would greatly increase the chances that students would spend most of their time with others much like themselves. Racial segregation has proven in the past to be extremely effective in undercutting justice, and voluntary segregation along racial, ethnic, class, sexual orientation, political, or religious lines would be harmful as well. Our society is strengthened by having most of our citizens educated in settings where they rub shoulders with people quite unlike themselves and where a common curriculum, with more or less consistent standards and with guaranteed access for all, prevails. Tax incentives for people to abandon this common education would unmistakably weaken it, making it most likely that public education would soon be reserved only for those with expensive problems and for those whose parents are too lazy or ignorant to move them. To those who say a common, standard curriculum, with free access to all, could be required as a condition of vouchers the question must be, how will that be any better or any freer than what we have now? Public schools need more resources and more public support, not less. A much more fractured society, with much less practical understanding of what other people are like, would be the result of vouchers.

And, as much as many secular parents might believe it would benefit our own children in some ways to be educated apart from others with irrational religious beliefs, it seems likely that even our own children would lose more than they would gain by being segregated—and for similar reasons.

Moral Education

All parents must of course have primary responsibility for the moral education of their children, including encouraging and supporting social institutions and organizations that have moral education as part of their purpose. While other essays in this book address moral education more generally, this essay will offer advice for secular parents on the role public schools should play in moral education. One frequent false belief is that public schools are prevented from engaging in moral education by separation of church and state. If moral education were dependent on religious beliefs, that might be true—but it isn't.

Religious believers often think morals come ultimately from God, but that ultimate basis need not be part of the education, and of course those of us without any religious beliefs don't agree about the source of morals anyway. No God is needed for—and it can even be reasonably argued that religion interferes with—moral development. How we treat each other, whether we lie or have integrity, whether we care about what is right and follow our code of right and wrong—all of this can and should be taught in public schools. Good teachers have always helped their students develop self-respect, an understanding of justice and fair play, respect for differences, and moral understanding. Good parents should encourage and appreciate this. Education certainly means more than making students acquire facts or information. The main goal of education should always be to learn how to learn, to become an independent thinker. While teaching students to think, any good teacher will always also teach them to treat themselves and others wisely and well. No secular parent can hope to do this alone, but every parent should consciously plan to do it.

> 66 Despite myths to the contrary, separation is not a matter of being careful not to offend either people without religion or people who follow a minority religion. 99

Supporting Separation of Church and State in Public Schools

Every citizen benefits from separation of church and state or, in the case of public schools, from the separation of religious education from common public education. Despite myths to the contrary, separation is not a matter of being careful not to offend either people without religion or people who follow a minority religion. Nor is separation of church and state an anti-religious principle. "Secular" means "not based on religion"—it doesn't mean "hostile to religion." As every public school teacher and every parent should know, the purpose of separation is to protect religious liberty. As government becomes involved in religion, interpretations of the true meaning of "God" and "faith" inevitably drift toward one narrowly defined denominational vision. Many Christian denominations in the United States, including Baptists and Catholics, have actively supported separation to prevent their own religious identities being pushed aside by a different concept of God.

> " "Secular" means "not based on religion"—it doesn't mean "hostile to religion." As every public school teacher and every parent should know, the purpose of separation is to *protect* religious liberty. "

The Southern Baptist Conference understood the point so well that it included separation of church and state as one of its founding principles. The Southern Baptists adopted, in their "Baptist Faith and Message," these words: "The church should not resort to the civil power to carry on its work. . . . The state has no right to impose penalties for religious opinions of any kind. The state has no right to impose taxes for the support of any form of religion." Only by consistently denying agents of government, including public school teachers, the right to make decisions about religion is our religious liberty secure.

There are four basic ideas that together form the basic logical underpinnings of separation of church and state:

1. Not all U.S. citizens hold the same opinions on religion and on important matters related to religion (like whether there is a God and, if so, what god's nature is; or, how or when or whether to worship God; or what God says to us about how to live). Everyone thinks he or she is right when it comes to religion. But not all citizens have the same beliefs on important religious matters.

2. Human judgment is imperfect. For Catholics, the Pope is sometimes considered an exception, with regard to official matters of doctrine, but even Catholics, like

all the rest of us, don't believe that human voters and human legislators always know what God wants us to do. The Bible is quite clear on this point: "Judge not, that ye be not judged" (Mt 7:1). Most other books held sacred by followers of different religions also make this clear. The question is not whether *God's* judgment is perfect—only whether *man's* is.

3. Religious truth cannot be determined by votes or by force. In the United States, neither a majority of citizens nor the government acting on the majority's behalf can make religious decisions for individuals. Anyone who might disagree with this idea should consider this question: If a nationwide vote were taken this fall and 99 percent of U.S. voters disagreed with you on a religious matter, would that change your mind? If 99 percent of the citizens wanted this country to adopt Catholicism or Methodism or Islam or atheism as the "right" religious point of view, would you accept their decision? Would that convince you? And it's not just voting, it's the law itself, the power of government, in question here. One need only consider the poor guy in Afghanistan who was almost convicted and put to death in 2006 for the "crime" of changing his religious beliefs.

4. Freedom, especially religious liberty, is worth having and protecting.

It would seem difficult if not impossible for any citizen who understands U.S. political philosophy to disagree with any of these four ideas, and it is equally hard to understand how anyone who agrees with all four would oppose separation of church and state. Since the fight waged in Virginia in 1784–1785 by James Madison and others—a struggle that almost certainly produced the archetype for the religious liberty established by the First Amendment—it has been clear that letting majorities or governments decide religious matters risks destroying religious liberty.

As a leader in that local battle, Madison wrote "A Memorial and Remonstrance," a petition signed by enough people all over Virginia to defeat "A Bill Establishing a Provision for Teachers of the Christian Religion." That bill, supported by a group led by Patrick Henry, was one designed to do what some claim the First Amendment does: support Christianity without choosing among denominations. The logic and facts that caused those wanting a "multiple establishment" to lose in Virginia are the best reasons for rejecting those interpretations of the First Amendment.

What does this have to do with separation in public schools? Keep in mind that the Virginia bill was intended to *support Christian teachers* and read a little of what Madison wrote:

> Who does not see that the same authority which can establish Christianity in exclusion of all other religions may establish, with the same ease, any particular sect of Christians in exclusion of all other sects? That the same authority which can force a citizen to contribute threepence only of his property for the support of any one establishment may force him to conform to any other establishment in all cases whatsoever?

Madison understood that governments must stay out of matters related to religion, or liberty is at peril, and this is at least as true regarding public schools as in any other case.

Many people do oppose separation of religion and public education, of course, but most do so because they lack good understanding of the principle and its purpose. The most common misunderstanding is that separation is designed to protect religious minorities, especially atheists, from being offended. Offending people without good reason isn't ever a good idea, but that *isn't* the point of separation. Separation is necessary to protect everyone's religious liberty.

> 66 Students can pray, including saying grace before lunch or praying that they'll pass the algebra test (though studying longer might be more effective). Students can bring a Bible or other religious book to school and can read it in free time at school. 99

Another set of misunderstandings relates to which behaviors are actually prohibited by separation, especially in public schools. Students can pray, including saying grace before lunch or praying that they'll pass the algebra test (though studying longer might be more effective). Students can bring a Bible or other religious book to school and can read it in free time at school. Teachers can also pray if they wish. Rules that do apply, reasonably enough, include the following:

- Students may not disrupt classes to pray or witness about their religious or anti-religious beliefs.
- Students may not proselytize others who don't want the attention.
- Teachers may not lead students in prayer or direct students to pray or not to pray.
- Teachers and administrators may not use government property or school time to promote or oppose religion.

Restrictions on teachers and administrators are the most important ones, and they are in every case intended to ensure that no one is using the power of government to impose religious decisions on students.[3]

Secular parents owe it to their children and to their society to support public schools, to plan thoughtfully for and support the moral education of their children, and to support separation of church and state—especially the separation of religion and education in public schools.

Chapter Two Endnotes

1. See Tanquist, "Choosing Your Battles" for another perspective on the mixed marriage.
2. See "Building the Secular Community" in Chapter 9.
3. Much more detailed information on the exact rules is available from Americans United for Separation of Church and State (*www.au.org* or 202-466-3234).

Additional Resources
Books

- Hamilton, Virginia. *In the Beginning—Creation Stories from Around the World.* Harcourt Children's Books, 1988. Probably the finest volume of comparative religion available for children, *In the Beginning* is just what is needed: a book that celebrates creation stories of all kinds as tales that are fascinating, imaginative—and mythic. The Judeo-Christian creation story is mixed among creation myths of Native American, Chinese, Tahitian, African, and Australian origin, among others. As no one story is denigrated or exalted, children can examine the concept of myth without indoctrination or objectionable overlays of punishment and reward. Heads up: The myths have (fortunately) not been scrubbed clean of anti-female or racist themes, which can and should generate even richer discussion. Exquisite watercolor illustrations by Barry Moser. Read aloud to children as young as early elementary age, or self-reading for grades 4 and up.
- Reed, Christine, with Patricia Hoertdoerfer. *Exploring World Religions with Junior High Youth.* Unitarian Universalist Association, 1997. Explores the development and features of different belief systems. Ages 11–15.
- Bennett, Helen. *Humanism—What's That? A Book for Curious Kids.* Prometheus, 2005. While learning about various religions, don't forget to learn a bit about disbelief as an authentic worldview. This book provides a good, accessible introduction to humanism for late-elementary-aged kids.
- Brockman, Chris. *What About Gods?* Prometheus, 1979. A classic, a bit dated, and at times overly pat in its answers, this book nonetheless gets into the reasons so many people believe in gods—an important part of building empathy and

understanding. Also addresses the fact that knowledge in recent centuries has made the god hypothesis ever less tenable.

- Armstrong, Karen. *A History of God.* Knopf, 1994. A brilliant exposition of the 4,000-year history of monotheism by one of the most lucid writers and thinkers of our time. Armstrong notes in the Introduction that after years as a nun, she "left the religious life, and, once freed of the burden of failure and inadequacy, I felt my belief in God slip quietly away." She retained her interest in religion, eventually returning to the idea of God as a pragmatic, self-created construct. Start with this one, then move on to *The Battle for God, The Spiral Staircase,* and the rest. Adults.
- Also recommended, by Karen Armstrong: *A Short History of Myth.* Canongate, 2005.
- DVD: *Jesus Christ Superstar* (1973). Music by Andrew Lloyd Webber, lyrics by Tim Rice. Directed by Norman Jewison. *The Ten Commandments* terrified and evangelized millions with an Angel of Death, rivers of blood, and an admittedly impressive (for 1956) parting of the Red Sea, while anti-Semitism and blood (is there a theme here?) got new life in Mel Gibson's *Passion.* So when it comes to family movie night, skip the indoctrination fests in favor of the rich, conflicted, and naturalistic retelling of the story of Jesus's final days in *Jesus Christ Superstar.* If you can endure the spastic-hippie choreography, you'll find a "passion" centered on a socially conscientious Judas who accuses Jesus of getting too enamored of himself and his supposed divinity—and ignoring their mission to help the poor. No miracles, no resurrection, and a balanced presentation of Christ, who is at turns wise, selfish, loving, raging, frightened, heartless, and courageous (not to mention, according to my daughter at one point, "a cutie"). Make sure kids know the basic story outline before hitting "play"—and keep a finger near "pause" for the many, many fabulous questions that pop up during showtime. Works for children ages 6–18.

Websites

- Religious Tolerance (www.religioustolerance.org)
  A comprehensive and evenhanded clearinghouse of information about belief systems. Includes definitions, histories, belief tenets, and practices of every significant belief system—even many insignificant ones—plus over 3,000 essays on a wide range of topics. Great resource for school projects that include a religious component (e.g., reports on conflict in the Mideast, stem cell research, or the abortion debate). Defines religious tolerance as "extending religious freedom to people of all religious traditions, even though you may disagree with their beliefs and/or practices." Notes that tolerance "does not require you to accept all

religions as equally true" and offers as one of its mottos, "When people deviate from reality, others often get hurt." Ages 12 and up.

- Beliefnet (www.beliefnet.com) Belief-O-Matic Quiz

  Home page has an "aura" of touchy-feely/spirituality/karma/aura/soul-healing/what's-your-sign—not my particular ball of cheese—but the site includes extensive information about all belief systems. BEST FEATURE: the Belief-O-Matic quiz. Asks twenty multiple choice worldview questions, then spits out a list of belief systems and your percentage of overlap. I for one come up 100% Secular Humanist, 98% Unitarian Universalist, 84% Liberal Quaker, and more Jewish (38%) than Catholic (16%). Fun and fascinating for age 14 and up.

- Bible Gateway (www.biblegateway.com)

  There are many times when quick access to the bible is useful to a secularist, whether self-education, weighing or defending against religious arguments, or understanding a religious incident or event. Bible Gateway is the best searchable database, even equipped with all major versions of the bible for comparisons. Well worth a peek and a bookmark.

Holidays and Celebrations

Introduction

Imagine life without cycles or landmarks of any kind—just birth, followed by a long, grey line of 27,941 days, then death.

Okay, it wouldn't be *that* bad. But fortunately it's not an issue: We live in wheels within wheels, cycling through weeks, months, seasons, and years, each of them marked with days and events we declare to be special. Some are fixed by nature, like birthdays, solstices, and equinoxes—which celebrate the return of the planet to a certain precise orbital spot—and seasons, a slower, more majestic ticking that (at my latitude, anyway) gives a person a glimpse at the cosmic wristwatch.

The recognition of life landmarks, such as naming, rites of passage, marriage, anniversaries, and death, evolved under religious auspices—but contributor Jane Wynne Willson shows that there's no problem finding secular expressions that are every bit as meaningful and satisfying in her essay "Humanist Ceremonies."

Then there is the wheel of holidays—which, more than anything else, is the one by which kids measure the passing of time. That her birthday is on November 17th means nothing to my 5-year-old, but "just after Halloween" works fine (until every November 1st, when she gets miffed at our lack of precision). Like the celebrations of personal landmarks, most of the holidays ("holy days") have religious origins—first pagan, then Christian—and most have developed entirely secular expressions. Add to those a few special days with purely secular roots and you have a calendar of secular celebrations introduced in the essay "Losing the 'Holy' and Keeping the 'Day.'"

The rest of the chapter is devoted to a question that's a constant source of lively debate in the freethought community: Isn't it better to simply skip holidays with loud religious overtones, like Easter and Christmas? And what exactly is to be done with (*gasp*) *The Santa Myth?* This latter kerfuffle is the subject of a lighthearted point/counterpoint titled "The Question of the Claus—Should the Santa Story Stay or Go in Secular Families?" Tom Flynn, editor of *Free Inquiry,* is counsel for the prosecution, and I take the side of truth and justice.

Ex-Mormon and blogger extraordinaire Noell Hyman (AgnosticMom. com) sees us out with her own take on the question in "To Easter Bunny or Not to Easter Bunny?"—and be sure to visit the Additional Resources for outstanding books and links for secular family celebrations.

Humanist Ceremonies

Jane Wynne Willson

CEREMONIES HAVE ALWAYS existed to mark important events in people's lives, even in quite primitive societies. Birth, puberty, marriage, and death can all be thought of as times of transition and, as such, have long been celebrated as "rites of passage" within families and communities all over the world.

As one would expect, the form these ceremonies take will naturally reflect the fundamental beliefs of a particular society and culture. In the Western world and beyond, Christianity has played an important role in ceremonial events, and religious procedures have come to dominate rites of passage.

For families who hold no supernatural beliefs, a religious wedding or funeral service is quite inappropriate and can be an uncomfortable and even distressing experience. Those humanists who want to mark an important event with a ceremony, to give the occasion some formality, feel the need for a secular alternative free of religious association. The growth in the popularity of humanist and nonreligious ceremonies in many countries at the present time is proof that there is a deep, though at times latent, need for such provision.

Terms and Definitions

Ceremony

Throughout this chapter I have decided to distinguish between the words *ceremony* and *celebration*. I use the term *ceremony* to describe an occasion when family and friends get together to mark an event of importance, such as a birth, marriage, or death, often called *rite of passage*.

Celebration

In the United States in particular, *celebration* is often used in the same sense, which can be confusing. *Celebration* originally denoted "observance" or "marking," as the corresponding verb is used in the sentence, "Do you celebrate Christmas in your family?" But in more general usage a *celebration* suggests a joyful occasion for congratulation and recognition or for thanks and appreciation. Celebrations are more in the nature of parties involving friends, colleagues, and family. They could include awards for academic, artistic, or sporting achievements or special awards for bravery.

Certainly there is often a celebratory element in the major rites of passage. Parents usually like to celebrate the arrival of a new baby (or sometimes an older child in the case of adoption) and to welcome him or her into the family. They are proud to celebrate the transition of their son or daughter from childhood to adulthood. Couples who have decided to share their lives want to celebrate the event among their family and friends. Even a funeral ceremony is an opportunity to celebrate a life that has ended. But there are exceptions. Couples who are getting divorced sometimes have a ceremony to mark a new stage in their lives as joint parents rather than partners. This is likely to be a dignified and moving statement of commitment and intent rather than a celebration.

In the widest sense of the word, celebrations can contribute to happiness and well-being in family life and in society so they are of particular importance to secular families. One of the basic ideals of Humanism is to make this life as pleasant as possible for everyone alive now and for generations as yet unborn. After all, it is the only life we expect to experience. In 1876, the great U.S. atheist and orator Robert G. Ingersoll wrote that "Happiness is the only good; the time to be happy is now, and the way to be happy is to make others so."

Ritual

Ritual is another term that is sometimes, although by no means always, used in a derogatory way. This describes a set framework and familiar series of actions that many people can find reassuring and helpful at moments of emotion or distress. The repetitive nature of church liturgy may have the same effect for religious people, but certainly not for humanists. The big difference in humanist ceremonies is that by their very nature they are personal and individual. The words are not texts from a religious book but are chosen to suit the personalities and circumstances of the people involved.

Humanist Ceremonies

For humanists, the decision to hold a ceremony is a very personal one. There is no obligation one way or the other. If parents want to investigate what is involved and to consider whether they would like to arrange one, the best thing to do is to meet up with other families and hear their views and experiences. National humanist, ethical, secular, and atheist organizations will furnish information about their availability in a particular country or state and will explain any legal requirements that may be necessary. If a humanist celebrant is not available locally, a family can usually arrange to organize a ceremony themselves. Alternatively, they can seek the help of a Unitarian or other liberal minister who is willing to conduct a nonreligious ceremony for them.

In a book about secular parenting, the most directly relevant ceremonies are those held to welcome new babies and those that mark the transition from childhood to adulthood. However, wedding ceremonies may be of interest, particularly in cases of remarriage, and funeral ceremonies are likely to occur at some time within families. The role children can play in these is important. So I shall write a brief account of all four rites of passage, stressing that this can only give a flavor of the kind of ceremonies that are already being enjoyed by humanists in many parts of the world. The beauty of our situation is that the way is wide open for any parents to create ceremonies that feel right for them and their children together as a family, if that is their wish. Humanists are not governed by convention or by church authorities.

> " The beauty of our situation [as humanists] is that the way is wide open for any parents to create ceremonies that feel right for them and their children together as a family, if that is their wish. "

Naming and Welcoming Ceremonies

Of the main rites of passage, the naming or welcoming ceremony is usually the least formal. Often these are more in the nature of parties for close family and friends, held perhaps in a grandparent's garden or living room, or in the parents' own home. It is a happy occasion that celebrates the baby or young child's arrival in the family, whether by birth or adoption. At the same time, the parents can express their commitment to the child's well being and their undertaking to care for him or her through the long years to adulthood, or for as long as is necessary. "Supporting adults," the equivalent of Christian godparents, are usually there and they can pledge that they will take a special interest in the child, through good times and bad. Sometimes older siblings are included in the ceremony. The giving of a name to the baby is usually part of the proceedings, even if the ceremony is held when the baby is several weeks or even months old and the name has been registered and in use for a while. There is often some symbolic act such as the lighting of a candle or planting of a tree. Music can be played and poems read.

Coming-of-Age Ceremonies

These are essentially ceremonies to mark the transition from childhood to adulthood. It is interesting that in Norway they are by far the most popular ceremonies, whereas in most other countries they do not exist. There was already a well-established religious coming-of-age ceremony for 14-year-old children in Norway, preceded by courses run by the established Lutheran church. The Norwegian Humanist Association campaigned hard for an alternative secular ceremony to be allowed, and this was achieved some years ago. Now, in town halls throughout Norway, many hundreds of humanist "ordinands," smartly dressed and glowing with pride, take part in a magnificent and popular ceremony each year, having attended a short course in citizenship and ethical matters run by humanist teachers and counselors in the weeks leading up to the occasion.

> 66 In town halls throughout Norway, many hundreds of humanist "ordinands," smartly dressed and glowing with pride, take part in a magnificent and popular ceremony each year, having attended a short course in citizenship and ethical matters run by humanist teachers. 99

This solemn but happy ceremony, held at a period in a young person's life that can often present difficulties, is especially valuable. The ceremony can provide a staging post on the child's road toward independence. At the same time it can help the parents adjust to their changing role and the prospect of their child's eventual departure from the family home. There is a clear challenge here for humanists in other countries to follow Norway's lead. Where one or both humanist parents have been brought up in cultures or religious traditions where ceremonies are held at puberty, this would be a natural progression. An example of such a situation might be for those from a Jewish background who would be familiar with the Bar/Bat Mitzvah ceremony. It might be a bit more difficult to introduce a secular coming-of-age ceremony from scratch where there is not already a tradition, but the benefits and beauty of such a rite would make such an effort well worth the undertaking.

Wedding Ceremonies

In most societies throughout history, weddings have taken place before the arrival of children in a family. At least that has been the theory! Nowadays, in Western societies, it is increasingly the case that children are present at, and even take part in, their parents' wedding ceremony. It is sometimes the arrival of one or more children that gives parents the idea that it might after all be sensible to establish a more stable family background than can usually be provided by two people living together without the security of marriage or an alternative legal framework. Sometimes the wedding may be the result of pressure from the extended family or friends. More often, it is at the remarriage of one or both parents after bereavement or divorce that children are present and can play an important role. This is particularly the case where stepfamilies are involved and the ceremony itself can go some way toward helping children adapt to new and at times difficult family situations.

In secular families, the form a wedding ceremony takes needs to be in keeping with the couple's deeply held beliefs. In a humanist ceremony, they can express their feelings for each other and their aspirations for their future together in their own words. They can do this in the presence of their families and friends in a place of their own choosing. The ceremony can reflect their serious commitment and their shared responsibility, particularly where children are involved.

In some countries and states, humanist weddings are now officially recognized and include registration; in others, official registration is separately performed and the humanist ceremony that follows still has no legal status. However, for the couple involved, it is the humanist wedding ceremony rather than the formal registration of their marriage that is the meaningful and memorable event, marking the start of their shared life together. This applies whether either or both have been married before and whether they are heterosexual or gay.

Funeral Ceremonies

Humanist funeral ceremonies provide an opportunity for families and friends to meet together to celebrate the life of someone they have loved, to say their last farewells, and, at the same time, to help each other by remembering and grieving together. This all applies equally to both adults and children.

Children need to be involved when someone close to them dies. The death and the funeral ceremony should be looked on as a family event, like other family events but this time rather a sad one. It is doing them no kindness at all to exclude them from the funeral and the preparations for the ceremony. They need something to occupy themselves during the unreal days leading up to the funeral. Even quite young children can enjoy helping in small practical ways such as making cakes or biscuits for the wake, or party afterwards, or picking and arranging flowers.

If a humanist celebrant is to take the funeral, he or she will visit the house to meet the family, to find out the kind of ceremony they would like and, most importantly, to listen and build up a picture of the deceased. Children can often help to choose an appropriate poem or song, contribute a touching or amusing anecdote, and sometimes they are keen to write something themselves to be read at the ceremony.

Children in secular families are likely to ask a lot of questions. They will need honest answers, particularly if well-intentioned religious friends have told them, for example, that their Grandpa has gone to Heaven and they will see him again one day. They will have to be told that they will be saying good-bye at the ceremony, but they will always be able to go on talking about Grandpa and remembering all the good times they had with him. They will need reassurance and comforting like anyone else.

Conclusion

Ceremonies can be seen as an important and enriching feature of life in many families throughout the world. In religious homes, they obviously follow the various religious traditions, but religions do not hold a monopoly of ceremonial practices that have existed since time immemorial. Once they have been disentangled from their religious packaging, ceremonies are as fitting in secular families as elsewhere. Humanist, ethical, and secular organizations can take pride in having gone some way toward restoring ceremonies and celebrations to their rightful place in society as a natural part of family life.

Losing the "Holy"
and Keeping the "Day"

Dale McGowan, Ph.D.

YEARS, DECADES, EVEN SEASONS are abstractions to most kids. It's holidays that mark the passing of time in childhood, letting kids know where they are and what's coming. Fall began sometime in the end of September, I knew, but it wasn't until I walked into the classroom on the first of October and saw that Mrs. Mawdsley[1] had festooned the place with orange and black felt that I felt the rhythm of the year begin. Those pumpkins and bats would be followed like clockwork a month later with turkeys and pilgrims, then (in olden tymes) by the Jolly Old Fat Man Himself. Then came New Year's, Valentine's Day, St. Patrick's Day—in addition to the various things they celebrate, the holidays shape the year.

There's not the slightest reason for secular families to forgo this lovely slow ticking of the calendar. Much to the consternation of a few fundamentalist wagon-circlers, many holidays that once had a religious overlay quickly find a nonreligious form as well, especially the fun and meaningful ones. St. Patrick's Day is said to have once been associated with a saint—can't recall which one—instead of just general Irishness. Same with St. Valentine's Day. And Easter, before it developed the admittedly weird tradition of colorful chicken eggs hidden by a rabbit, supposedly had some religious tie-in as well.

Christmas, though—I'm pretty sure that one's always been ours.

Now now, uncircle those wagons, believers. It's *good* that you've found a way to use old pagan rituals to articulate your worldview. It's what we all do, and should do: borrow and redefine the inheritances of the past to suit our changing human needs. It's beautiful. It's fun. I wouldn't want to take away your right to do that for *anything*—just as I'm sure you support my right to do it *my* way. So we're cool, right?

Okay then. Happy holidays.

There have been many attempts to forge new holidays free of religious overtones, with mixed results. The most effective and meaningful attempts seem to be those connected to the past in some way. Something that redefines instead of creating from scratch always seems somehow more authentically grounded. On the other hand, new perspectives, especially the wonder of the universe illuminated by science, can offer new things to celebrate and contemplate, and new ways to do so.

Below is a list of eleven holidays that lend themselves to secular celebration. If you do it right, your family can experience all the wonder, spirit, fun, and goodwill that religious holidays provide, with a little something extra thrown in.

1. DARWIN DAY (February 12)

Charles Darwin was born on the same afternoon as another worldshaking freethinker, Abraham Lincoln—February 12, 1809. The celebration of Darwin Day has been picking up steam as we approach 2009, the bicentennial of his birth and sesquicentennial (150th) of the publication of the book that changed the world, the *Origin*. Darwin Day events celebrate the wonder of science and the glory of human achievement. Some outstanding Darwin Day websites are listed at the end of the chapter, with games, activities, and readings for kids of all ages. Not to demean any particular other February holidays, but a little celebration of science beats the heck out of cherry trees and log cabins.

2. VERNAL EQUINOX (March 20-21, Northern Hemisphere) and EASTER (first Sunday after the full moon following the vernal equinox, I kid you not. Pagan enough for ya?)

Easter lends itself perfectly well to the aforementioned unholy marriage of rabbit and hen—but there's another option, and quite an intriguing one. The vernal equinox is a bona fide celestial event. Because our planet spins like a tipping top as it orbits the sun, the days grow longer and the nights shorter for half of the year, then reverse for the other half. On just two days a year, in the middle of those two cycles, day and night are balanced at twelve hours each—the equinoxes of spring and fall. The mid-March moment of equipoise, when the North Pole begins tipping back toward the sun, has been observed for thousands of years with rites of spring rejoicing in the resurrection of the natural world. The outstanding website Secular Seasons[2] notes that "many [Mediterranean] religions had stories of a man-god, born of a virgin, who was killed and reborn at this time each year, and this day was often connected to the worship of many fertility goddesses with names like Eostre, Ishtar, and Ostra (hence "Easter"). All the same incentives for celebration are present for secular families, as well as an additional opportunity to grasp the poetry of the top-like whirling of our planetary path through the solar system. See Secular Seasons for great family activities.[3]

3. APRIL FOOL'S DAY (June 3)

Who says holidays can only be built around gratitude, introspection, and group hugs? Fine, no one says that. But if we're going to celebrate what it means to be human, why not celebrate foolishness? We are a silly species, after all, every one of us prone to self-deception, gullibility, and boneheadedness. *Every one of us.* If you exclude yourself from that fine company, all I can say is, "Oh, look—there's something on your shirt." I know ultra-rationalists who follow a skeptical tirade with the news that their moon is ascending through Virgo. I believed for *years* that M&Ms wouldn't melt in my hands, despite daily evidence to the contrary. We are *all* fools. Accepting the fact that witlessness is our unanimous birthright is a fine reason to celebrate April Fool's Day in a big way. Fall for the traps your kids set for you and set a few for them as well. Just be sure to laugh at yourself twice as much as you laugh at anyone else.

4. EARTH DAY (date in committee)

Poor Earth Day. Organizers can't even agree on an official date and have now hunkered into the Always April 22nd camp and the Vernal Equinoxers, with a third contingent lobbying for a move to the summer solstice. (See? Silly species.) Doesn't matter—choose your favorite date and recognize the fragility and beauty of our planet as a family by planting trees, cleaning up a park, rafting a river, climbing a tree, hiking a trail, writing an indignant letter to a newspaper editor or politician, working in the garden, visiting a farm or zoo or aquarium . . . the possibilities are endless.

5. SUMMER SOLSTICE (around June 21 in the Northern Hemisphere)

Also known as Midsummer, this is the day with the longest period of daylight. For thousands of years it has been a celebration of happiness, contentment, and security. The crops are in the ground, the snow is long gone, hunting's good, and the baseball season's in full swing. Weddings and (other) fertility rituals have traditionally been associated with Midsummer Day, which is why June is still the biggest month for tying the knot. Call your local Humanist celebrant for a secular wedding—or just have a family picnic and keep living in sin!

6. AUTUMNAL EQUINOX (around September 23 in the Northern Hemisphere)

The first day of spring is a time of rebirth, so it's natural to look at first day of autumn as a time of slowing down, of reflection on the preciousness of life as the natural world moves into dormancy. Like the Vernal Equinox, the Autumnal is a moment when daylight and dark are balanced at twelve hours each—but this time the North Pole is beginning its tip *away* from the sun. Temperatures start their descent and daylight begins its retreat. This, not Thanksgiving (when the harvest is generally two months past and snow is often flying) is the sensible time for a dinner to celebrate the harvest and to recognize the changes associated with autumn: the first changing leaves, that first chilly wind in the evening, squirrels turning from tree-trunk tag to serious nut-gathering, geese consulting their Lonely Planet Guide to the Southern States. By Thanksgiving, after all, these things are done deals.

It's a natural (and beautiful) time to visit a cemetery to remember those who are no longer with us or to take a nature walk to appreciate the changing leaves. Hold a fresh-food harvest potluck in your neighborhood. Find a bridge or high building and (after taking all necessary precautions, people) do a pumpkin drop. Line up an online penpal in the Southern Hemisphere to exchange greetings and observations as he or she celebrates the coming of spring.

7. THANKSGIVING (fourth Thursday in November)

There should be no difficulty in secularly observing a holiday dedicated to gratitude. We can express to each other our thankfulness *for* each other, for our good fortune, and for life itself. No eavesdropping deity required. There is an additional opportunity to note that the Puritan pilgrims were pursuing the kind of freedom of religious observance to which secularists should be devoted—fleeing harassment and religious persecution in England and heading to the New World where they were free at last to burn witches. Okay, leave that part out.

8. WINTER SOLSTICE (December 21–22 in the Northern Hemisphere)

I wouldn't be completely surprised if Jamaicans were still flat-earthers. You could conceivably disbelieve the spherical earth in the low latitudes. But up where I sit in the northern plains, it's a whirling ball we're on for sure, and in late December it gets to feeling like the atmosphere itself has been pared away, leaving nothing at all between our chapped, upturned faces and the brilliant stars. Awesome, that. Downright humbling. Many traditions recognized the winter solstice—the shortest day of the year—as a time for celebration and anticipation. It was at this point each year that the sun would end its long retreat and begin moving toward us again. This "return" of the sun was good reason for celebration, for it meant that spring, though a long way off, was inevitable.

Freethought communities in recent years have begun to adopt the winter solstice celebration as a favorite, probably to have a Hanukkah/Kwanzaa/Ramadanesque alternative to the Christmas juggernaut. Whatever the reason, it makes a great excuse for a midwinter bash. Most of the accoutrements of secular Christmas celebrations transfer over just fine—gifts, cards, goodwill, peace on Earth, family, even a solstice tree. Online resources and books are growing.

9. FESTIVUS (December 23 . . . or whenever)

The most promising new holiday in centuries, Festivus was invented (despite the stern denial of "Festivus historians") for a 1997 Christmas episode of *Seinfeld* as "a Festivus for the rest of us!"—an alternative to the commercialism and other agonies of the Christmas season. Though there is no central Festivian doctrine, typical elements include gathering around the aluminum Festivus Pole with those you *really* want to be with (as opposed to many other holiday gatherings) for such heartwarming traditions as the Airing of Grievances and the Feats of Strength.

The idea of a completely satirical holiday has taken off like a shot, with books, websites, and celebrations around the world—and around the calendar. Some celebrate Festivus on the summer solstice, the vernal equinox, or a randomly selected Thursday in July—or as many as six times a year. Why not? Unorthodoxy is the only dogma, so have a ball.

10. CHRISTMAS (December 25)

Yikes! A flaming arrow just went by my ear—and I don't even know from which side. But it's true. Christmas has an entirely secular persona parallel to the sacred one. No, not the excesses of buying and greed—I'm talking about the joyful humanistic spirit that sets in that time of year. It's surely no coincidence that holy days emphasizing family and charity and peace and goodwill are sprinkled through the shortest and latest and coldest days of the year, when we have to rely on each other to make it through. Despite the shopping and insanity, if only for a few moments, just about everyone succumbs gladly to the best of human impulses at this time of year. The thin veneer of religion is easily stripped away to reveal natural, honest, human virtues of which religion is just one articulation. That's why the "holy days" have so naturally and easily secularized to "holidays," these celebrations of human hope and goodness in the midst of sometimes painful realities. So have yourself a merry little Christmas, without getting too hung up on whether this or that symbol or ritual has religious roots.

11. HOLIDAYS FROM OTHER TRADITIONS AND CULTURES

Why not celebrate a holiday from somewhere else? It's a great way to knock down walls of culture and nationality and *especially* valuable for removing our home-grown Isms and Anities from the center of the universe. Have a Chinese New Year party. Celebrate Boxing Day, whatever that is (the British don't even seem to know for sure). Halloween not creepy enough? Try Mexico's Day of the Dead (November 1–2). Observe X-Day on July 5, the day the world did *not* end in 1998, despite satirical predictions that it would, or toast Queen Elizabeth on her birthday (April 21—makes a nice merge with Earth Day), or Buddha on his (celebrated on the full moon of the month Baisakh—sometime in April or May). For a nice exercise in comparative religion, consider joining Cubans on December 17 as they somehow celebrate both the Catholic Saint Lazarus and the African god Babalú Ayé.

There's a reason this kind of cultural stewpotting drives the religious right insane. By recognizing the validity of the many, you make the one less and less sacred—the very sort of thing that could end us up with a more reasonable world.

Some of these holidays may seem artificial and forced at first. I'm sure the bunny-and-egg thing crossed a few eyes at the start, too, not to mention a virgin giving birth. If you want to stick with the traditional holidays, no sweat. If you want to give something else a try, as well or instead, knock yourself out. Find the right fit for your family and friends. If you find a new holiday that feels satisfying and enjoyable, do it again the next year. And there's the key to turning a new holiday into a beloved family tradition: Make it fun, make it meaningful, and do it twice. Keep it up, and who knows—twenty years from now we might all be singing Festivus carols on the White House lawn around the National Pole.

Point/Counterpoint

The Question of the Claus—Should the Santa Story Stay or Go in Secular Families?

Point: Put the Claus Away

Tom Flynn

Eighty-five percent of U.S. 4-year-olds believe in Santa Claus. But does the myth hurt or help in raising independent thinkers? Amazingly, science offers little guidance. Although it has become a nearly universal rite of passage for U.S. preadolescents to discover that the most cherished belief of their childhoods was an elaborate parental lie, few researchers have studied the phenomenon—or, perhaps more precisely, have opted to publish what they have found.

Hard data are so sparse that Santa's defenders still trot out a famous child psychologist's 1971 pronouncement that "the small child should be able to believe in Santa . . . to hate reality is a likely consequence of being forced to give up fantasies too early." This appeared not in a scientific publication, but in the mainstream women's magazine *Ladies' Home Journal;* the famous psychologist in question was Bruno Bettelheim, who would later be discredited for concocting psychiatric principles and diagnoses out of whole cloth, allegedly causing some of his young patients enduring harm. Anyway, if you like unsubstantiated assertions, I'll go with one by Canada's George Brock Chisholm (1896–1971), first director of the World Health Organization, who warned that believing in the Santa myth with its many physical impossibilities could "seriously damage" a child's "whole relationship with reality and whole ability to think clearly in terms of cause and effect."

Still, when the moral arguments are weighed in light of the meager available research, the best course seems clear: "Just say no" to "ho, ho, ho." Here's why:

1. To perpetuate the Santa myth, parents must lie to their kids. We know there's no old man at the North Pole who visits all the world's households in a single night, but that's not what we tell our kids. Yes, Virginia, that's lying. Some parents rationalize it as an innocent sharing of fantasy, but a

1978 study suggested otherwise: It found that children relate to Santa as real, quite differently than they relate to, say, storybook or movie characters. Children relate to Santa as a mundane reality as prosaic—and undeniable—as "a wheelbarrow in the back yard." Clearly, for parents to pass on the Santa myth isn't like passing on a Brothers Grimm fairy tale. It's lying, plain and simple. So don't be surprised if the child who caught you lying about Santa tunes out your other guidance on other issues as adolescence blooms.

There is no excuse for deceiving children. And when, as must happen in conventional families, they find that their parents have lied, they lose confidence in them and feel justified in lying to them.

—Bertrand Russell

2. To buoy belief, adults often stage elaborate deceptions, laying traps for the child's developing intellect. Questioning Santa is the first attempt at critical thinking many children make. Yet parents often smokescreen curious children for asking why there are so many Santas at the mall, or wondering why Santa and Aunt Nell use the same wrapping paper. Frequently, parents punish youngsters for sharing their suspicions injudiciously with schoolmates or siblings. Ambitious parents may go to enormous lengths to bamboozle an inquisitive child into believing for another few months. Whatever else we might say about such parenting strategies, clearly they represent no way to teach critical thinking!

3. The myth encourages lazy parenting and promotes unhealthy fear. Hectoring kids to be good because Santa will detect any transgression that parents may miss is equivalent to warning children to behave because God is watching. The establishment of such parental "coalitions with God" defines a parenting technique that research correlates with negative child development outcomes. Meanwhile a child who's "been bad" (itself a questionable concept) may dread Christmas Eve, expecting a telltale lump of coal to alert parents to some hitherto-overlooked misconduct. (A grade school classmate of mine dreaded the holiday because he expected to be exposed in a misbehavior he had up until then "gotten away with." When Santa failed to "blow him in" with a stocking full of coal, that imposed further corrosive pressure on his naïve view of the world.) Some parents

who recognize the danger in leaning too hard on "You better watch out, you better not cry" may strive to engender belief in Santa while avoiding the myth's "Big Brother" aspects. To those parents I can say only "good luck"; a single hearing of "Santa Claus Is Coming to Town" on the minivan radio en route to the mall can instantly undo all that careful work.

4. The myth makes kids more acquisitive, not less so. Proponents argue that belief in Santa teaches children the "spirit of giving," whatever that is. But a 1982 study, one of few to address this issue, showed conclusively that the myth actually *encourages* selfishness. In that study, children who in other contexts requested unselfish benefits such as health or long life for family members invariably demanded material things when writing to Santa.

5. The Santa myth appears to exploit age-appropriate cognitive patterns that religious children use in forming their ideas of God. Santa—a magical being who sees all and whose judgment can be swayed by shows of good behavior—uncomfortably resembles the way theistic children understand God at the same ages. The secular parent should worry that Santa belief in early childhood *might* bias youngsters toward later uncritical faith.

Some parents say the opposite, arguing that unmasking Santa actually inoculates kids against supernatural beliefs. Again, the available research offers inconclusive guidance. But I can't help noticing that the relationship I suspect between belief in Santa and later religious faith —namely, that belief in the first makes belief in the second more likely—is direct and straightforward. In contrast, the proposed relationship between belief in Santa and later religious disbelief seems contrary, even tortuous. Lacking solid evidence that holding an unsupported belief now makes a child *less* likely to hold another unsupported belief later, why take the risk? Secular parents have a choice . . . and a chance. Research shows that dissuasion works. Children whose parents explicitly, consistently discourage belief in Santa are unlikely to form the belief. So do your kids a favor. Make a conscious decision not to support irresponsible beliefs, and brick up that chimney!

Counterpoint: Santa Claus—the Ultimate Dry Run

Dale McGowan

It's hard to even consider the possibility that Santa isn't real. Everyone seems to believe he is. As a kid, I heard his name in songs and stories and saw him in movies with very high production values. My mom and dad seemed to believe, batted down my doubts, told me he wanted me to be good and that he always knew if I wasn't. And what wonderful gifts I received! Except when they were crappy, which I always figured was my fault somehow. All in all, despite the multiple incredible improbabilities involved in believing he was real, I believed—until the day I decided I cared enough about the truth to ask serious questions, at which point the whole façade fell to pieces. Fortunately, the good things I had credited him with continued coming, but now I knew they came from the people around me, whom I could now properly thank.

Now go back and read that paragraph again, changing the ninth word from *Santa* to *God*. Santa Claus, my secular friends, is the greatest gift a rational worldview ever had. Our culture has constructed a silly and temporary myth parallel to its silly and permanent one. They share a striking number of characteristics, yet the one is cast aside halfway through childhood. And a good thing, too: A middle-aged father looking mournfully up the chimbly along with his sobbing children on yet another giftless Christmas morning would be a sure candidate for a very soft room. *This* culturally pervasive myth is *meant* to be figured out, designed with an expiration date, after which consumption is universally frowned upon.

I'll admit to having stumbled backward into the issue as a parent. My wife and I defaulted into raising our kids with the same myth we'd been raised in (I know, I *know*), considering it ever-so-harmless and fun. Neither of us had experienced the least trauma as kids when the jig was up. To the contrary: We both recall the heady feeling of at last being in on the secret to which so many others, including our younger siblings, were still oblivious. Ahh, the sweet, smug smell of superiority.

But as our son Connor began to exhibit the incipient inklings of Kringledoubt, it occurred to me that something powerful was going on. I began to see the Santa paradigm as an unmissable opportunity—the ultimate dry run for a developing inquiring mind.

My boy was 8 years old when he started in with the classic interrogation: *How does Santa get to all those houses in one night? How does he get in when we don't have a chimney and all the windows are locked and the alarm system is on? Why does he use the same wrapping paper as Mom? All those cookies in one night—his LDL cholesterol must be through the roof!* This is the moment, at the threshold of the question, that the natural inquiry of a child can be primed or choked off. With questions of belief, you have three choices: Feed the child a confirmation, feed the child a disconfirmation—or teach the child to fish.

The "Yes, Virginia" crowd will heap implausible nonsense on the poor child, dismissing her doubts with invocations of magic or mystery or the willful suspension of physical law. Only slightly less problematic is the second choice, the debunker who simply informs the child that, yes, Santa is a big fat fraud.

"Gee," the child can say to either of them. "Thanks. I'll let you know if I need any more authoritative pronouncements."

I for one chose door number three.

"Some people believe the sleigh is magic," I said. "Does that sound right to you?" Initially, boy howdy, did it *ever*. He *wanted* to believe and so was willing to swallow any explanation, no matter how implausible or how tentatively offered. "Some people say it isn't a *literal* single night," I once said, naughtily priming the pump for later inquiries. But little by little, the questions got tougher, and he started to answer that second part—*Does that sound right to you?*—a bit more agnostically.

I avoided both lying and setting myself up as a godlike authority, determined as I was to let him sort this one out himself. And when at last, at the age of 9, in the snowy parking lot of the Target store, to the sound of a Salvation Army bellringer, he asked me point blank if Santa was real—I demurred, just a bit, one last time.

"What do you think?" I said.

"Well . . . I think all the moms and dads are Santa." He smiled at me. "Am I right?"

I smiled back. It was the first time he'd asked me directly, and I answered his question.

"So," I asked, "how do you feel about that?"

He shrugged. "That's fine. Actually, it's good. The world kind of . . . I don't know . . . makes *sense* again."

That's my boy. He wasn't betrayed, he wasn't angry, he wasn't bereft of hope. He was *relieved*. It reminded me of the feeling I had when at last I realized God was fictional. The world actually made *sense* again.

And when Connor started asking skeptical questions about God, I didn't debunk it for him by fiat. I told him what various people believe and asked if that sounded right to him. It all rang a bell, of course. He'd been through the ultimate dry run.

By allowing our children to participate in the Santa myth and find their *own* way out of it through skeptical inquiry, we give them a priceless opportunity to see a mass cultural illusion first from the inside, then from the outside. A very casual line of post-Santa questioning can lead kids to recognize how completely we *all* can snow ourselves if the enticements are attractive enough. Such a lesson, viewed from the top of the hill after exiting a belief system under their own power, can gird kids against the best efforts of the evangelists—and far better than second-hand knowledge could ever hope to do.

■ ■ ■ ■ ■ ■

To Easter Bunny or Not to Easter Bunny?

Noell Hyman

THE LAST THING I EXPECTED when I got married was to face the possibility of giving up Santa and the Easter Bunny. Deny my future children the magic of believing in those imaginary characters, of staying up late into the night, hoping to catch a glimpse of what no child has seen before? Of knowing that the most popular person in the world thinks of you every year? The truth is, I knew they weren't real for one or two years before I finally admitted it to myself. I made the joy last as long as I could.

My husband's siblings, though, did not grow up "being lied to," as they put it. My mother-in-law insists that learning about Santa devastated her as a child. She felt her mother betrayed her trust and lied to her. While some of the family members are still staunch against the tradition, a few of the others agreed

---

First appeared on the weblog www.AgnosticMom.com, April 19, 2006. Used with permission.

to go along with their spouses, including my own husband. One question that enters the minds of some young atheist and agnostic parents is whether to have Santa and the Easter Bunny, if you decide to celebrate those holidays at all. How do we justify giving our children the fantasy of an Easter Bunny while denying them the security of a Jesus?

> " I love Santa and the Easter Bunny. I cannot imagine my childhood without those wonderful nights of exhilarating anticipation. They brought a joy that only Disneyland could match. Discovering they were not real did no damage to my psyche. It was more like discovering the secret to a great magic trick. "

I love Santa and the Easter Bunny. I cannot imagine my childhood without those wonderful nights of exhilarating anticipation. They brought a joy that only Disneyland could match. Discovering they were not real did no damage to my psyche. It was more like discovering the secret to a great magic trick.

Having considered my mother-in-law's experience, I set up a number of guidelines regarding the fantasy characters that grace our holidays. Hopefully, the use of these guidelines will not only prevent the rare devastation that a handful of children feel, they will also demonstrate the difference between imagination and reality; between our perceptions and the facts, between the stories humans tell and the actual truths they represent.

First, parents need to take into consideration the child's character. For example, my mother-in-law has an inner drive to get her facts accurate. In her mind, you don't move forward on something without first verifying each detail. Most children are not this way, which is why most children walk away from their Santa beliefs with a smile and a tradition to pass on to their children. If you, yourself, are more like my mother-in-law, then you can guess that some of your children are likely to be the same way, as well. If this is the case with you, then you may consider banning Santa and the Easter Bunny altogether. But I think revealing the truth at a younger-than-average-age is also an option.

Age, in general, is another factor to consider. For most children, somewhere between 6 and 8 is a good time. Part of the devastation, if it happens, is because the child has been defending Santa's existence to friends. It is socially humiliating for an older child to learn he or she has been asserting something that everyone else knew was wrong. A good way to know it is time to reveal the secret is when the child asks you directly, "Is Santa real?"

So how do we make the Santa/Bunny scenario work to our advantage as atheists and agnostics? I figured it out as I was trying to avoid my mother-in-law's mishap of my children's perceiving us as lying. I made a decision at the beginning that I would not tell elaborate stories of how Santa gets his belly down the chimney or how the bunny gets those baskets into the house.

When my oldest son, Blake, starting asking these questions, I replied with my most common of all replies: "What do you think?" I encouraged Blake to think the problems through. The Santa/Bunny scenario provides an opportunity for both critical thinking and imaginary play. At the younger ages, imagination really goes to work. As children get older, they adopt critical thinking. As skepticism creeps into the questions, you know revelation time is near.

I prefer to wait until the child asks straight out, "Is Santa really real?" With many children, like myself and my first child, the desire to believe hangs on longer than the actual belief. We should allow them to believe for as long as they want. But when they want the truth, parents must give it.

> " With many children, the desire to believe hangs on longer than the actual belief. We should allow them to believe for as long as they want. But when they want the truth, parents must give it. "

And how do we handle the truth? We could say, "No, Santa and the Easter Bunny aren't real." But I don't think that answer demonstrates the reality, nor the reason for the stories. As Joseph Campbell taught, humans have always couched real principles into stories we tell over and over and pass on through generations. Santa and the Easter Bunny are stories of life, love, and the joy of giving. Parents are Santa to kids in ways they won't understand until they become parents themselves. Like the Easter Bunny, parents bring life and hope to their children.

So when it comes time to answer the golden question, a more meaningful reply is, "Do you know who Santa is? Mom and Dad are Santa and the Easter Bunny."

Parents can use this revealing of truth to explain how humans are a storytelling people. We have always told stories to express ideas. Some stories generate more belief and conviction than others. The Bible is a compilation of stories that many people have come to believe as literally true. Santa is a good analogy of how people want to believe in the stories of gods. Most stories have an amount of truth within them, as well as an amount of embellishment.

I finally told my oldest child the truth before Christmas last year as he was turning 8 years old. When the day ended, I asked Blake if Christmas felt different now that he knows Mom and Dad are Santa. He told me that maybe it did a little. But that somehow, seeing the unwrapped Santa gifts, and going along with the game for the younger siblings, the magic still felt real.

Chapter Three Endnotes

1. I am currently accepting nominations in the unlikely event anyone has ever had a more perfectly named schoolmarm than my Mrs. Mawdsley.
2. See link at end of chapter.
3. Or, for a neat twist on the Easter egg hunt, check out the activity titled "Camouflage Egg Hunt" in "The Idea That Changed the World" (Chapter 8).

Additional Resources

Books

- Willson, Jane Wynne. *Funerals Without God: A Practical Guide to Non-Religious Funerals.* British Humanist Association, 1990. A concise and practical guide to meaningful recognition of the end of life without religious symbols, rituals, or readings.
- Willson, Jane Wynne. *Sharing the Future: A Practical Guide to Non-Religious Wedding Ceremonies.* British Humanist Association, 1996. Available through Amazon UK (www.amazon.co.uk).
- Willson, Jane Wynne. *New Arrivals: Guide to Non-Religious Naming Ceremonies.* British Humanist Association, 1991. Also at www.amazon.co.uk.
- Shragg, Karen. *A Solstice Tree for Jenny.* Prometheus, 2001. The young daughter of archaeologists wants to know if their secular family believes in the "same good things" as those around them who celebrate Christmas, Hanukkah, and other holidays. Of course, her mother replies, though we don't believe a god created the world. "We think we can be very good people and know what is right to do," Mom explains, without relying on commandments supposedly handed down from a god. Jenny continues with thoughtful questions, finally deciding she wants a celebration too. Her family creates their own winter solstice celebration, complete with the ancient solstice tree. Ages 4–8.
- Pfeffer, Wendy. *The Shortest Day: Celebrating the Winter Solstice.* Dutton Juvenile, 2003.
  One of many science-oriented titles by Wendy Pfeffer, this accessible and poetic book gives the history of the solstice, notes how many winter holidays derived from it, and offers several science activities and ideas for celebrating the solstice at school and at home.

Other outstanding solstice and equinox titles for kids — all for elementary ages:

- Jackson, Ellen. *The Winter Solstice; The Summer Solstice; The Autumn Equinox; The Spring Equinox.* Millbrook, 1994–2003.
- Conrad, Heather. *Lights of Winter: Winter Celebrations Around the World.* Lightport Books, 2001.
- Haven, Kendell. *New Year's to Kwanzaa: Original Stories of Celebration.* Fulcrum, 1999. Thirty brief fictionalized tales of children celebrating everything from the Day of the Dead to April Fool's to Passover in cultures around the world. Ages 4–8.

Websites for Secular Celebrations and Holidays

- Secular Seasons (www.secularseasons.org). The best of the best—a comprehensive, beautiful, and well-designed site with the names and descriptions of secular holidays organized by month, from obscure (Ingersoll Day) to the equinoxes and solstices, the National Day of Reason, April Fool's, and much more. Includes additional links and activities for each holiday.
- Secular Celebrations (www.secular-celebrations.com).
- The Darwin Day Program (www.darwinday.org).
- Earth Day Network (www.earthday.org).
- National Geographic Xpeditions (www.nationalgeographic.com/xpeditions). Includes activities related to seasons that can be used in conjunction with solstice celebrations.
- Freedom From Religion Foundation (www.ffrf.org). The Foundation offers several CDs of music for the winter solstice and other secular holidays.
- Family Education's "Build Your Own Stonehenge" (http://fun.familyeducation.com/outdoor-activities/winter/35028.html). A fun and educational way to understand planetary astronomy and the procession of seasons. Build a simple viewing circle on the solstice, then add markers once per week for a year—and you'll have a tourist destination for the ages! Bonus: No fifty-ton slabs of granite or ritual sacrifice required. Ages 8 and up.
- Festivus: The Website for the Rest of Us (www.festivusbook.com). Website for the book of almost the same name, with links, activities, and a faux history of the holiday.

Secular Holiday Cards

- Council For Secular Humanism (www.secularhumanism.org/cards/).
- Abundant Earth (www.abundantearth.com).
- Blue Mountain Arts (www.bluemountain.com).

Humanist Celebrants and Ceremonies
  • The Humanist Society (www.humanist-society.org).
  • The British Humanist Association (www.humanism.org.uk—click on Cere-
    monies).

[N.B. Many humanist celebrants affiliate with local humanist organizations and can be found by searching
online for "humanist celebrant" and the name of your city, state, or locality.]

On Being and Doing Good

Introduction

I attended a debate between a theist and an atheist last year, though I try hard to avoid these things. They are usually all heat, and—since the audiences generally consist of recruited partisans of the two sides—very little effective light. There are always better ways for the two sides of the issue to learn about each other, if they are so inclined.

This one took place in one of the new teen Christian centers now appearing in suburban strip malls. Before the debate began, loud Christian rock thumped and bright lights flashed as juice-drinking teenagers welcomed each and every comer with a genuine smile and handshake.

The presenters were old friends and so were more respectful of each other than is sometimes the case. The theist made several points that I thought were well-taken. But when the discussion turned to morality, he said something I will never forget. "We need divine commandments to distinguish between right and wrong," he said. "If not for the seventh commandment . . ." He pointed to his wife in the front row. ". . . there would be nothing keeping me from walking out the door every night and cheating on my wife!"

His wife, to my shock, nodded in agreement. The room full of evangelical teens nodded, wide-eyed at the thin scriptural thread that keeps us from falling into the abyss.

I sat dumbfounded. *Nothing* keeps him from cheating on his wife but the seventh commandment? Really?

Not *love?*

How about respect? I thought. *And the promise you made when you married her? And the fact that doing to her what you wouldn't want done to you is wrong in every moral system on Earth? Or the possibility that you simply find your marriage satisfying and don't need to fling yourself at your secretary? Are respect and love and integrity and fulfillment really so inadequate that you need to have it specifically prohibited in stone?*

Of course not. There are good *reasons* to be and do good. And I'm pretty confident that the debater has all of those additional reasons but simply hasn't recognized that they are in play as well as the commandment—and that removing the finger-shaking commandment would in fact change nothing in his marriage or in his moral action, except maybe increasing his appreciation of how strong and beautiful his marriage actually is, just between the two of them. Just as our children benefit more from hearing *why* they need sleep than hearing, "Go to bed because I said so," the development of a meaningful moral sense is better served by understanding moral principles than by numbly receiving commandments.

Fortunately, very few people have a sense of right and wrong so hobbled that they do not know right from wrong on their own and are reliant on received orders. Even religious believers who claim their morality relies on scriptural commands are putting the cart before the horse. Commandments can reinforce and remind us, but it's hard to believe that anyone really saw the sixth commandment for the first time and said, "Wow. Killing is bad. Didn't see *that* one coming. Well okay, if You say so." Think about it: Not actually knowing right from wrong is so rare that it is considered a mentally altered state and a legal defense in criminal cases. If the debater's claim was true, a defendant could mount a complete defense by taking the stand and saying, "I'm sorry . . . the Ten *what?*"

Yet this inaccurate view of moral development persists. Advocates of placing the commandments in public schools have argued that a prominent display of the sixth commandment at the entrance to Columbine High School would have stopped Klebold and Harris in their tracks. "Wait just a minute!" you can hear the killers saying. "This murdering we're about to do—it's apparently *wrong!*"

It is important for children to learn the difference between right and wrong. But *knowing* what is right is much less than half the battle. Much more important is providing the incentive to do what you *already* know is right. It's here that the wrath of God comes into play in some denominations, with very mixed results. A more meaningful and reliable groundwork is laid by discussing the "why." This chapter begins with the insights of one of the great advocates of developing reflective thinking in children, Dr. Gareth Matthews, who addresses the complex concept of evil. Developmental psychologist Dr. Jean Mercer describes how moral development *actually* occurs in children, and Dr. David Koepsell examines the relative merits of commandments and principles.

This chapter also introduces the first of several poems by nonbeliever and secular parent E.Y. "Yip" Harburg. Yip authored all of the lyrics and much of the screenplay of *The Wizard of Oz,* making in the process one of the greatest contributions of the past century to the imaginative landscape of modern childhood.

Morality and Evil

Gareth B. Matthews, Ph.D.

SECULAR PARENTS MAY FEEL that they have a special advantage over religious parents in not having to discuss the problem of evil with their children. That is, since they do not believe there is such a thing as a divine being who is both all-good and all-powerful, they do not have to try to explain to their children why terrible things sometimes happen to innocent or even good people—tsunamis that kill thousands of innocent victims, or terrible illnesses that make babies and small children suffer unbearable pains before they then die. These parents, like most all parents, may want to shield their children from news about the horrors of the world. But, if the children see something heartbreaking on TV, at least they do not have the burden of explaining how a loving and all-powerful being could allow such a thing to happen.

On the other hand, religious parents may feel that they have an advantage over secular parents when it comes to moral upbringing. These parents may be upset at the moral relativism they and their children see in the movies or hear in their favorite music, but they may feel confident that they have an answer to all moral relativism: Morality, they believe, rests on the unshakable commands of God.

In fact, I shall argue, both assumed advantages are illusory. The idea that it is God's commands that justify morality is not as much of an advantage in helping our children to become morally good people as one might think. And the idea that the problem of evil is only a problem for religious believers is mistaken. But my counsel is not a counsel of despair. It is rather that parents, whether religious or secular, should have open discussions with their children, including discussions about morality and about evil. Children need to work out their own answers to the fascinatingly difficult questions of life. With encouragement from their elders, they will do this. I begin with the problem of evil.

My grandson Julian has always loved trucks. When he was barely fifteen months old, and just learning to talk, he would take my hand and lead me to one of his father's trucks, most likely to his father's dump-truck, which was then his favorite. He would stand by the dump-truck in an almost ecstatic trance, quiver all over, and pronounce, very carefully, perhaps several times, those magic words, "dump-truck."

Julian continued to like dump-trucks through early childhood. But his primary allegiance shifted from dump-trucks to *bucket-loaders*. I remember seeing him at 2½, in the same trance-like state, literally shaking all over, as he watched the magical actions of a bucket-loader.

Julian was also, and remains so to this day, an ardent nature-lover. Even at age 3 he could recognize a large number of bird varieties, more than many of us adults. He also knew much, much more about frogs and turtles than I have ever dreamt of knowing. He was especially passionate about frogs. While he was still 2, he and his mother, my daughter, Sarah, had heard wood frogs quacking in the wetlands across the street from their house. So, in the following spring, just as Julian was turning 3, Sarah took Julian, and Julian's older sister, Pearl, onto the land across the street in the hopes of hearing wood frogs again, and maybe getting a look at one.

Unfortunately, a developer had recently cleared a huge tract of land adjacent to the wetlands and had filled in some of the wetlands. Julian had enjoyed watching the big trucks do this work. But now, when Julian and his sister and mother went to look for wood frogs, none could be found. Instead of the quacking sound of wood frogs, which Julian could clearly distinguish from the call of tree frogs, they heard nothing but the sound of bucket-loaders. Without thinking about what effect her words might have on Julian, Sarah blurted out, "The bucket-loaders have killed the wood frogs."

Sarah's remark stunned Julian. He kept repeating, "Oh my God! You're kidding, Mama! The bucket-loaders have killed the wood frogs?" Sarah tried to console Julian, but nothing helped.

In that experience Julian encountered the problem of evil. It is not that he wondered how it is possible that God, who is all-good and all-powerful, could allow evil to exist in the world. He was relatively innocent of any explicitly theological framework for thought. But he had to face the shattering realization that one pre-eminent good in life, a bucket-loader, could destroy another pre-eminent good in life, a colony of wood frogs.

Later on, in a move somewhat reminiscent of Immanuel Kant's argument from justice for human immortality, Julian developed the conviction that mother wood frogs have babies, then die, and then later come to life again. In this way he reassured himself that his beloved wood frogs had not, after all, been completely obliterated by his equally beloved bucket-loaders. They would be born again.

Evil does come from good. This is a metaphysical problem. This is also, as it was for Julian, an existential problem. There is no particular age, or stage in life, when we have to confront the problem of evil. It may hit us when we first read David Hume in a philosophy class. It may hit us when we read the Book of Job in church or temple. It may hit us when we read about the torture of prisoners in Iraq or Guantánamo. Or it may hit us when we have seen what a bucket-loader, or perhaps a developer, who may, of course, be a very good person, has done to the wetlands, and to the wood frogs who had inhabited it.

The religious parent who teaches her children about God's love and unlimited power should be prepared to think freshly with her children about the problem of evil. It is not easy for anyone to do that. Yet, I maintain, it is part of the responsibility of a religious parent to have an honest discussion with her children about the problem of evil.

Surprisingly, perhaps, the challenge for secular parents is not entirely different. They might hope to avoid having to deal with any form of the problem of evil with their children. But for parents who have a genuine respect for their children and for the hard questions their children ask the hope of evading the problem of evil may well be frustrated. After all, evil does sometimes come from good.

> For parents who have a genuine respect for their children and for the hard questions their children ask, the hope of evading the problem of evil may well be frustrated. After all, evil does sometimes come from good.

Parents may not want their children to think of either frogs or bucket-loaders as inherently good things. Yet, one could argue, it is an impoverished childhood in which nothing seems to be unqualifiedly good. Julian's consuming love of nature, and of trucks, gave his childhood an especially magical quality. But it also gave him the problem of evil.

I turn now to my second topic, the issue of whether the idea of morality as something commanded by God can help ward off the threats of nihilism and moral relativism so pervasive in our society. No doubt many religious parents feel they have a distinct advantage over their secular counterparts when it comes to moral education. After all, they can teach their children that it is God, no less, who commands us not to kill, lie or steal, and it is God who commands us to love our neighbors as ourselves.

Secular parents who are conscientious about raising their children to be morally good people may also wish they had an easy way to ground morality and protect their children from cynicism and moral relativism. They may even harbor the secret wish that they could pull out the divine trump card to fend off the attractions of immorality their children will have to face.

Yet the divine trump card is not fully effective in the way religious parents may expect. This was shown a long time ago by Plato in his dialogue, *Euthyphro.* In that dialogue Socrates asks what the holy is. After several failed efforts to answer the question, Euthyphro offers the suggestion that the holy is doing what the gods love. Socrates then asks, "Is it holy because the gods love it, or do the gods love it because it is holy?"

We can translate Socrates's famous question into the theology of monotheism by asking, "Is is morally right (for example) to tell the truth simply because God commands it ('Do not bear false witness!'), or does God command us to tell the truth because that is the morally right thing to do?" If we say it is right simply because God commands it, we leave open the possibility that moral rightness could be a mere matter of divine whim. For most religious believers, that doesn't seem right. But, if we say that God commands us to be truthful because that is the morally right thing to do, then it seems we should be able to understand what is morally required of us independently of the fact that God commands it.

I once discussed the *Euthyphro* problem with two classes of seventh graders in a Hebrew day school. We were discussing whether the things God commands in Leviticus 19 are holy because God commands them or whether instead God commands them because they are holy. One student said this: "God wants us to do these things because they are holy. If God [had] told us to kill, steal, and commit adultery, would [those] be holy thing[s] to do? I don't think so. I think these things are holy and God wants us to do them *because* they are holy."

If what this seventh grader said is right, and I am inclined to agree that the religious person should say this, then the religious parent and the secular parent are in much the same boat when it comes to raising their children to be morally good people. Moral development will have to include cultivating moral feelings, such as empathy and a sense of fairness, developing habits of telling the truth and keeping promises, nurturing attitudes of

> The religious parent and the secular parent are in much the same boat when it comes to raising their children to be morally good people.

generosity and loyalty, and reflecting on how to resolve moral dilemmas when, for example, the duty to tell the truth or keep a promise conflicts with the duty to help someone in need, or under threat of assault.

Whether the ideal of a moral life has a divine sanction is not a trivial question. But once one sees the implications of the *Euthyphro* problem, the question of divine sanction does not offer much enlightenment about what morality requires, or about how to become a moral person. Unless what God commands us to do is what we morally ought to do anyway, then the very idea of a divine sanction for the moral law seems to threaten the rationality of trying to be moral.

So where does this leave the secular parent with respect to issues about the problem of evil and the nature of morality? It seems to leave the thoughtful secular parent in roughly the same situation as the thoughtful religious parent. Children cannot be shielded from the problem of evil, even by trying to keep them innocent of theology. Evil does come from good. And as for helping one's children to become caring, fair-minded, and responsible moral agents, the primary resources open to religious parents are much the same as those open to secular ones.

If one believes that God is supremely just, merciful, and good, then it will follow that God also wants us to be just, merciful, and good. But we will have the very same reasons for being just, merciful, and good as God has, even if, as the religious among us may suppose, we don't understand those reasons as well as we think God does, or even as well as we ourselves would like to.

Behaving Yourself: Moral Development in the Secular Family

Jean Mercer, Ph.D.

A 5-YEAR-OLD BOY SWIPES the coins his mother has left on her desk. As it happens, the mother knows exactly how much she has put there in preparation for a trip to the laundromat. She confronts the little boy, who says he didn't take the money—but there lies the exact amount of the missing money, right on his pillow. The mother gives him a serious talking-to, then sends him to his room, telling him to come out only when he can say why he should not have taken the coins. After some minutes, he emerges in tears, but is able to state what was wrong with what he did: "Ya get in TROUBLE!"

This vignette contains many elements common to the moral instruction of secular and religious families alike. The child did not plan to break any rules, but was not able to resist temptation when it occurred. The offense was only a minor inconvenience to the mother at the time, but she wanted to respond appropriately because she was concerned that the child not take other people's property in the future. She was influenced by what she feared was the development of an undesirable pattern of behavior and so was unwilling to let the incident pass. She believed the child was old enough to think through the situation, but she was also willing to accept a very simple rationale when the child offered it.

The early development of moral thinking and moral behavior choices is largely based on brief interactions like this one. Children do childish wrong things, and parents provide *ad hoc* corrections. In early and middle childhood, parents are quite unlikely to instruct children on major moral issues, because the children are unlikely to do things that obviously involve major issues in a direct way. It is probably safe to say that no parent gives direct training on avoiding the most serious moral lapses—"Sally, when you go out to play, I don't want you to murder anybody. And Timmy, no raping—I don't care what the other boys do, it's not nice to rape people." Nevertheless, few adults do commit murder or rape, in part because they did receive direct instruction about related minor matters like hitting or pulling another child's pants down—instruction from which abstract moral principles may be derived as the child's reasoning ability matures. The whole process is a gradual one involving repeated experiences, rather than memorization of a list of "right things" and "wrong things," or the early mastery of universal principles.

Whether a family is secular or religious in beliefs, the basic processes of moral training and development are probably pretty similar. One college student, brought up in a devout Catholic family, responded to this idea with a disbelieving exclamation: "How can they develop morally if they're brought up without any values?" Of course, every family has a set of values, although the parents might have trouble stating just what they are, and every family has an interest in passing on a value system to the next generation. Although some families admire criminal or simply underhanded behavior and encourage it in their children, most families in a cultural group want to foster socially desirable behaviors: some degree of truthfulness, some willingness to sacrifice for others, some concern with others' property rights, and, later on, some caution about sexual activity. Background values are different, however. In many non-secular families, supernatural entities and events are presented as reasons for complying with rules about behavior; in secular families, compliance is connected with overarching principles related to human needs and experiences, such as individual autonomy, equal rights of human beings, and freedom of conscience.[1] Religious families may find it easier to state the connection between values and behavior than do secular families, who are generally thinking in terms of highly abstract principles rather than of nonhuman entities who can be presented as having personal wishes and emotions. But all families function to help establish children's ways of thinking about moral issues, emotions connected with morality, and behavior patterns related to value judgments.

The Development of Moral Reasoning

The term *moral development* describes the fact that children's moral behavior and thinking change with age in predictable ways. Developmental changes of all kinds can be studied empirically, and many aspects of development have proven to follow systematic pathways, so that most human beings go through the same developmental steps, often at similar ages. Empirical studies of moral development have most often focused on changes in moral reasoning, the kind of thinking that underlies decisions about moral issues. The best-known theory of developmental change in moral reasoning comes from the work of

Lawrence Kohlberg,[2] who studied the process by presenting children with "moral dilemmas"—problems where two decisions seemed equally desirable—and asking them to explain why they made the choice they did. Kohlberg felt that the development of moral reasoning could be described as involving six stages. (Because Kohlberg's method involved talking about a problem, the first stage could not be identified until the child could talk well, which would not occur until at least age 3 for most children.)

The earliest stage Kohlberg described was one in which right and wrong are defined by punishment rather than by any larger principle. If something is followed by punishment, it was wrong; if it is not, it was right. The light-fingered 5-year-old mentioned before was at this stage. A second stage considers reward as an important indication that something is right. The stress in these early stages is on works, not faith—rightness or wrongness is identified in terms of what a person actually does, not what he or she intended but was unable to perform.

A third stage described by Kohlberg involves social approval and disapproval. By this point, the child separates moral correctness from specific punishment or reward. The moral choice is instead the one that makes other people consider someone a nice boy or a good girl. Continuing with the stress on community approval, a fourth stage emphasizes the existence of laws or rules that are valuable in themselves; breaking a rule is morally wrong simply because it is a rule, not because of the possible consequences for the rule-breaker or for others.

Very few individuals would move beyond this fourth stage during childhood, but in adolescence or afterward a number of people will achieve a "social contract" level of moral reasoning, in which laws and rules are seen as desirable for the comfort of the community, but potentially changeable if they do not work well. Moral decisions can involve complying with rules or working to change them. A final stage, not likely to be reached before late adolescence, involves thinking in terms of universal ethical principles such as the value of human life; decisions to support a universal principle could be made in spite of others' finding one "not nice" or even in the face of certain punishment under the laws.

Most descriptions of developmental change involve steps that are typical of all human beings. Kohlberg's theory is somewhat different, however. This approach suggests everyone follows moral development in the same sequence, but that people do not necessarily arrive at the same step at the same age and that some may never reach the higher stages. Certainly, a number of adults do not appear ever to go beyond the second stage posited by Kohlberg, and the "official morality" of the United States appears to be somewhere between the fourth ("law and order") and the fifth ("social contract") stages. These facts raise questions about advanced development in moral reasoning: Are there experiences that help people achieve these higher stages?

> ❝ Contrary to traditional beliefs, frequent punishment and the assertion of parental authority are not factors that facilitate growth in moral reasoning. ❞

Family actions do seem to be related to the development of moral reasoning. Contrary to traditional beliefs, frequent punishment and the assertion of parental authority are not factors that facilitate growth in moral reasoning. Parents of children with advanced moral reasoning are more likely to be authoritative (taking charge, but without an overly strict or punitive approach) than authoritarian. Authoritative parenting fosters cognitive development in general, so it is not surprising that moral reasoning, a type of cognitive skill, is also facilitated. Advances in moral reasoning are also associated with exposure to parental discussion of moral uncertainties and to equal sharing of power between parents, which leads to frequent negotiation and compromise.[3]

Intriguing as it is, Kohlberg's theory is far from a complete description of moral development; for example, women and girls are not usually assessed as highly advanced moral reasoners in Kohlberg's model. And, of course, moral reasoning is not the whole story of moral development. Decisions about moral behavior involve motivation to do what is right as well as the ability to apply moral principles in thought.

Emotion and Moral Development

Looking at moral development from the viewpoint of moral reasoning showed us stages of morality beginning in the nursery school years. When we consider the emotional aspects of morality, however, we must go back to an astonishingly early period of development—even as far back as early infancy, when the first social relationships begin to form. This statement is particularly true of values based on human needs and rights, because events during infancy provide the foundation for our understanding of others' feelings and our wish to comfort and help them.

Infants in the first few months of life have little ability to understand facial expressions or other indications of emotion, but they already react very differently to human beings than they do to inanimate objects, even moving ones.

If they have frequent experiences with sensitive, responsive adult caregivers, infants soon begin to notice emotional cues. For example, an infant responds by beginning to cry if an adult simply turns a blank face toward the baby and does not respond to smiles or vocal sounds. By seven or eight months, an infant confronted with some surprising new object turns to look at a familiar caregiver's face; if the caregiver looks frightened, the baby backs away from the object, but if the caregiver looks happy, the baby goes on to investigate. The baby is beginning to develop an essential set of skills, sometimes categorized as Theory of Mind.[4] Theory of Mind allows each person to be aware that behind every human face is an individual set of experiences, wishes, beliefs, and thoughts; that each of these sets is in some ways similar to and in other ways different from one's own set; and that facial expressions and other cues can enable each of us to know something of how others feel and what they are going to do. The development of Theory of Mind has already begun by nine or ten months, when a well-developed baby can already show the important step of joint attention. In this behavior, the child uses eye contact and movement of the gaze to get an adult to look at some sight that interests the baby and then to look back again, to gaze at each other and smile with mutual pleasure. Importantly, not only *can* the child do this, but he or she *wants* to do it, demonstrating the very early motivation to share our happiness with others— surely the foundation of empathic responses. Without this early development, it would hardly be possible to achieve secular values such as a concern with equal rights, a principle based on the understanding that all human beings have similar experiences of pleasure and pain.

How does this complex and early developmental process occur? Does it simply unfold, or does experience with others play an important role? This question is more complicated than it appears, because some individuals, often characterized as autistic, do not seem to develop Theory of Mind, even though they have normal experiences.[5] For most infants, however, there seems to be an initial component of being especially interested in human beings, and this is followed by many experiences of predictable interactions with caregivers, so that a facial expression or tone of voice becomes a signal that the adult is about to do certain things. Ideally, the caregiver also responds in a predictable way to the baby's signals of smiling or reaching or turning the eyes away. Unfortunately, many babies are exposed to the much less responsive and predictable demeanor of a mother who suffers from a perinatal mood disorder or who is involved with drugs or alcohol. They may also spend many hours in poor-quality child care arrangements, with repeated changes of foster family so that no one learns to "read" the baby's expression, or with caregivers who mistakenly believe that responding to the baby's emotional expressions will cause "spoiling." Theory of Mind is facilitated by responsive nurturing and the devoted care of adults who value infants as members of the human species. Early steps in Theory of Mind seem to be essential to the growth of the empathic attitudes that are a basic part of humanistic values.

However, the first steps are not the end of the process. Experiences in the toddler and early preschool period provide a watershed for the development of empathic behavior. It is important to realize that the distress of another person does not provide a simple signal calling for a simple response. Distress causes complex facial expressions and behavior patterns that call out ambivalent reactions in young children and in adults. People who like clowns find their sad faces funny; many of us have horrified ourselves by laughing quite inappropriately at a funeral; a common trigger for child abuse is the child's crying. The appearance of distress can call out an impulse to help, but can also create amusement or even the wish to attack the troubled person. What makes some human beings more likely to respond compassionately to distress, others more likely to laugh or attack? This is a difficult topic to study systematically, but it is thought that experience with caregivers helps to establish an individual's compassionate or aggressive response to distress signals. When the young child is distressed himself or herself, a caregiver's kind or hostile response models the appropriate way to act when others are uncomfortable. Nurturing, responsive caregivers are likely to help children become compassionate, and unsympathetic caregivers guide children toward an aggressive response to others' distress. Perhaps the worst model is the adult who teases and torments a child into a tearful rage and then dismisses or even punishes the distressed child as "a big baby."

Guidance, Discipline, and Moral Development

As a child develops Theory of Mind and the capacity for emotional empathy, and as moral reasoning progresses to more advanced stages, parental guidance provides specific information about right and wrong behavior. (Incidentally, the actions that are considered right or wrong will change as the child gets older—for example, a toddler might be punished for trying to pick up a crying infant, but a 10-year-old praised.) Such guidance helps to establish knowledge about specific behaviors that can eventually be used to derive abstract principles of morality.

Although the behavior of parents serves as an important role model for children, few families rely on modeling alone as a way to shape children's behavior. And, although parents may prefer to praise and reward approved behavior, few manage to raise children without some use of punishment. For secular families, this fact may be problematic, because the use of punishment by persons in authority appears to be in conflict with humanistic principles such as the autonomy of the individual. Nevertheless, it is clear that when a parent is dealing with a young, relatively nonverbal child who is doing something dangerous to himself or painful to others, punishment may be the quickest, most effective way to stop the behavior, and thus to work toward understanding of related moral issues.

Punishment need not be physical in nature, although physical restraint or removal of the child from the scene may be part of the parent's action. Punishment may simply involve the parent's communication of anger or sadness and interruption of the behavior (which the child presumably wanted to carry out). To be effective, punishment must be highly consistent—if there is a rule, it always applies. The timing of punishment is critical, and it is by far the most effective if it occurs just as the undesirable behavior begins. If punishment is swift and sure, it need not be severe, and in fact milder forms of punishment, which do not trigger an intense emotional reaction, are more likely to teach effectively. These points about punishment suggest that the most effective parents will be those who plan their use of guidance techniques, who are consistently attentive to the child's behavior, and who respond predictably even when they find it inconvenient or boring to do so.

Parental guidance techniques are also associated with moral development as factors in the establishment of the social emotions. These emotions occur in response to the child's awareness of others' evaluation of her, and they appear in the late toddler/early preschool period. One approach to the social emotions classifies these feelings as either positive or negative, and as either global or specific, yielding four basic social emotions that occur in response to awareness of others' opinions.[6] The child may experience *guilt,* an unpleasant feeling of having failed in some specific way; *shame,* an unpleasant feeling of having been judged as globally bad or wrong; *pride,* a pleasant sense of having received approval for a specific action or characteristic; and *hubris,* a pleasant but unrealistic feeling of global approval by others. Of these emotions, guilt and pride are useful guides to good behavior, because they involve specific acts that can be avoided or repeated in future. Shame and hubris are far less useful, because the individual has no control over the nature of the self and cannot change the basic self to gain approval or avoid disapproval. In fact, the response to shame may be one of helpless terror and rage, as destruction of the self seems to be the only way of escape from the judgment. In older children and adults, shame experiences may be triggered easily by events that imply "disrespect," and extreme antisocial reactions may result.

This view of the social emotions suggests that moral development would be fostered best by parenting that stresses pride and guilt rather than hubris and shame. Such parenting involves mild punishment that does not overwhelm the child with fear and anger and careful verbal communication that clarifies for the child exactly what was bad or good in his behavior. Parents who work toward desirable social emotions need to have insight into their own reactions of approval or disapproval. Parental reactions of contempt or disgust toward the child are difficult for the child to process as connected with specific actions, and they may pass unexplained if the parent is only vaguely aware of his or her attitude; a pervasive sense of shame is a likely outcome if there are many experiences of this type.

As a general rule, parenting practices seem to support desirable behavior and moral development best when they involve mild emotion that does not threaten the child's autonomy. Messages to the child are most effective when they are understandable but indirect and have some humorous component.[7] Parenting practices are less successful when they involve a high degree of psychological intrusiveness or attempts to control the child's beliefs and emotions through psychological means such as threatened withdrawal of love. Although effective parental control of children's behavior (like demanding mature behavior) has positive outcomes, psychological intrusiveness results in a higher number of emotional and behavior problems, and this is, surprisingly, particularly true when a high level of parental affection is also present.[8]

Advantages and Disadvantages of a Secular Approach to Moral Development

Are there differences between secular and nonsecular families in the fostering of children's moral development? There is no recent evidence that seems to support the superiority of one group or the other. The development of emotional components of morality, such as empathy, begins so early that it is doubtful that family beliefs play a significant role. As for discipline and guidance practices, these are probably similar in families with various beliefs, except that a small number of religious fundamentalists stress "breaking the child's will" and try to establish complete obedience from the age of a few months.[9] It is possible that secular humanist principles such as individual autonomy and equal rights may reduce secular families' use of punishment, or at least point up the need for reasoning and discussion of behavior issues in addition to reward and punishment.

The major difference that might be expected to result from contrasting beliefs has to do with moral reasoning. Whereas nonsecular families may choose to stress reasoning in terms of the punishments or rewards available from supernatural entities or their agents (which they do not necessarily do), such ploys would be most unlikely among secular parents. Secular families base their standards on overarching ethical principles that may be highly abstract and that are connected to specific behaviors through extensive reasoning. Because discussion of moral issues in the family encourages advanced moral development, it is possible that children of secular families have an advantage here.

> " Secular families base their standards on overarching ethical principles that are connected to specific behaviors through extensive reasoning. Because discussion of moral issues in the family encourages advanced moral development, it is possible that children of secular families have an advantage. "

Are there disadvantages in a secular approach to moral development? The one obvious problem has to do with the need for a community that shares and reinforces the family's values. Although the earliest steps in moral development occur within the family, older children and adolescents come into increasing contact with the standards of the surrounding community. The issue here is not so much that the children will abandon the family's values as that family members may feel isolated or even beleaguered by value conflicts with neighbors. Nevertheless, if this situation is handled well by secular parents, value disagreements may be turned to advantage through family discussion and opportunities to model advanced moral reasoning.

Take Two Tablets and Call Me in the Morning

a poem by Edgar "Yip" Harburg

If the Lord, who could surely afford it,
Were a little bit more democratic,
That is, if the Lord didn't lord it
And weren't so doggone dogmatic,
The world would be one bed of roses,
Sweet psyches and better digestions
If the tablets he handed to Moses
Were inscribed not commands but suggestions.

■ ■ ■ ■ ■ ■

On Being Good for Good Reasons: Commandments vs. Principles

David Koepsell, JD, Ph.D.

IT ALL STARTED ABOUT *2000 years ago* . . .

Many people, when confronted with the fact of a friend's atheism, will exclaim something like "Well, we need religion so we know how to behave," which puzzles most of us. Though we nonbelievers are not god-fearing, we seem to behave well, to be civil, to not run rampant through the streets robbing, stealing, pillaging, and raping. How odd, then, that most religious people feel that the foundation for morality is a set of commandments they barely know from a book most of them have not read. Since we are living proof we can be good without god, the question will inevitably arise when Johnny or Sally comes home one day from school after being accused by classmates of being evil—and Mommy and Daddy will have to explain why their friends say they are going to hell.

> " Though we nonbelievers are not god-fearing, we seem to behave well. How odd, then, that most religious people feel that the foundation for morality is a set of commandments they barely know from a book most of them have not read. "

I suggest we teach our children to respond that they are simply not going to hell (a) because there is no such place, and (b) because they act ethically in ways that even Jesus would approve of. And that's not because of some moribund commandment, but because Jesus's second favorite rule, to love one's neighbor as one would wish to be loved, is just good old-fashioned rational behavior from a liberal freethinking Essene. And by the way, he borrowed that from a number of philosophers who predated him, but no matter. Of course, Jesus mentioned his preference for this commandment when queried by his followers as to which of the famous "Ten" Commandments he liked best. In many ways, this dispute between the ethics of the Golden Rule and the morals allegedly displayed by the Old Testament commandments echoes disputes

> " Jesus's second favorite rule, to love one's neighbor as one would wish to be loved, is just good old-fashioned rational behavior from a liberal freethinking Essene. "

about the nature of ethics that have been underway for thousands of years. Recognizing this "commandments vs. principles" dispute can help us think about how to make ethical principles resonate in kids in a way that will help them make good ethical judgments on their own.

Commandments vs. Principles

Philosophers have debated for centuries where the foundations for ethical behavior might lie. There are two predominant schools of thought, though their expressions are many, varied, and nuanced. The two major views are roughly (a) that morals are unchangeable laws inherent in nature or divinely sanctioned and (b) that morals are man-made creations based upon reason and intended to produce certain consequences that generally improve our lives. Even while these two competing schools of thought have duked it out for centuries, humans have never acted as though the choice is a zero-sum game. Rather, we tend to employ both the "received-wisdom" model and the "best-consequences" model in our ethical decision making. Getting this point straight when educating our children about ethics could save years of questioning, disillusionment, and distrust. You can do this all without even mentioning a single philosopher or ethical theory by name. But introducing kids (in developmentally appropriate ways) to the basics of ethical theory *is,* in my opinion, essential to making children capable of making moral judgments. As free inquirers, disposed to using reason and science to help us solve human problems, we can more or less agree that an essential tool is knowledge, and knowledge about the rudiments of ethical theory is just the sort of knowledge that can help enable us and our children to choose to act ethically.

As anyone with a 2-year-old knows by now, it isn't enough to tell them what to do, since the inevitable next question is "why." At some point, "cuz I say so" won't cut it any more with a little free inquirer, so let's explore some reasons to do the right thing beyond that offered by a mere appeal to authority. Good reasons can be expressed, in logical and accessible ways, according to each of the two major schools of ethical thought. Here is one good "commandment"-type reason for acting ethically: *As a general rule, we should not treat others as we would not wish to be treated.*

Now some may cringe that this is the Golden Rule to which the biblical Jesus refers when he admonishes us to love our neighbors as we wish them to love us. It is—and it isn't. Jesus did not invent it. It dates at least as far back as Confucius, and possibly much further back in philosophies as distinct as Zoroastrianism, Buddhism, and Judaism. The rule continued to stimulate ethical reflection in philosophy. Immanuel Kant provided an excellent secular defense of the rule, adding his own version—*"Follow only those principles you would wish to be made universal"*—to the formulations of the others, while providing a comprehensive framework of argument to demonstrate the reasoned roots of ethics.

Recent studies indicate that the Golden Rule is naturalistically based. Studies of ape culture, and other animals, have shown that reciprocal altruism abounds in the natural world. This makes a certain amount of sense. If one's species is to survive, one has to help one's fellow monkey, armadillo, or human, and so on. This general rule, simply stated, makes good sense, although there are also certain common-sense exceptions. Teaching it may not only make good sense, but is already acceptable to most children once they develop the psychological capacity for *empathy* and can envision themselves in the shoes of another. "Now how would *you* feel, Rayna, if Jordan did X to *you?*"

A second good reason for acting ethically—this one of the "best-consequences" variety: *We ought to generally act in ways that maximize happiness.*

This one is most familiar and friendly to your average secular humanist. Under the general banner of "Utilitarianism," this kind of moral system focuses on the net *effect* of our acts to determine their moral value. The British philosopher John Stuart Mill is credited with updating Utilitarianism and can be thought of as giving it a more humanistic bent. At the core of Utilitarianism is the notion that the goal of all moral behavior is to maximize happiness generally. This certainly seems to be a pretty commonsensical criterion for our day-to-day ethical and moral judgments. When we make everyday decisions about how to act, we often ask ourselves: What will be the consequences for the people I care about? Will this make so-and-so happy?

This can become rather complex. One of the shortcomings of Utilitarianism is the difficulty in assessing the results of any particular action. How many people will become happier due to a particular action, and to what degree? Moreover, in its original form, there is no distinction among types of happiness. Does the happiness in question involve simple bodily pleasures, or are some pleasures better, objectively, than others? Mill values intellectual and aesthetic pleasures above "base" bodily pleasures, but on what basis can he make that distinction hold?

Another significant problem with Utilitarianism is that is can justify certain things that none of us would be very happy with, if carried to its logical extreme. The most common example is Utilitarian justification for enslaving a small segment of a population if overall happiness could be increased. Much worse examples could be devised. It has been suggested that instead of making utilitarian calculations on an act-by-act basis, we should devise general rules of behavior that, when followed, tend to increase happiness. This, again, is both complicated and difficult to base philosophically on firm ground. Ultimately, many Utilitarians have to ground their ethical judgments not upon calculations of best consequences, but upon what is really a type of received wisdom: that happiness is itself good.

Practical Ethics

So where does that leave us, in learning ethics, in devising moral modes of behavior, and in educating our children about right and wrong? When ethical theories so divergent exist, and are followed to some degree by most people, what does this say about their truth or use? I think it demonstrates that there is something to ethics. There is a real grounding for our making ethical judgments, and despite divergent theories of the basis for that grounding, we tend to come to similar conclusions in all but the toughest cases about what we should or should not do. The only remaining unsolved question is the one that 2-year-olds habitually and rightly ask as budding philosophers: *Why?*

The "why" is very important and remains fertile ground for investigation. Moreover, as free inquirers interested in understanding the world, we cannot stop asking this question. While we may be able to derive some good normative ethical rules, we cannot stop there, and must always ask ourselves whether those rules make sense. To do anything less would be to fall into the trap of dogmatic thinking and to reject the use of philosophy in ordinary life. Free inquiry demands that we put to the test, on a regular basis, our judgments and those of others, asking always what the principles we employ are. Let's encourage this in ourselves and our children, because it is truly the stuff of reason, and quintessentially human.

Chapter Four Endnotes

1. A. Dacey, "Believing in doubt," *New York Times* (2006, February 3), A23.
2. L. Kohlberg, C. Levine, & A. Hewer, *Moral Stages: A Current Formulation and a Response to Critics* (Basel, Switzerland: Karger, 1983).
3. R. Dobert, & G. Nunner-Winkler, "Interplay of Formal and Material Role-Taking in the Understanding of Suicide among Adolescents and Young Adults. I. Formal and Material Role-Taking." *Human Development,* 28 (1985), 225–239.
4. S. Baron-Cohen, "From Attention-Goal Psychology to Belief-Desire Psychology: The Development of a Theory of Mind, and its Dysfunction," in S. Baron-Cohen, H. Tager-Flusberg, & D. Cohen, eds., *Understanding Other Minds* (New York: Oxford University Press, 1993), 59–82.
5. S. Baron-Cohen & P. Howlin, "The Theory of Mind Deficit in Autism: Some Questions for Teaching and Diagnosis." In S. Baron-Cohen, H. Tager-Flusberg, & D. Cohen, eds., *Understanding Other Minds* (New York: Oxford University Press, 1993), 228–291.
6. M. Lewis, *Shame: The Exposed Self* (New York: Free Press, 1992).
7. J. Grusec & J. Goodnow, "Impact of Parent Discipline Methods on the Child's Internalization of Values: A Reconceptualization of Current Points of View," *Developmental Psychology* 30 (1994), 4–19; G. Kochanska, "Beyond Cognition: Expanding the Search for the Early Roots of Internalization and Conscience," *Developmental Psychology* 30 (1994), 20–22.
8. K. Aunola & J.-E. Nurmi, "The Role of Parenting Styles in Children's Problem Behavior." *Child Development* 76 (2005), 1144–1159.

9. G. Ezzo & R. Bucknam, *On Becoming Babywise* (Sisters, Oregon: Multnomah Books, 1995).

Additional Resources
Books

- Humphrey, Sandra Mcleod. *If You Had to Choose, What Would You Do?* Prometheus, 1995. A well-conceived attempt to present the youngest children with situations requiring moral decision making. Twenty-five short scenarios are presented in which a child grapples with questions of right and wrong in a commonplace setting. Each parable is followed by the basic question "What would you do?" along with a few corollary questions. Parents can and should scan the stories to find those best matched to his or her own child's level. Some are eye-rollingly simple, others more complex and interesting—including some that can even get the parent headscratching. Do you turn in a good friend for petty shoplifting? At the age of 6, my son had a quick answer—"yup"—until I suggested the shoplifter was Sean, his dearest friend in the world. He offered to rat out half a dozen less precious acquaintances, but not Sean. The ensuing discussion was rich and rewarding, finally resulting in a nuanced solution of his own making (Sean gets one last warning before my boy drops a dime)—followed by an insistence that we read another of the stories, then another, then another.

  In another story, two sisters gather pledges to participate in a walk for the World Hunger Drive. Niki sprains her ankle halfway through and pleads with Leslie to go with her to the doctor. Leslie must decide whether to refund the money she collected from her friends and neighbors or to send it on to the World Hunger Drive, even though she hadn't finished.

  Now that's a brow-knitter worth pondering, a wonderfully complex, multidimensional, real-world situation that demonstrates the ineffectiveness of a commandments approach to morality. Ages 6–12.
- Barker, Dan. *Maybe Right, Maybe Wrong: A Guide for Young Thinkers.* Prometheus, 1992. A good, well-presented introduction to principles-based morality for kids. Ages 8–12.
- Berry, Joy. *A Children's Book About Lying,* from Grolier's Help Me Be Good series, 1988. Ages 4–8.
- Borba, Michele, PhD. *Building Moral Intelligence.* Jossey-Bass, 2002.

[N. B. See Additional Resources in Chapter 5 for more morality/values resources.]

■ ■ ■ CHAPTER 5 ■ ■ ■

Values and Virtues, Meaning and Purpose

Introduction

In a book devoted to helping parents raise ethical and caring kids, the four words in this chapter title loom large. Whose values? Whose virtues? Whose definition of meaning and purpose?

For those who believe our values, virtues, and purpose are dictated by God, the conclusions drawn by the contributors to this chapter may seem surprising. For with some notable exceptions, most of us share the same basic values, recognize the same virtues, and find meaning and purpose in the same things, regardless of our worldview. Even when we seem at opposite poles, there is most often an underlying commonality. We all tend to think that treating others as we would like to be treated is a good foundation for ethics—which explains why every ethical system on Earth includes some form of that notion. We can be counted upon to find killing reprehensible and lying a thing to discourage, even if we differ on when exceptions are called for. We tend to admire those who overcome adversity to achieve great things, though we sometimes disagree on what constitutes adversity and greatness. Our differences, then, though they can seem intractable, are less fundamental than we tend to think. The secular view simply recognizes that these values, virtues, and purposes have human origins.

We start this diverse chapter with Shannon and Matt Cherry's thoughts on raising their young twin girls to embrace the "twin" virtues of pride and respect—or, you might say, self-respect and other-respect. The essay "Seven Secular Virtues" proposes a set of admirable qualities to which secularists should aspire—including a few that don't always come easy.

The irrepressible Dr. Donald B. Ardell is our guide to secular meaning and purpose in "Supporting Your Children in Their Quest for the Meaning of Life!" How do you find your meaning and purpose? Try a few on for size, he suggests, and stop when you find one that's fulfilling. It's all we've ever done. And what if your meaning and purpose is serial killing? Let's worry about that when more than 0.00001 percent of the population finds that a fulfilling activity.

What better way to articulate your values and virtues than recognizing those who have embodied them? And when you're a freethinker, why not include a few of the men and women who've had the courage and integrity to challenge the dominant religious views of their day? Annie Laurie Gaylor offers a light-speed introduction to some of the great freethinking figures of the past and present, followed by "A Sixty-Second Reckoned Roll of Freethinkers Historical" and Yip Harburg's "Enemy List"—inspired, no doubt, by his own blacklisting during the McCarthy era. Next time your son or daughter needs a great historical figure for a report or presentation, make a quick scan of the names in these three pieces.

The chapter concludes with author James Herrick's exploration of one of the great avenues for the expression of human meaning and purpose—the arts—focusing especially on the place of literature in understanding the human condition.

Double Vision: Teaching Our Twins Pride and Respect

Shannon and Matthew Cherry

We will build a home that is compassionate to all,
full of respect and honor for others and each other.
May our home be forever filled with peace, love, and happiness.

WHEN WE SAID THESE WORDS at our humanist wedding ceremony four years ago, we didn't even know if we would have children. Now that we have twin baby daughters this vow has taken on a whole new importance.

Yes, Lyra and Sophia have changed our lives, but not our values.

We are raising our children in an explicitly humanist family. *Chambers Pocket Dictionary* defines humanism as "seeking, without religion, the best in, and for, human beings." That's really how we see our job as parents: seeking to bring out the best in our children so that they can have the best in life.

The humanist tradition in the West has its roots in the Ancient Greek ideal of cultivating human excellence. There are many principles needed to bring out the best in people. But there is one value mentioned in our wedding vows that keeps coming up in our discussions of how to raise good kids: respect.

"Respect" is more than an Aretha Franklin song. It means treating the world around us—and everyone in it—as valuable. It also means self-respect, or pride. We want to raise our girls to respect themselves, their surroundings, their pets; to value families, friends, and neighbors. And we don't just mean an attitude of respect, but respectful behavior: We see too many people who boast all the tolerant opinions required in liberal society, but don't actually accomplish much with their lives.

Perhaps, most challenging of all, will be teaching respect for people who have different values—even people with beliefs we think are daft and behaviors we fear as dangerous. Philosophically, respect is at the heart of the major systems of morality: from the Golden Rule (treating others with the same respect with which we would want them to treat us) to Kant's Categorical Imperative (that we must always treat people as ends in themselves and not merely as means to our own ends). But philosophy won't cut it with our infant girls. Even though they can't speak a word yet, their big blue eyes are constantly watching and learning from us. What matters to them is not the philosophy we preach, but how we practice those lofty principles.

To teach them respect, we need to model the right behavior. "Do what I say, not what I do" is not only unfair but just doesn't work. Sooner or later, children see through hypocrisy, and will lose their respect for you or copy your hypocrisy—or both.

It all sounds good on paper, but in reality it can be hard. That's why, as parents, we work on respect every day. It's in the little things . . .

It's when we volunteer for social justice groups or do the shopping for an elderly neighbor.

It's when we're waiting in line, and see an opening to cut ahead of others. Even though the girls may be too young to realize it, we do the right thing and wait our turn—though waiting in line with twins gives you both motive and excuse to jump ahead!

And it's in the big things . . .

It's having their mother create a successful public relations business that allows her to work at home, while helping other women pursue their business goals. This shows the girls that with hard work, women have choices—many choices. And they can choose the options that work for them.

It's making the choice to live in an urban—not suburban—neighborhood, where diversity reigns and people of all races, beliefs, classes, and sexual preferences live together. When we sit on our stoop with our girls—along with the cats and dog—we talk with everyone, including the men living in the halfway house, the politicians, the families, the old, the young, and the homeless.

The girls will realize early on that living downtown isn't always an episode from *Sesame Street*. Seeing disrespect out in public will open the door to interesting conversations around the dinner table about how we feel it was wrong and what we can do. And yes, having dinner together, with conversation, is another of our family goals.

Modeling respect means that we need to set a high standard for ourselves as parents. But we're only human; not saints or superheroes. So when we screw up, we will need to admit it, apologize to everyone affected by it, and correct the situation to the best of our ability.

Sure, God isn't watching us—but our children certainly are!

We believe that the best foundation for respecting others is respect for oneself. Once the girls value themselves, it's easier to teach them to respect their possessions, family, friends, and the world around them. We want our daughters to have compassion, courage, and creativity, but to do that the girls need to develop a fourth C—confidence.

> 66 Sure, God isn't watching us—but our children certainly are! 99

The Ancient Greeks taught that pride was a virtue; indeed, Aristotle said it was the crown of all the virtues. Yet many religions treat pride as a sin—especially for women and girls—and this attitude has seeped deep into our everyday culture. Maybe that's why educators and parenting books use long-winded synonyms for pride, such as "self-confidence" and "self-esteem." Pride may be the virtue that dare not speak its name, but all the children's experts agree that "self-esteem" has been grievously neglected in our society.

Raising confident girls means encouraging them to explore their potential. Fulfilling their potential will take ambition, hard work, and deferred gratification; it requires self-discipline. We expect confident children to enjoy their accomplishments: They will have earned it. This kind of justified pride is very different from *hubris* or arrogance, with its overconfidence and disrespect for others.

The recipe for instilling self-confidence is well known. Every day we give our girls opportunities for success and then praise them when they achieve it—though it's important to respond with genuine appreciation, rather than just rote flattery. When they struggle, we help them face their challenges. When they fail, we help them cope with their defeats and learn from them.

In reading about how to raise children with strong self-esteem, we've noticed that humanist values are emphasized again and again. For example, teaching children to critically examine their options and giving them the freedom and responsibility to act on their choices are among the best ways to build self-esteem.

Again, modeling plays a role as well; as parents, we celebrate our individual successes and when faced with a problem, help each other find a way to get through it. After all, it's what a family is really about.

We also model both independence and collaboration. While pursuing separate careers we try to find ways to work together: like writing this book chapter!

We have been focusing on the positive, but we know we will face some tough issues as a secular family in a predominantly religious society.

Perhaps one of the first situations our girls will face is how to deal with the Pledge of Allegiance when they go to school. If they are not comfortable using the phrase "under God," how will they deal with the ever-present peer pressure when their classmates say it and they don't? And if they do say it, will we (perhaps unconsciously) pressure them not to?

While we want to raise our children to have the courage of their convictions, it's a lot to ask from a 5-year-old.

One of the biggest challenges we will face as the girls get older is teaching respect for those who not only have different beliefs but actually hold opposing values. Unlike most other nonreligious families, our beliefs are at the forefront of our lives, since one of us runs an international humanist organization, the Institute for Humanist Studies. We cannot hide this—nor should we, because that would teach our girls that we don't respect our own beliefs and values.

Fortunately, we live in a very diverse and liberal neighborhood in one of the most progressive corners of the country. Still, our children are going to meet a lot of people who don't like their father's work. Even in the most friendly of environments, they are likely to find themselves explaining what humanism is far more than most kids! So they will find themselves discussing why their parents don't believe in God and other charged issues—like the interesting news that Lyra is named after a fictional hero who overthrows God to establish a Republic of Heaven![1]

Let's be honest here. We want our daughters to be intelligent, discerning individuals who are willing to demand answers to their questions and not afraid to criticize bad ideas.

We don't believe that all ideas have equal merit. Some are right; some are wrong. Some are good and some are bad. So we cannot say that we want our children to respect all beliefs equally.

> We don't believe that all ideas have equal merit, so we cannot say that we want our children to respect all beliefs equally. And yet we do want them to treat all believers with respect and dignity, even if they disagree with our family values.

And yet we do want them to treat all believers with respect and dignity, just as we want everyone to treat our daughters with respect, even if they disagree with our family values. How do we teach our children to respect others whose values they disagree with?

We don't claim to have the perfect, pat answer to this. We do know, however, that we are able to do this, for the most part, in our own lives.

The girls' mother has parents who consciously brought their children to different religious events—from a Jewish Seder to a Muslim wedding, as well as the family's own Catholic ceremonies—to help them appreciate diversity. We hope to be able to involve our daughters in such events as well, so they can appreciate others' traditions and points of view. Their father serves as the president of the United Nations NGO Committee on Freedom of Religion or Belief, which works with hundreds of groups, both religious and secular, to defend the UN's agreements on freedom of conscience. This models the idea that even when you disagree profoundly on major issues, you can still find common ground to work together respectfully.

It won't always be easy, especially as humanists in such a religious society. We want our children to respect others, but we won't let our daughters' self-esteem be damaged by asking them to defer to people who openly disrespect them or their family's values.

These issues may not arise until the girls are older. We hope the foundation of pride and respect that we're building will empower our daughters to rise to these challenges.

We started this chapter with vows and are ending it with uncertain hopes and unanswered questions. Yet as humanists, we relish questions to which we haven't worked out all the answers. If we do a decent job raising Sophia and Lyra, we expect they will work out answers for themselves, as well as posing questions that never occurred to us. We can respect that. In fact, it would make us proud.

Seven Secular Virtues: Humility, Empathy, Courage, Honesty, Openness, Generosity, and Gratitude

Dale McGowan, Ph.D.

THE IDEA OF VIRTUE IS A noble one: Identify those qualities that make for an admirable person, then work hard to attain them and encourage others to do the same. Identifying virtues and building a collective desire to achieve them can go a long way toward making a better world. And it's a very good idea for parents of any stripe to have a firm grasp of those qualities they want to encourage in their children.

The trick, of course, is naming the right virtues. The early Christian church named seven (faith, hope, charity, courage, justice, temperance, and wisdom), placing them in opposition to seven deadly sins (pride, avarice, lust, anger, gluttony, envy, and sloth) for command of the human soul. Once Thomas Aquinas weighed in, the list of virtues was set in stone.

Freethinkers don't take kindly to stone-carved lists. We know that the best possible rules, principles, ideas, and theories result when we continually reconsider, rethink, and challenge them.

This is not a comprehensive list of human virtues, nor a list that applies only to secularists. Nor do they represent qualities that always come easy to secularists. On the contrary, like traditional virtues, they are qualities to which we can aspire—often with great difficulty. They are not carved in stone, but in butter, meant to stimulate your own thinking about virtue rather than to dictate an immutable set of commandments.

Humility

Pride, properly understood as self-esteem, is something to nurture in our kids. Arrogance, on the other hand—extreme self-importance mixed with a dose of contempt for others—is something to guard against, for two good reasons: It's unbearable to be around, and it makes no sense.

Think of people you've known who were just unbearable to be with. Now think of those whose company made you feel at ease, people you could spend all day with and come back for more. Odds are good that arrogance was a big part of the personalities of those unstandables, and *humility*—a decent dose of modesty and self-deprecation—was a common characteristic of the others.

Humility, like so many of these virtues, is about caring what others think and feel, about giving validation to others instead of seeking it all for yourself. The best way for parents to teach this, of course, is to model humility ourselves. Monitor your next conversation. How often can you catch yourself saying, "I may be wrong about that"—no one should know more than a skeptic that everything includes an element of doubt—and how often do your kids *hear* you saying it? How often do you invite someone else's opinion? Do you spend at least half of the conversation asking about the other person, or are you mostly yakking about you? Do you find something to validate in the other person's thoughts, or is it wall-to-wall correction?

If being a bearable member of society isn't incentive enough, try this one: Humility is the natural consequence of religious disbelief. The Christian view holds humans to be specially created repositories of the divine spark, molded in the image of the Creator of the Universe, granted dominion over "mere beasts," and promised immortal life in God's loving embrace.

Wow. Hard to be humble when you're the center of it all.

But we're not the center, of course. Perhaps the greatest contribution of science has been its humbling recasting of our role in the universe. Instead of the main event in a young, small universe, we have come to realize that we are a blink in time and a speck in space. And instead of having dominion over the animals, we find that we are simply one group among them, special only in the development of one organ—which we too often underuse.

> 66 Everything about the scientifically informed world view cries out for humility. We are trousered apes. Yet many nonbelievers arrogantly strut and crow about having figured *out* that they are apes. That's pretty hilarious if you think about it. 99

Everything about the scientifically informed world view cries out for humility. We are trousered apes. Yet many nonbelievers arrogantly strut and crow about having figured *out* that they are apes. That's pretty hilarious if you think about it.

Next time you look in the mirror, scratch under your arms a bit. Say *hoo hoo hoo*. Let your kids see you doing it and invite them to do the same. We've done some pretty amazing things, we trousered apes, but genetically we're still less than 2 percent away from our fellow chimps. When we get a little too full of ourselves, a little pit-scratching in the mirror can do wonders for restoring some humility.

Empathy

Empathy is the ability to understand how someone else feels—and, by implication, to care. It is the ultimate sign of maturity. Infants are, for their own adaptive good, entirely self-centered. But as we grow, our circle of concern and understanding enlarges, including first family, then one's own community. But having developed empathy for those who are most like us, we too often stop cold, leaving the empathy boundary at the boundary of our own nation, race, or creed—a recipe for disaster. Statements of concern for "the loss of American lives" in armed conflict, for example, carry an unspoken judgment that American lives are more precious than others, a serious failure of empathy.

Continually pushing out the empathy boundary is a life's work. We can help our kids begin that critical work as early as possible not by preaching it but by embodying it. Allow your children to see poverty up close. Travel to other countries if you can, staying as long as possible until our shared humanity becomes unmistakable. Engage other cultures and races not just to value difference but to *recognize sameness*. It's difficult to hate when you begin to see yourself in the other. And why stop at the species? Knowing that we are just one part of the incredible interwoven network of life on Earth should engender a profound empathy for those who just happen to be across the (relatively arbitrary) boundary of species.

Secular parents must be on guard against a particular failure of empathy—the failure to recognize and understand the religious impulse. Too many nonbelievers shake their heads contemptuously at the very idea of religious belief, failing to recognize religion for what it is—an understandable response to the human condition. Let me repeat that: If the religious impulse seems completely incomprehensible to you, I humbly suggest that you don't fully grasp the human condition.

Let me explain. I have been very fortunate. I grew up in a stable home, never at risk of starvation, violence, or death. I had a world-class education and parents who encouraged me to develop my mind and refused to dictate my beliefs. My life expectancy is in the late seventies, and I'll probably make it. Those circumstances, and a few dozen others, have given me the freedom—the luxury, if you will—of seeing my way out of superstition. But it would be incredibly pig-headed of me to fail to understand why others, living more tangibly in the shadow of death or without access to education or freedom of inquiry, would find comfort in religious belief. That doesn't mean I can't challenge the many ill effects of that belief—I can and I do, without apology—but we *must* begin by understanding the realities that gave birth to religion and keep it alive. The best thing we can do is work hard to remedy those realities, to give *everyone* the benefits for which we should be grateful. Until then, we must give ourselves a good hard mental swat every time we feel inclined to mock, sneer, or roll our eyes at those whose beliefs differ from our own. You'll know you've failed at this the first time you see your kids mocking or sneering at religious belief. Be thoroughly ashamed when that happens, since they will almost certainly have learned it from you. 'Fess up and fix it on the spot, not because it's not nice, but because a lack of empathy is literal ignorance.

> " We must give ourselves a good hard mental swat every time we feel inclined to mock, sneer, or roll our eyes at those whose beliefs differ from our own. You'll know you've failed at this the first time you see your kids mocking or sneering at religious belief. "

Courage

The philosopher Paul Kurtz called courage "the first humanistic virtue." For no good reason but to demonstrate a little stubborn freethinking independence, I've placed it third. Secularists need courage for two main reasons: to live in a religious world that marginalizes and demonizes disbelief and to face the realities of human existence honestly.

It takes very little courage to live in the mainstream. As long as you embrace the norms and beliefs of the majority, you'll encounter little difficulty, little resistance. Go with the flow and the world will pat you on the head and coo. Protest what is "normal"—dress differently, believe differently, speak differently—and you'll create problems for the Machine. And the Machine, in return, will create problems for you.

Kids need to know that nonconformity requires courage. There are plenty of nonconformists to draw upon as examples, secular and religious people alike, from Socrates to Martin Luther King to Michael Newdow—people whose strength of conviction led them to face with dignity and courage the consequences of stepping outside of the norm in the name of heartfelt principles. It isn't easy, but doing what's right can be well worth it.

The second reason is even more daunting. As noted above, religion primarily evolved not to provide answers but to console fears. The idea of death (if I may jump right to the big one) is terrifying to a living being. Evolution has made sure of that—the more indifferent an animal is to death, the more quickly it will achieve it, and the less such unwise indifference will appear in the next generation. An afterlife illusion addresses the fear of death by simply denying it really happens. Not much integrity in such a plan, but if you can get yourself to believe it, the comfort would be undeniable.

Secularists, God bless us, have opted for the honest truth. In doing so, we face the ultimate terror of existence: our eventual *non*-existence. Philosophy has its consolations, of course, but I'm not convinced they do the whole job. If you've come happily to terms with oblivion, well bully for you. You're way ahead of me, and 99.8 percent of the species. For the rest of us, courage, in the face of mortality and the other genuinely challenging aspects of being human, is a virtue well worth cultivating.

Honesty

Honesty is the essence of secularism. It is a willingness to set aside any and every comfort in order to know the truth that allowed us to see our way out of religious belief. Somewhat more difficult is ensuring that we practice the same level of honesty in all other aspects of our lives. I say "somewhat more difficult" because in truth most of the humanists and atheists I know are relentlessly, exhaustively honest, sometimes to a comical extent. We are often *paralyzed* by our obsession with honesty—yet in one of the greatest ironies I know, nonbelievers consistently rate as the least trustworthy minority in the United States.

Yet in one aspect of honesty, we too often fall flat. How many of us have stuttered or stammered when a pollster asked our religious preference, or when a new neighbor asked what church we attend? It may not be surprising that we blanch at revealing our disbelief to someone who may after all have heard once a week for 800 consecutive weeks that disbelief is the ultimate, unforgivably hell-bound sin. But what better way to overturn culturally ingrained misconceptions about nonbelievers than by revealing that hey, this guy or gal you've known and liked for years, your friend, your neighbor, is a nonbeliever? What is accomplished by continuing to "pass"?

Teach your children to choose their beliefs honestly and then to honestly and proudly own them.

Openness

Openness has several facets, but all are rooted in the same two principles: embracing your own fallibility and embracing diversity.

Secularists, being human, are as prone as anyone to cling stubbornly to our opinions once they're established. Openness includes recognizing our own fallibility: No matter how thoroughly we have examined a question, we could still be wrong. The best way to avoid being wrong is to keep our opinions and ideas open to challenge and potential disconfirmation.

The other principle—which often goes by the awful name of "tolerance"— is the very fundament of liberal philosophy. A student in an honors seminar once asked me to define the difference between liberalism and conservatism in a few words—one of the best questions I'd heard in fifteen years. I stared at the floor for what seemed like an hour, then was struck by what I still believe is a darn good answer: The key distinction is the attitude toward difference.

Conservative philosophy tends to believe that there is one "best way" to be and that our job as individuals and as a society is to find that one way and to unify around it—united we stand, you're with us or you're against us, join the saved, and to hell with the damned. Liberal philosophy holds that there are many "good ways" to be and that our job as individuals and as a society is to embrace that diversity of approaches to life. Different strokes for different folks.

One student immediately raised the usual concern that the liberal view looks like an "anything goes" position. But it isn't, of course—it embraces *many* ways, but not *all* ways. Someone whose choices harm others would not be permitted by the society to choose that way. So liberals tend to oppose war, which invariably inflicts harm on innocents, and to support the right of gay marriage, which harms no one and would make many people happy.

My concern with the conservative position is that we humans tend to each define *our* way as the "one true way"—and quickly end up facing each other in armed camps, coalesced around our various "best ways," determined to eradicate the others, with God on our side. (For reference, see MIDDLE EAST, NORTHERN IRELAND, ABORTION DEBATE.)

A conservative secularist might declare our way of believing the "one true way," dreaming of a day without religion. That would be as boring and undesirable a world to me as a Planet Evangelical. We shouldn't even *wish* for everyone to be like us—and fortunately, few secularists do. Our worldview is inherently liberal philosophically. We should therefore look toward a world in which our view is one legitimate voice among many and teach our kids openness of spirit and embrace of diversity as a fundamental virtue.

Generosity

Hear enough "deconversion" stories and you'll begin to see a pattern. Many feel sadness and confusion as their faith begins to flag—only to describe a feeling of peaceful relief once it is finally gone, followed by a sense of personal freedom. But then—despite the dire warnings of the evangelists—instead of picking up a machine gun, we are hit with what I'll call the Humanist Epiphany: In the absence of a god, *we are all we've got.* Freedom is joined by an awesome sense of responsibility.

Christians could be forgiven if they took an entirely hands-off approach to charity. God is all-just, after all. He will provide for the needy, if not in this world, then in the next. Yet plenty of Christians are out there doing good works for others as a direct and visible expression of their values.

Atheists, however, have no excuse to sit passively. We know there's no divine safety net, no universal justice, no Great Caretaker, no afterlife reward. We have the full responsibility to create a just world and care for the less fortunate because there's no one else to do so. So why are Christians doing most of the charity?

They're not.

I was shocked to learn that myself. That churchgoers do the lion's share of the charitable work in our communities is simply untrue. They get credit for it because they do a better job of tying the good works they do to their creed. But according to a 1998 study,[2] 82 percent of volunteerism by churchgoers falls under the rubric of "church maintenance" activities—volunteerism entirely within, and for the benefit of, the church building and immediate church community. As a result of this siphoning of volunteer energy into the care and feeding of churches themselves, most of the volunteering that happens out in the larger community—from AIDS hospices to food shelves to international aid workers to those feeding the hungry and housing the homeless and caring for the elderly—comes from the category of "unchurched" volunteers. The same pattern is apparent on the international stage. The Center for Global Development (CGD) reports that the developed countries that rank highest in terms of generosity to poor countries are those in which church attendance is lowest. Denmark, Norway, Sweden, and the Netherlands consistently top the list, all of which have regular church attendance below 15 percent. The idea of a religious monopoly on charity and community service is clearly a myth.[3]

> 66 Our shortcoming is not in doing good, but in making it clear that charity without church is not a stretch but a logical outgrowth of a nontheistic worldview. 99

Our shortcoming is not in doing good, but in making it clear that charity without church is not a stretch but a logical outgrowth of a nontheistic worldview.

Generosity goes far beyond organized charity, of course. We must also model the kind of generosity of spiriit that improves everyone's experience of daily life. Giving a compliment is an act of generosity. Allowing a car to merge in front of you is an act of generosity. Spending time with an isolated person, expressing love, interest, concern, or support, allowing someone else to take credit for something done together—these acts of generosity are all better modeled than "taught" to our children, and represent a virtue that fits hand-in-glove with the nonreligious worldview.

Gratitude

The most terrible moment for an atheist, someone once said, is when he feels grateful and has no one to thank. I suppose it was meant to be witty, but it's pretty silly. Nonbelievers of all stripes should and do indeed feel enormously grateful for many things, and I'm not aware of any terrible moments. Whereas religious folks teach their children to funnel all gratitude skyward, humanists and atheists can thank the *actual* sources of the good things we experience, those who *actually* deserve praise but too often see it deflected past them and on to an imaginary being.

We have no difficulty reminding the 4-year-old to "say thank you" when Grandma hands her an ice cream cone, but in other situations—especially when a religious turn-of-phrase is generally used—we often pass up the chance to teach our kids to express gratitude in naturalistic terms. Instead of thanking God for the food on your table, thank those who really put it there—the farmers, the truckers, the produce workers, and Mom or Dad or Aunt Millicent. They deserve it. Maybe you'd like to lean toward the Native American and honor the animals for the sacrifice of their lives—a nice way to underline our connection to them. You can give thanks to those around the table for being present, and for their health, and for family and friendship itself. There is no limit. Even when abstract, like gratitude for health, the simple expression of gratitude is all that is needed. No divine ear is necessary—we are surrounded by real ears and by real hearers.

I read recently of a woman who had lost her husband unexpectedly. She was devastated and bereft of hope—until her neighbors and friends began to arrive. Over the course of several days, they brought food, kept her company, laughed and cried, hugged her, and reassured her that the pain would ease with time and that they would be there every step of the way. "I was so grateful for their love and kindness during those dark days," she said. "Through them, I could feel the loving embrace of God."

She was most comfortable expressing her gratitude to an idea of God, but the love and kindness came entirely from those generous and caring human beings. Humanists and atheists are not impoverished by the lack of that god idea; they must simply notice who truly deserves thanks, and not be shy about expressing it.

Supporting Your Children in Their Quest for the Meaning of Life!

Donald B. Ardell, Ph.D.

O Karma, Dharma, pudding and pie, gimme a break before I die:
grant me wisdom, will and wit, purity, probity, pluck and grit.
Trustworthy, loyal, helpful, kind, gimme great abs and a steel-trap mind,
and forgive, Ye Gods, some humble advice—these little blessings would suffice
to beget an earthly paradise:
make the bad people good—and the good people nice;
and before our world goes over the brink, teach the believers how to think.

"O Karma, Dharma, Pudding and Pie" by Philip Appleman

Reprinted from Appleman, Philip, Selected Poems (University of Arkansas Press, 1996). Used with permission.

IT WOULD BE NICE if we could all contribute to helping "teach believers how to think before our world goes over the brink." However, let's be realistic. Unless you are a gifted orator like Robert Green Ingersoll,[4] a writer like Sam Harris, a philosopher like Paul Kurtz, or other great talent with *wisdom, will and wit, purity, probity, pluck and grit and all the rest*—including *great abs and a steel-trap mind*—saving the world might be a bit of a reach. Maybe it's quite enough to focus your efforts on the children, specifically, your own.

At a time when religion seems to permeate our culture as never before, from the White House down, it's important to help our children develop the skills and predispositions to resist indoctrination and think for themselves.

Creating not just an interest but also a fascination with the great questions about our meaning and purpose is, to quote Dr. McGowan, "a perfectly normal option for raising healthy, ethical, well-rounded kids in a loving and honest environment."

Recently, I asked my parents if they recalled my first words. Surprisingly, they did. At the tender age they estimated at around six minutes, I remarked, totally out of the blue and with no coaching, "Gaaaaa waabooooaaaaaaaa." Yes, I was a precocious little bugger. My proud mom and dad may or may not have understood what I said, but I remember the moment quite clearly. I wanted to know why I was here, who made me, and what was expected. In short, I was curious about my purpose and what, exactly, was the meaning of life.

Well, I don't think I understood their response, but sooner or later (probably a great deal later, since I was raised Catholic), I realized I was going to have to figure out this one myself. Why? Because the packaged response—"You are here to serve God, God made you, and you are expected to follow His rules"—did not compute by the time I was around, oh, maybe 10.

This essay is designed to contribute a few ideas about secular parenting related to life's great questions. Not all children start out asking existential biggies, but many teachable moments contain openings for nourishing such curiosities. You never know when a meaningless gurgle that sounds like "Gaaaaa waabooooaaaaaaaa" is actually the start of a lifelong search for answers. Or, at least an insight or two about the great mysteries.

We all want what's best for our kids, whether we believe in a Grand Wazoo by one name or another, or choose to shape meaning and purposes without reference to an Imaginary Friend.

Alas, "what's best" is yet another of life's great mysteries, not to be determined (beyond the earliest years) by the parents. Both religious and secular parents must recognize, at some level, this cold fact: With regard to how your

135

child will turn out, there are no sure things. Even under ideal, utopian, or near-perfect conditions over time (the right mix of love, supportive environments, positive peers, quality education, and so on), things might not turn out as you wish. Despite all manner of advantage and caring investments over time, the little tyrants might still grow up to be cowboys! Or, your sweet, precious, beautiful, and brilliant little girl with such vast promise for a life free and epic, the treasure you fantasized would become president some day and change the course of history, might end up a nun. But, who knows—maybe she's happy, at one with the universe, and quite clear about her meaning and purpose. Maybe you succeeded after all. Who can say?

So, do your best, hope for good things, but recognize that, if you are really fortunate, he or she will eventually do what is best for him- or herself.

Considerations for Secular Parents

I'll go out on a limb here and guess that most of us agree on what is NOT the meaning of life. It is not, to give a few examples, to avoid illness, accidents, and suffering. Nor is it to seek and find pleasure, to gain riches, or live a stress-free life. It's not to acquire more stuff, however attractive certain stuff may seem at times. You agree with all this, right?

Well—what then? What IS the bloody meaning of life, or MOL? Everyone's entitled to an opinion. I'd guess you believe as I do—that there is none, save what we invent. By saying there is no meaning of life, I mean no universal, inherent meaning that applies for everyone. What is called for, then, is a *conscious* quest for meaning, the kind of self-directed meaning-making urged by such great existential thinkers as Viktor Frankl. Psychiatrists like Irving Yalom suggest that pondering such questions is important for good mental health, even if the answer is ultimately unknowable. While Frankl fascinated us in *Man's Search for Meaning* with accounts of finding meaning amid the horrors of the Nazi death camps, most of us face less daunting obstacles. Yet I suspect Frankl's reflections, though drawn from worst cases, apply even in favored or (pardon the term, here intended in a secular way) "blessed" circumstances.

> " Viktor Frankl identified selfless service to others as the surest path to finding a fulfilling sense of meaning. On a less dramatic level than Frankl endured, we build meaning from an accumulation of modest, nondramatic services over time. "

Frankl identified selfless service to others as the surest path to finding a fulfilling sense of meaning. On a less dramatic level than Frankl endured, we build meaning from an accumulation of modest, nondramatic services over time. Carrying an organ donor card, for instance, might someday improve or even save the life of another, and a discussion about becoming a donor could be a parental teachable moment. Such brief, low-key communications with a child often stimulate early existential reflections in the informed, supportive atmosphere of a loving family context.

I carry a donor card myself, by the way—else I would not have the gall to urge you to do so. Provided I am certifiably deceased, anyone is cordially welcome to one or both of my kidneys and lungs, my quite excellent (so far) triathlete heart, my pretty good liver, pancreas, and intestines, as well as my skin and bone marrow, heart valves, connective tissue, eyes, ears—you get the picture. (I'm reminded of one of Ashleigh Brilliant's wonderful Potshots—"I'm Not Perfect, But Parts of Me Are Excellent!") And Frankl was right: That conscious decision to serve others even after I'm gone is a very fulfilling part of my self-constructed sense of meaning and purpose while I'm still here.

Where might you look then for a starter set of ideas about finding more satisfaction in terms of meaning and purpose (henceforth M&P) than you already possess? I recommend a low-key, unhurried quest for your own tentative answers, or at least possibilities.

No Inherent Meaning

A sense of meaning and purpose is important for mental and emotional wellness. But life is without *inherent* meaning, so to be optimally well, we must *invest* life with meaning and purpose and teach our kids to do the same.

By receiving M&P in prepackaged parcels, the children of religious parents gain less experience in self-directed meaning-making. In my first grade, back around 1944, the answer to "Who made me?" was, of course, "God made me," and the next M&P question ("Why did God make me?") made clear what I was here for and what life was all about: "To love and to serve Him."

There it was. An inherent meaning of life, same for me as for all my classmates and, presumably, everyone else in the whole wide world—including, presumably, the Nazis who were tearing about Europe at the time.

Later, I began to consider it more likely that M&P was what you made it to be, not a cosmic given. At least that's my view now. Carl Sagan expressed it this way: "We are the custodians of life's meaning. We would prefer it to be otherwise, of course, but there is no compelling evidence for a cosmic parent who will care for us and save us from ourselves. It is up to us." Had he said that in first grade in 1944 at St. Barnabas in Philadelphia, PA, little Carl would have been severely disciplined. Of course, such schools were not organized to teach (or encourage or even *tolerate)* critical thinking skills, to promote free inquiry, or to reinforce reason and skepticism about unsupported assertions. We're all entitled to opinions, and reflections and opinions on this mystery could foster enriching discussions at your family's dinner table. Such discussions can be endlessly rewarding, elements of a rich family intellectual life during all phases of a child's wonder years. Of course, staying alert for new ideas and possibilities about M&P should never end until the final curtain call.

Of course (to quote comedian Dennis Miller), "I could be wrong about this." Certainty has its drawbacks, as I learned later in life about the required answers to those M&P questions posed in first grade. This is seen as well in modern times in the words of the cartoon character Calvin, who said, "The meaning of life is that people should do what I want!"

Is there a link between M&P and human happiness? Well, as Jack Palance told Billy Crystal in the movie *City Slickers* after an exchange about the meaning of life, "That's for you to find out." For those who choose to parent their children in secular, reason-based ways, "that's for you to find out" might come in handy on many occasions, until such times as they conclude for themselves that such is and always will be the case.

So what do the Tooth Fairy, Big Foot, the Loch Ness Monster, and the meaning of life have in common? Answer: None of these things exists! I think people make them up, for various reasons, for better or worse.

You can get by quite nicely without the Tooth Fairy, Big Foot, and the Loch Ness Monster, but meaning is another thing. If you suspect, as I do, that there's not a single meaning to life applicable to all, you'll want to find something that's really meaningful to you.

One of the Many Possible Roads to M&P—Volunteering

Volunteering for a consequential cause is a meaning-building activity that many find fulfilling. I say "hail to volunteers" who do good work and to the organizations that utilize and channel their exceptional energies. Great causes have been advanced and countless lives improved by those willing to donate their time and effort.

> Only a life lived for others is worthwhile.
>
> — Albert Einstein

There are a few caveats to consider in volunteering. Sometimes volunteering includes a strong element of self-interest, even beyond the fulfillment of M&P. Students, for example, need volunteer service for admittance to prestigious universities, and many volunteering in programs sponsored by religious organizations are in part seeking admission to Paradise! There's no harm in such self-interest, of course, provided it's above board and recognized by all concerned. Volunteers should also be careful not to increase the dependency of those they serve.

These caveats shouldn't dissuade you from volunteering, but acknowledging all sides of the issue is a vital part of the examined life. And the unexamined life, as Socrates put it, is not worth living. The most satisfying meaning is the meaning we build with our eyes wide open.

> " The unexamined life, as Socrates put it, is not worth living. The most satisfying meaning is the meaning we build with our eyes wide open. "

If *you* plan to volunteer, look for ways to involve your children. Few experiences are as rewarding and eye-opening. Just balance the usual talk about the importance of helping others with a discussion of motives—especially the importance of avoiding a "holier-than-thou" syndrome where the volunteer expects to be hailed or honored for doing what is basically personally satisfying.

This is only one of endless possibilities for building a meaningful and purposeful life. You'll know when you've found the right fit for you—the feeling is unmistakable. Trust it, and teach your kids to look for and trust that feeling as well. But whatever you do, please don't find your M&P by starting another religion, adding to the amount of myth-information in the world!

Be well. Always look on the bright side of life.

What Your Kids Won't Learn in School

Annie Laurie Gaylor

MOST PEOPLE, EVEN ATHEISTS and agnostics, do not realize how many admired figures in history have been nonreligious. Many icons in U.S. history and literature were skeptics or outright scoffers. Yet when schoolchildren read about inventor **Thomas Alva Edison,** they won't encounter his view that religion was all bunk. When they read about **Thomas Paine** and his influence in fomenting the American Revolution, it is unlikely they will be taught that Paine's book, *The Age of Reason,* is one of the most devastating critiques of the bible ever written. A growing number of references ensure that a thoughtful parent can readily introduce children to the heady history of freethought heroes and heroines they won't learn about in school. Any time is the right time to introduce your children to freethinking and its heritage.

Ensuring that your child grows up free from religion—from such unwholesome ideas as original sin or everlasting punishment—might be the greatest gift you can offer. Yet the absence of religion in a household may not be enough. Are you equipping your child to survive and thrive as a freethinker in one of the most religious nations in the world?

In today's United States, atheism is the least acceptable minority position. The increasing U.S. acceptance of religious diversity does not extend to atheists, according to a national survey released in March 2006 by the University of Minnesota's department of sociology. The survey found that in this country atheists are rated below Muslims, recent immigrants, gays and lesbians, and other minority groups as not "sharing their vision of American society." Atheists are the minority group most Americans are least willing to allow their children to marry into. The kneejerk reaction of most religionists is that atheists and agnostics do not even have a moral sense of right or wrong! Given society's demonization of atheism, how can we teach our children to think for themselves, be proud if they choose to belong to the category of "none of the above," and respectful of nonbelievers if they do not? While freethought must be a position one arrives at intellectually and independently, it is still vital to affirm secular values as a parent. Just as we would take steps to prevent our children from growing up homophobic, violent, racist, or sexist, we do not want our children to fall prey to superstition and religious dogma. Part of producing healthy children may require inoculating our children against dogma. With the religious right in full attack against the Enlightenment, now is not the time to hide or downplay your freethinking views, especially in front of your children. Humanity has progressed as religious power has diminished, often as a result of courageous battles fought by secular heroes and heroines. Acquainting your child with the truly impressive contributions of freethinkers will help instill a sense of history and a respect for freethought—the formation of opinions about religion based on reason, rather than tradition, authority or established belief.

Take advantage of life experiences, news events, and school assignments to share interesting tidbits about freethinkers. The next time super-athlete **Lance Armstrong** is in the news, why not mention that Armstrong rejected religion and prayer during his fight with cancer? If your child is learning to play **Johannes Brahms'** "Lullaby," by all means let her know that the composer, a much-admired philanthropist, had no use for religion. Next time you take your kids with you on Election Day when you vote, explain that it was nonreligious women who were the first to work for women's right to vote. When a **Cole Porter** song comes on during a movie sound track, let your kids know that Porter was out of the closet both as a gay man and an atheist. Be sure your children know that much of the screenplay and all of the lyrics in *The Wizard of Oz,* a movie that is a magical benchmark in most young lives, were written by freethinker **E.Y. "Yip" Harburg.**

Suggesting a freethought topic, when your child comes to you with a school assignment or essay, can turn a young mind on. Suggest that your child research the forgotten nineteenth century freethinker **Robert Green Ingersoll,** for example. If your student must select a poem to memorize or parse, direct them to something freethinking by the plethora of skeptical poets, including **William Blake, Robert Burns, Lord Byron, Samuel Coleridge, e.e. cummings, Robert Frost, Goethe, Langston Hughes, John Keats, Amy Lowell, James Russell Lowell, Robert Lowell, Molière, Edgar Allan Poe, Alexander Pope, Carl Sandburg, Percy Bysshe Shelley, Gertrude Stein, Algernon Swinburne, Alfred Tennyson,** and **Walt Whitman.**

Most children who like to read discover Tom Sawyer by themselves. And most schoolchildren are still assigned *The Adventures of Huckleberry Finn,* with its freethinking denouement, in which Huck vows he would rather burn in hell forever than send his friend back into slavery. What a perfect opportunity to discuss the freethought views and contributions of **Mark Twain!** Parents have great influence through the books, journals, and movies found in their homes. Parents of older elementary school-aged children who like fantasy such as *Harry Potter* have a perfect winter solstice present in the *Dark Materials* trilogy of **Philip Pullman,** which the British atheist author wrote directly to counter the influence of C. S. Lewis's pious *Narnia* series. A painless way to introduce your children to freethought concepts while entertaining them is by screening movies, such as *Contact,* based on **Carl Sagan's** novel, which stars Jodie Foster, a freethinking actress, as a nonreligious scientist. *Chocolat* is a direct challenge of the repression of the Catholic Church and contains an appealing child character. A surprising number of classic films contain laudable freethinking characters, such as the movie based on **Lorraine Hansberry's** play *A Raisin in the Sun.* Teenagers may be ready for nonfiction by and about freethinkers, including readings of the great skeptics or philosophers, such as **Hobbes, Spinoza, Hume, Diderot, Nietzsche, Freud, Santayana, Mencken,** and **Russell.**

Below follows a brief but representative sampling of famous freethinkers and their contributions.

American Revolutionaries

Thomas Paine, who named the United States of America and fanned the flames of the Revolution, believed "My own mind is my own church." U.S. patriot Col. **Ethan Allen** (1737–1789), who organized the Green Mountain Boys in Vermont during the American Revolution, wrote what is believed to be the first rationalist book published in America: *Reason: The Only Oracle of Man* (1785). **Benjamin Franklin** (1706–1790), one of the more orthodox deists of the American Revolution, nevertheless believed there should be no government support for religion. Deist and President **Thomas Jefferson** (1743–1826) urged the adoption of the First Amendment, separating church from state. Jefferson passionately rejected the Trinity and a supernatural Jesus, urging instead the use of reason. **James Madison** (1751–1836), the fourth U.S. president, was the primary architect of the secular U.S. Constitution, which drew inspiration from such deists **Montesquieu** and **John Locke.** Madison believed religion shackles the mind, and that a union between church and state had produced only "torrents of blood."

Celebrities

Celebrities make freethinking a little more fun. Among the actors who have made public statements expressing doubt or disbelief are: **Charlie Chaplin, George Clooney, W.C. Fields, Harrison Ford, Katharine Hepburn, Angelina Jolie, John Malkovich, Butterfly McQueen, Jack Nicholson, Uma Thurman, Marlene Dietrich, Jodie Foster, Julianne Moore, Tony Randall, Christopher Reeve, Julia Sweeney,** and **Bruce Willis.** Disbelieving movie directors include **Woody Allen, Ingmar Bergman,** and **Steven Soderbergh.** Composers who were deists, questioners, or unbelievers include **Beethoven, Bizet, Brahms, Debussy, Gershwin, Mahler, Mozart, Schumann, Strauss,** and **Verdi.** Popular songwriters and lyricists include **Irving Berlin, Yip Harburg, Tom Lehrer, Cole Porter, Richard Rodgers,** and **Stephen Sondheim.** Musicians include **Bjork, Ani DiFranco, John Lennon,** and **Frank Zappa. Andy Rooney** of television's *60 Minutes* is a well-known scoffer. TV commentator **Ron Reagan,** the son of the late president Ronald Reagan, has pointed out that he could not realistically run for office as an atheist.

Novelists

Have a child looking for a book report? The list of well-known novelists who have questioned or openly rejected religion is lengthy, including **Margaret Atwood, Pearl Buck, Joseph Conrad, Charles Dickens, F. Scott Fitzgerald, John Fowles, Robert A. Heinlein, Joseph Heller, Langston Hughes, Victor Hugo, Aldous Huxley, John Irving, James Joyce, John Le Carré, Ursula LeGuin, Sinclair Lewis, Jack London, Herman Melville, Joyce Carol Oates, George Orwell, Edgar Allan Poe, Ayn Rand, Tom Robbins, Salmon Rushdie, Upton Sinclair, John Steinbeck, Mark Twain, Gore Vidal, Kurt Vonnegut, Alice Walker, H.G. Wells,** and **Virginia Woolf.** A writer your children might recognize is **Gene Roddenberry,** creator of Star Trek. **Isaac Asimov,** a sci-fi and nonfiction writer, perhaps the world's most prolific, was a strong atheist.

Reformers
Abolition

Without the bible's sanction of slavery, the long, shameful legacy of slavery in the United States might have been curtailed, perhaps averting the bloody Civil War. A widely accepted myth is that Christian churches led the fight against slavery. Yet with the exception of Quakers and Unitarians, most Christian denominations were johnny-come-latelies. The words "infidel" and "abolitionist" were considered interchangeable insults in the early 1800s. The first in America to publicly call for an outright end to slavery was deist Thomas Paine. Deist **William Lloyd Garrison** (1805–1879), founder of the abolitionist newspaper *The Liberator* and the American Anti-Slavery Society in 1833, famously called churches "bulwarks" of slavery. We still sing the words penned by **Lydia Maria Child** (1802–1880), "Over the river and through the woods," but few of us realize this influential abolitionist was a pariah in Boston society for her early abolitionist book, *An Appeal in Favor of That Class of Americans Called Africans.* Abolitionist and former slave **Frederick Douglass** (1817?–1895), who became editor of the *North Star* (1847), noted in one of his autobiographies: "I prayed for twenty years but received no answer until I prayed with my legs." President **Abraham Lincoln,** who signed the Emancipation Proclamation, was likely not more than a deist. His observation that the North and South "both read the same Bible, and pray to the same God" is inscribed on the Lincoln Memorial.

General Reformers

The ranks of reformers are full of nonconformists and unbelievers, whose willingness to challenge prevailing dogma made them courageous advocates of democracy, abolition of the death penalty, and educational reforms. Among the greatest was deist **Voltaire** (1694–1778), father of the Enlightenment, and the world's first civil libertarian. Nineteenth-century British freethought produced many reformers who fought censorship and blasphemy laws, such as **Welsh Robert Owen** (1771–1858), who worked to improve laborers' lives during the Industrial Revolution, championing women's rights and progressive causes. British utilitarian **Jeremy Bentham** (1749–1832) believed in "the greatest happiness of the greatest number" and worked for political, legal, prison and educational reforms. **J. S. Mill** (1806–1873), who wrote *On Liberty,* worked for reforms such as sexual equality and public ownership of national resources. The nineteeth-century United States was awash in freethinking utopians and abolitionists who, after the Civil War, turned to suffrage, labor, or other radical reform movements. Founder of the American Red Cross **Clara Barton** (1821–1912) was a deistic Universalist. Twentieth-century nonreligious reformers include radical "Red" anarchist **Emma Goldman** (1869–1940), who shook up U.S. smugness in her quest for labor, human, and women's rights, **W.E.B. DuBois** (1868–1963), founder of the NAACP, and **Jane Addams** (1860–1935), founder of the strictly secular Hull House.

Feminist Reformers

Where would feminism be without its freethinking founders—who braved scriptural prohibitions ordaining women to keep silent and be in subjection? The first influential feminist book, *A Vindication of the Rights of Woman,* was written by deist-turned-agnostic **Mary Wollstonecraft** (1759–1797) in 1792, urging that women be treated as "rational creatures." Scottish-born **Frances Wright** (1795–1852), an abolitionist, became the first to lecture before audiences of men and women in North America in the 1820s, calling for women's educational rights and castigating the clergy. "Serene agnostic" **Elizabeth Cady Stanton** (1815–1902) was the first woman, in 1848, to call for woman suffrage, launching the women's movement. She was joined by sister agnostic **Susan B. Anthony** (1820–1906). The ranks of the suffrage movement were filled by freethinkers, who were its most radical thinkers, espousing marriage and divorce reform, birth control, and self-autonomy. **Margaret Sanger** (1879–1966), whose motto was "No Gods—No Masters," overcame insuperable barriers to free women by making birth control legal and accessible.

Scientists

A majority of elite U.S. scientists admit to personal disbelief, doubt, or agnosticism and reject belief in human immortality. A landmark 1914 survey by James H. Leuba found that 70 percent of the "great" scientists of the time disbelieved in a god. Twenty years later, when Leuba replicated the survey, he found that doubt among the top tier of scientists had increased to 85 percent. In 1996–1998, when Edward J. Larson and Larry Witham repeated the survey among today's top tier—members of the National Academy of Sciences—fully 93 percent expressed disbelief.[5]

The long warfare between science and religion is best represented by the fate of Spanish physician **Michael Servetus** (1511–1553), who first accurately described pulmonary circulation. Calvin personally ordered Servetus' execution for writing an anti-trinitarian book. Italian mathematician **Galileo Galilei** (1562–1642), pioneer of the experimental scientific method, whose research described inertia, momentum, and gravity, was forced to abjure his Copernican theory that the sun does not revolve around the earth. He died under house arrest. British astronomer **Edmund Halley** (1656–1741), known as the "infidel mathematician," had his career threatened by religious critics.

Irreligious science giants include **Charles Darwin** (1809–1882), an agnostic who rejected Christianity. The British genius delayed publishing *Origin of Species* (1859), from which the religious world is still reeling, anticipating the backlash. German-born **Albert Einstein** (1879–1955), whose papers explaining photoelectric effect and the special theory of relativity revolutionized science, rejected belief in a personal god or immortality. Freethinking American **James Watson** (born 1928) and British atheist **Francis Crick** (1916–2004), along with Maurice Wilkins, unraveled the DNA code. Watson went on to head the human genome project. A sampling of prominent Nobel-award winning scientists who have rejected religion include Polish-born physicist **Marie Curie** (1867–1934), U.S. physicist and popular science writer **Steven Weinberg** (born 1933), physicist **Richard P. Feynman** (1918–1988), and chemist **Linus Pauling** (1901–1994). Astronomer and space scientist **Carl Sagan** (1934–1996), one of the greatest popularizers of science through his television program, *Cosmos,* wrote of his rejection of religion in *The Demon-Haunted World. Selfish Gene* author and British biologist **Richard Dawkins** is one of the world's most outspoken atheists and freethinking authors (*The God Delusion,* 2006).

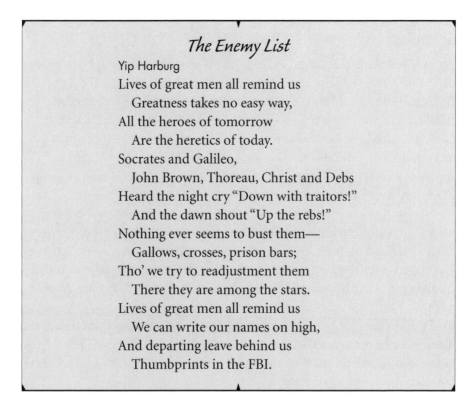

The Enemy List

Yip Harburg

Lives of great men all remind us
    Greatness takes no easy way,
All the heroes of tomorrow
    Are the heretics of today.
Socrates and Galileo,
    John Brown, Thoreau, Christ and Debs
Heard the night cry "Down with traitors!"
    And the dawn shout "Up the rebs!"
Nothing ever seems to bust them—
    Gallows, crosses, prison bars;
Tho' we try to readjustment them
    There they are among the stars.
Lives of great men all remind us
    We can write our names on high,
And departing leave behind us
    Thumbprints in the FBI.

When, as a fifth-grader, I happened to ask my mother for more information about our family's agnostic views, she opened a volume by **Bertrand Russell** and had me read a chapter titled, "Why I Am an Agnostic." I was enchanted. A world of reason opened for me. A parent cannot force that "aha!" moment (and would not want to), but an astute suggestion, book, or guidance at the right moment can change a life—or at the very least provide a much-needed antidote to the assumption that religious belief is universal among those we admire.

■ ■ ■ ■ ■ ■

A Sixty-Second Reckoned Roll of Freethinkers Historical

Dale McGowan, Ph.D.

(SPONTANEOUSLY COMPOSED, SUNG, and copyrighted at the dinner table in response to my 6-year-old's statement that everyone outside of our family believes in God, this song lists famous figures who challenged the dominant religious beliefs of their times—atheists, agnostics, humanists, deists, and other freethinkers. Sung (very fast) to "I Am the Very Model of a Modern Major-General" from *HMS Pinafore*, or, if you prefer, "The Elements" by freethinker Tom Lehrer.)

There's Celsus and Confucius and Lucretius and Epictetus
Thucydides and Socrates and Marcus A. Aurelius
And Seneca and Diderot who lived a long long time ago
But still were smart enough to know, no God above, no Hell below.

Thomas Paine and old Mark Twain had no religion on the brain
And Sigmund Freud would be annoyed if someone asked him to explain
The ludicrous psychology of someone whose theology
Suggests we're damned eternally for munching apples off a tree.

Inventors and biologists and people skilled in medicine
Like Thomas Henry Huxley and like Thomas Alva Edison
And while we're on the Thomases you have my solemn promises
That yet another Thomas is the one named Thomas Jefferson.

Few Christians know these people, so they simply try to pass 'em off
As Bible-thumpin' Christians—even guys like Isaac Asimov!
I hate to have to tattle but they'll have an uphill battle,
That'll be the day when Isaac thumps a Bible (in a Christian way).

Henry Louis Mencken, he was really quite a thinkin' man
And Abraham a-Lincoln no communion wine was drinkin', man
And possibly the best of all, a man named Robert Ingersoll
Who had the unrelenting gall to call religion falderal.

Then there's the man whose *nom de plume* was nothing less than David Hume,
He didn't buy the virgin womb and chuckled at the empty tomb
He laughed and laughed and laughed and laughed
and laughed and laughed and laughed and laughed
and laughed and laughed and laughed and laughed . . .
And so did Mary Wollstonecraft.

We haven't even broken into people in the sciences
Who've written and have spoken their heretical defiances
Of seven-day creation and our sacred obligation
I begin to lose my patien(ce)—and start throwing small appliances.

I'd better stop, I'm obviously losing my ability
To set these noble names in rhyme with metrical facility
I only hope my little song has shown you that the list is long
Of folks who've given God the gong—by thinking with agility.

■ ■ ■ ■ ■ ■

Parenting and the Arts

James Herrick

NOTICE

Persons attempting to find a motive in this narrative will be prosecuted;
persons attempting to find a moral in it will be banished;
persons attempting to find a plot in it will be shot.

BY ORDER OF THE AUTHOR

PER

G. G., CHIEF OF ORDINANCE
(On the forepage of Mark Twain's *Huckleberry Finn*)

IF YOU ARE LOOKING FOR comfort, if you are looking for consolation, if you want the meaning of life handed to you on a plate—don't go to the arts. Whether it is for parents or children, or their interaction, the arts can disturb and should not avoid the difficult areas of life. But art is not to be feared, for it can also stretch the imagination—art is wonderfully elastic, and it can stir creativity. Art is a wonderful stirrer, and a stirrer of wonder.

I intend to consider art and its effect and value, looking particularly at literature, the art with which I am most engaged. I will refer to four children's/adult texts that seem relevant—*Huckleberry Finn* by Mark Twain, *A Gathering Light* by Jennifer Donnelly, *Northern Lights* by Philip Pullman and folk tales—a phrase I prefer to "fairy tales," which sounds effete when in fact the tales are often knotty and tough. I shall consider the range of arts and the range of their practice particularly to children. And I shall conclude by returning to the value in art that we can all take—parents, children, citizens.

For a nonreligious parent or child, art can become an integral part of under-

> 66 Art is not a substitute for religion—no such thing is necessary. But it brings to us all the excitement and danger of being alive, the intensity and delight of love and human relationships, the lasting enhancement of beauty and the perception of extraordinary wonder. 99

149

standing the world and other people and of creating a meaning in life. Art is not a substitute for religion—no such thing is necessary. But it brings to us all the excitement and danger of being alive, the intensity and delight of love and human relationships, the lasting enhancement of beauty, and the perception of extraordinary wonder.

Art is not just challenging—it can be dangerous. Do not enter if you feel queasy. Kafka wrote in his diary of 1916 that "If I am condemned, then I am not only condemned to die, but also condemned to struggle till I die." The artist is then condemned to struggle, and to some extent the reader or observer may need to struggle too. Potted biographies of artists are not much use, but an understanding of the Herculean struggle through which some artists go to hammer out their art is worth having. Humanism is a questing, questioning attitude to life, which may not always be easy.

Humanism in the arts involves looking at communality, diversity, human sympathy, otherness, freedom, and truth.

We are essentially social animals: It is our place in the community that establishes us as living, feeling, thinking people. Some art is social in nature—joining with others to watch a play or a film, which gives a very different experience from watching television or a PlayStation on one's own. Laughter together is a liberating force, and no harm if the laughter is subversive. Singing in a choir or playing in an orchestra or a band or group (both experiences I have had at some stage in my life) are social experiences that require intellectual discipline and deep feeling at the same time.

George Eliot, perhaps the greatest of all British nineteenth-century novelists, created a complete community in *Middlemarch:* There is a reality to that place and those people that compares with the complete reality of a Dutch painting. Within that town are people struggling: to change the medical establishment, to come to terms with their own dishonesty, to allow great idealism to clash with dry pedantry. George Eliot was an agnostic, but one who believed deeply in human values, the power of good. In contrast, Mikhail Bulgakov, a Russian novelist of the first half of the twentieth century who fought against repression and censorship, portrayed in *The White Guard* a city in disarray, with civil disorder in the face of the Bolsheviks. But Bulgakov has the long perspective of the artist: "Everything passes away—suffering, pain, blood, hunger and pestilence."

These literary masters create worlds in which human values, ambitions, loyalties, and longings compete—worlds that may then be compared quite meaningfully to our own place and time. In this way, literature can serve much the same purpose for secular audiences as scriptural tales do for the religious, providing narratives upon which we reflect and against which we view our own lives and choices.

Equally important to art are the more individual qualities of "universal sympathy" and human diversity. If we cannot enlarge our understanding by the scrutiny of others—depicted on screen or canvas, on printed page or raised platform—there is a failure of communication. It is the "otherness" of the world around that is so important. We are easily immersed in ourselves, and this leads to a diminishment of our identity. To be aware of the "other," the other people, the other places, the other events, is a creative act: It enhances a sense of awe at the world and, indeed, the universe.

Human diversity is seen abundantly in the texts we will shortly consider. Huck's friendship with the black Jim in *Huckleberry Finn* and the two gay angels in the trilogy *His Dark Materials* by Pullman illustrate the need for children and adults to accept the variety of the human race. Attempts to stifle this are found in Arthur Miller's play *The Crucible*, where the persecution of supposed witches represents the unacceptability of those who are different and the hysteria in response to threats. Miller wrote of that play: "The tranquility of the bad man lies at the heart of not only moral philosophy but dramaturgy as well." Art does not propose moral answers but does offer moral issues for our consideration.

Art cannot be cheery—it must face the depths. Consider for instance the brilliant *If This is a Man* in which Italian author Primo Levi gives an account of his experiences in a World War Two concentration camp. He has to tell the truth of his awful experience. If parents can face this, so can their children at some stage in their development.

This seems a long way from Twain's *Huckleberry Finn*, but growth and development are characteristics of the three central characters in the three texts I shall look at. Huck, who is certainly not of a good background (his father's a drunk), through his travels along the river, through the types that he meets, through his friendship with the "nigger" Jim, develops an awareness of people and the process of living that he had not had at the beginning. The fact that Jim is described as a "nigger"—now a taboo word, but used regularly at the period of the novel—does not signal a derogatory attitude, for Jim is of pure gold and when Huck thinks Jim has disappeared "he set down and cried." Weaver, the black youth in *A Gathering Light*, living fifty years later, is outraged by being called a "nigger." Thus we see the development of language and understanding. And language is important to all the texts, Twain being particularly good at expressing the vernacular and Mattie in *A Gathering Light* being a person to whom words are life.

Although Twain wants no moral to his story, he is excellent at portraying the ethical ambivalence that Huck inhabits, especially when he decides to help Jim escape from slavery. It is worth remembering that *Huckleberry Finn* was regarded as a subversive book in its day. Pullman's trilogy has likewise caused controversy, particularly in the opposition to religion. The river that is Huck's highway has a largeness and a power that we hold in awe. And Huck and Jim, when they lie looking at the stars, discuss whether they are made or "just happened."

A Gathering Light by Jennifer Donnelly is a remarkable recent novel set at the beginning of the twentieth century in a subsistence farming community in New York State. The central character is Mattie, who plays with words and wants to be a writer. A teacher encourages her and tells her that books are dangerous. We need to focus on the fact that art is dangerous. The teacher is herself a poet who has fallen foul of Comstock and faced censorship. (I am reminded of a recent report of the banning of the Cassell *Dictionary of Slang* in a North Carolina school, under pressure from conservative Christian groups.) Parents, *let your children explore*—and especially explore words.

Like Huck, Mattie has an important interracial friendship. Hers is with Weaver, who like Mattie wants a college education. She asks him: "Why aren't people plain and uncomplicated? Why don't they do what you expect them to do, like characters in a novel?" The best novels are not like that. Mattie is unexpected in many ways: her falling in love with a simple would-be farmer, her toughness in seeing her family through illness, her choice of a new word every day from a dictionary, her loyalty to the poor in the community. Rightly, because novels should leave questions, not answer them, we do not know for sure what success she will have.

Northern Lights, the first of Pullman's trilogy, is an "other world" novel, where all the characters have demons attached to them for support and where the enemy is the church—and at the end of this volume there is the hope of the end of centuries of darkness. Lyra, the central character, is resourceful, imaginative, and determined.[6] One of the novel's strengths is the great diversity of characters. In a later volume, there are several gay angels of great charm. Just as Huck is aware of the power of the river, so Lyra, when looking at the Aurora, the northern lights, feels "it was so beautiful it was almost holy."

Folk tales are often told to young children, but they have resonance for parents as well. Tales such as *The Arabian Nights* have stories that are of a richness and wonder, delineating the magic and unexpected in life and reminding of the richness of Islamic culture. Grimm's tales are much darker—children who might be shoved in the oven and eaten, the threat of being boiled to death by a witch, the loss of sight when jumping from a tower into thorns. Freud and his disciples had a field day with these tales. Some say they are too grim for children—but children do have dark fantasies and dreams, and it helps them to accept them, or make sense of them, to have them read to them in a controlled way—and the darkness is often followed with an ingenious rescue. Angela Carter, the novelist and storyteller, has praised Peril the French fairy story writer for his "consummate craftsmanship and his good-natured cynicism. . . . From the work of this humane, tolerant and kind-hearted Frenchman, children can learn enlightened self-interest . . . and gain much pleasure besides."

Other arts are equally important. Music and theatre and film and the visual arts are all valuable for young and old alike. There have been increasing attempts at outreach by professional artists into schools and community groups. As an example, a group of difficult adolescent youths were taken for some weeks dancing—creating a dance drama. They came back to class completely transformed and ready to learn. Journalist Will Hutton has pointed out that "today's society does not equip boys with the emotional intelligence to come to terms with their feelings." Schools and families can be harsh and lacking in understanding. They need more democracy and participation and listening—and more artistic activity. Music, for example, teaches self-discipline, working together with others, perseverance, cooperation—and gives great rewards. Why then has musical education declined? The state should encourage arts in schools and homes, partly because it pays off in producing balanced, imaginative citizens, but partly because it leads to fulfilled individuals.

> " Schools and families can be harsh and lacking in understanding. They need more democracy and participation and listening—and more artistic activity. "

I finish with Thoreau on the value of knowledge and the arts and sciences—and then ultimately the value of not-knowing.

Knowledge
Men say they know many things;
But lo! They have taken wings,—
The arts and sciences,
And a thousand appliances;
The wind that blows
Is all that anybody knows.

Chapter Five Endnotes

1. See Jim Herrick's essay "Secular Parenting and the Arts" at the end of this chapter for more on the character Lyra.
2. "Religion and Volunteering in America," paper presented at the Conference on Religion, Social Capital, and Democratic Life at Calvin College by Steven J. Yonish (University of Wisconsin-Madison) and David E. Campbell (Harvard University), October 1998.
3. *Foreign Policy* and the Center for Global Development, "Ranking the Rich," *Foreign Policy Magazine,* May/June 2005.
4. That makes five times Robert Ingersoll's been mentioned in this book—the only five times most readers have probably heard his name. Ingersoll was attorney general of Illinois in the late 1860s, but his further political ambitions were thwarted by his anti-religious views. He then pursued a career as a traveling orator, delivering sparkling, brilliant public lectures around the country in support of nontheistic morality and against the harmful effects of religion. Called "The Great Agnostic," Ingersoll was an influential voice in the nineteenth century but quickly faded into undeserved obscurity after his death in 1899.
5. E.J. Larson & L. Witham, "Leading Scientists Still Reject God." *Nature* 394 (July 1998), 313.
6. See Cherry and Cherry, "Double Vision," for another appearance of Lyra.

Additional Resources

Books

- Ardell, Don. *The Book of Wellness: A Secular Approach to Spirit, Meaning and Purpose.* Prometheus, 1996. A founder and leader of the wellness movement, Dr. Donald B. Ardell suggests that doctors turn more attention to encouraging the contemplation of meaning and purpose in their patients—and that they do so without any religious overlay.
- Heelas, Paul, with Linda Woodhead. *Spiritual Revolution: Why Religion is Giving Way to Spirituality.* Blackwell, 2004. Strong mostly in establishing the fact that organized religion is losing its appeal in favor of a more personal, nondogmatic spirituality for the expression of meaning and purpose. Very interesting reading—but go elsewhere for specific recommendations or practices.
- Grayling, A.C. *Meditations for the Humanist: Ethics for a Secular Age.* Oxford, 2003. A beautifully written and thought-provoking set of reflections on values and ethics without religion.

- Cortesi, David. *Secular Wholeness: A Skeptic's Paths to a Richer Life.* Trafford, 2002.
- Mather, Anne, and Louise Weldon. *Character Building Day by Day: 180 Quick Read-Alouds for Elementary School and Home.* Free Spirit, 2006. The title says it all. "Faith" and "reverence" blissfully absent from the list of virtues.

Four great introductions to "secular heroes":

- Allen, Norm R., *African-American Humanism: An Anthology,* Prometheus Books, 1991.
- Gaylor, Annie Laurie, ed., *Women Without Superstition: No Gods—No Masters. The Writings of 19th & 20th Century Women Freethinkers,* FFRF, 1997.
- Haught, James A., *2000 Years of Disbelief: Famous People with the Courage to Doubt,* Prometheus Books, 1996.
- Freethought of the Day at www.ffrf.org/day. A searchable database of free-thinkers.

- Medhus, Elisa, MD. *Raising Children Who Think for Themselves.* Beyond Words, 2001. Recipient of numerous awards, this book encourages the eponymous value of freethought: thinking for one's self. Medhus offers suggestions for raising children who are inner-directed by self-defined values rather than externally driven by peer pressure, pop culture influences, and authority.
- Also by Elisa Medhus: *Raising Everyday Heroes: Parenting Children to be Self-Reliant.* Beyond Words Publishing, 2003.
- Wykoff, Jerry. *20 Teachable Virtues.* Perigee Trade, 1995. Twenty chapters, each offering parents tips for teaching a single virtue—and more importantly, a warning that what you don't model yourself will not be learned. The spotlighted virtues, including empathy, fairness, tolerance, caring, courage, humor, respect, and self-reliance, should warm the secular heart.
- Espeland, Pamela, with Elizabeth Verdick. *Knowing And Doing What's Right: The Positive Values Assets* (The Free Spirit Adding Assets Series for Kids) 2006. One of a large series of excellent books by Espeland for parents and children, *Knowing and Doing What's Right* focuses on six positive values assets: Caring, Equality and Social Justice, Integrity, Honesty, Responsibility, and Healthy Lifestyle.

[N.B. Note that several of the virtue-related resources are listed in the Additional Resources section of Chapter 4, "On Doing and Being Good"]

CHAPTER 6

Death and Consolation

Introduction

We are going to die, and that makes us the lucky ones. Most people are never going to die because they are never going to be born. The potential people who could have been here in my place but who will in fact never see the light of day outnumber the sand grains of Arabia. Certainly those unborn ghosts include greater poets than Keats, scientists greater than Newton. We know this because the set of possible people allowed by our DNA so massively exceeds the set of actual people. In the teeth of these stupefying odds it is you and I, in our ordinariness, that are here.

Richard Dawkins, *Unweaving the Rainbow*

When one of the great living science writers first heard this book was being prepared, she offered a little advice. Sure, religions give their members rites of passage and structure and all that, she said—but the afterlife myth is the big prize. "Unless you tackle the subject of death head-on," she said, "you'll be leaving your readers in the lurch at what are likely to be some of the darkest moments of their unchurched parenthood."

She was right, of course. So—how are *you* doing with the idea of death?

Forgive me for asking. But since you are reading this, I assume that you've set aside the consolations of theology and are asking your children to do the same. Nonbelievers tend to focus on how and what we know without spending much time acknowledging the gaping existential questions that are, after all, the real reasons religion was born and persists. We are, each and every one of us in turn, going to die. There is every reason to believe our consciousnesses will vanish into nothingness. We live a very short while, then are dead forever.

So how *are* you doing with that? And if the answer is "not too well," how are you going to help your kids resist the temptations of the heavenly illusion?

I often wonder, especially here at midlife, what it really means to cease to exist. I can't imagine it myself. It is beyond our ability to form a conscious notion of our own utter nonexistence. Hence the alternative so many choose—to simply deny it. We don't really die after all: We ascend to a higher reality.

It works! Try it. You'll feel ever so much better. And you won't find out that you're mistaken until . . . well, you'll never find out! That's the beauty of the thing.

But most of us became nonbelievers once we decided honesty was better than comfort. We fell in love with the idea of knowing what *is* and learning to deal with that, rather than hiding behind comforting illusions. Seems the grownup way to be a conscious thing, doesn't it? But that doesn't make it easy. So how can we turn away from the consolations of religion in the face of death?

After his beloved 4-year-old son succumbed to scarlet fever, the nineteenth-century biologist and agnostic Thomas Huxley asked himself much the same question. The Reverend Canon Kingsley had urged Huxley to renounce his agnosticism in the face of his loss and to embrace the consolations of faith. Huxley politely declined, replying with moving candor in a letter that many consider the single greatest and most profoundly moving testament to intellectual integrity:

> My convictions, positive and negative, on all the matters of which you speak, are of long and slow growth and are firmly rooted. But the great blow which fell upon me seemed to stir them to their foundation, and had I lived a couple of centuries earlier I could have fancied a devil scoffing at me and them and asking me what profit it was to have stripped myself of the hopes and consolations of the mass of mankind? To which my only reply was and is *Oh devil!* Truth is better than much profit. I have searched over the grounds of my belief, and if wife and child and name and fame were all to be lost to me one after the other as the penalty, still I will not lie.

Huxley is among my greatest heroes. But even Huxley, turning from false consolations in the midst of his grief, offered little in the way of compensation other than a picture of breathtaking intellectual courage. Yes, I want to reject the false consolations of theology—but might there be *true* consolations out there somewhere?

Yes indeed. They are the consolations of philosophy.

Science has worked wonders in recent centuries when it comes to replacing superstition with reason. But when it comes to setting aside superstition in less concrete areas—such as morality, attitudes toward death, and the like—progress has taken place not in the bright light of scientific inquiry but in the quiet, reflective works of philosophy. And it is to these works we can turn for true consolation.

The Greek philosopher Epicurus thought that we are afraid of death mainly because we fail to really grasp nonexistence. Creatures of consciousness, we can only picture it as "me-floating-in-darkness-forever." Is it really surprising that that horrific idea sends people racing to the kneelers to pray to someone who is said to have conquered it for us? Heck, if the darkness was really the thing, I'd be wearing out my own knees. But it isn't. The key, Epicurus says, is to really get that death is the *end* of experience. One can only experience life, up to its final moment, not beyond. "As long as I exist," he said, "death does not. Once death exists, I will not. Why should I fear something I will never experience?"

Thinking hard about that simple fact can make for real consolation—and give parents one more small way to help children deal with death without immersing them in dishonest fables.

Epicurus also offered the "symmetry argument." If you fear death, he said, consider the expanse of time before you were conceived. The "past infinity" of nonexistence before your conception is just the same as the "future infinity" of nonexistence after death. "You" have already been there, in other words—though that is really just exactly the wrong way to phrase it. We don't consider having not existed for an eternity before our conception to be a terrible thing, so we shouldn't think of not existing for an eternity *after* our deaths as a terrible thing. There is literally no difference in the two other than our ability to contemplate and anticipate the future. (See Yip Harburg's "Before and After," coming up next, for a poetic take on the idea.)

Though it may take a lifetime to grasp, it should be possible to come peacefully to terms with our mortality by fully understanding it. And it never hurts to recall that life is made immeasurably more precious by the fact that it ends. Life as a preamble to afterlife would be just a warmup. But understanding this existence as an unimaginably lucky shot at consciousness—*in the teeth of these stupefying odds, it is you and I, in our ordinariness, who are here*—has the power to make every moment unspeakably precious. We should wake up every morning laughing with amazed delight that we are here at all, not weeping because it won't last forever. Easier said than done, I know. Believe me, I know.

■ ■ ■ ■ ■ ■

Yip Harburg starts us off by giving death a philosophical raspberry in "Before and After," followed by Noell Hyman with a touching description of helping her young children understand and accept the end of life.

The largest portion of this chapter is the work of one author—the Reverend Dr. Kendyl Gibbons, senior minister of the First Unitarian Society of Minneapolis. Kendyl is among the most articulate and thoughtful of a very articulate and thoughtful breed—Unitarian humanists. If the idea of a minister who doesn't believe in God is new to you, Kendyl is a marvelous introduction to the concept.

The modern Unitarian Universalist movement, as noted in Chapter Two, is a fascinating post-Christian institution consisting almost entirely of humanists and atheists. Despite having set aside theistic beliefs, they still seek the other benefits of religious institutions: the shared search for meaning, a sense of community, the consolation of others in time of need, and dedication to the good. Among her many gifts, Kendyl Gibbons brings the wisdom of a counselor who has provided solace in time of loss to countless secularists without benefit of the easy answers available in theistic religion. From the loss of a pet to the loss of a grandparent, from "ordinary" death to sudden or tragic loss, from the contemplation of death in the abstract to the awesome realization that we ourselves must die, Kendyl offers advice and suggestions for helping children deal with and understand death without reliance on illusions.

Before and After

Yip Harburg

I cannot for the life of me
Recall at all, at all
The life I led
Before I tread
This small terrestrial ball.
Why then should I ponder
On the mystery of my kind?
Why bother with my great beyond
Without my great behind?

The End, As We Know It

Noell Hyman

To live at all is miracle enough.

—Mervyn Peake, *The Glassblower*

AMONG THE WIND-BLOWN blossoms that flew around our feet, my 3-year-old, Aiden, spotted a yellow butterfly that lay dead on the parking lot of my doctor's office.

I paused to let my Mr. Curiosity examine it. "It's dead," he muttered.

This concerned him.

I suppressed my initial inclination to comfort Aiden with the words, *Yes, it's dead and in heaven now.* Instead I explained, "His brain stopped working. His life is all done now."

My concept of death has reincarnated into an entirely new animal since leaving religion.

Years ago my father-in-law made a vocal recording of the story of his conversion from Judaism to Mormonism. I transcribed that story at least seven years ago, and I remember how his reason for considering Christianity made an impression in my mind.

At that time, the war in Vietnam was alive and killing many of America's youth. The war stopped the breath of a number of my father-in-law's friends. He said in his recording that the reformed Jewish temple that he grew up in didn't provide many answers about death. He said that most Jewish people focus on the memories of the person. They emphasize that what you are after death is what you leave behind for those who are still alive.

This answer was inadequate for my father-in-law in his time of loss.

Such a concept of death was foreign to me, a Mormon. The explanation impacted me because Mormons and other Christians place so much emphasis on life after death. My thoughts of death during my religious days were images of enhanced life.

How ironic that I now embrace the concept my father-in-law abandoned.

First appeared as a column in *Humanist Network News,* June 14, 2006. Used with permission.

Parenting Beyond Belief

Transferring that concept to my children was a task I avoided for a long time. My kids held on to our previous idea of heaven when we left religion.

Last month, Blake realized there was a dilemma between my assertions that there are no such things as ghosts and his belief that people become spirits when they die.

"Aren't spirits actually ghosts?" he questioned.

"Yes," I explained. "Religions say we become spirits. And if that were true, then there would be ghosts. But from all the scientific searching there is no evidence of it. We can't find any reason to think there actually are ghosts or spirits. And we only rely on evidence. We don't hold beliefs that have no evidence."

Later, the kids asked about death, wondering if people are sad or hurt when they are dead.

"When someone dies, their brain shuts off," I told them. "So they can't be sad. And they can't feel pain. And we have all the memories of that person and the things they did and how they made us feel."

Recently I was reading an article in a scrapbooking magazine about the healing process of sharing stories of loved ones who have passed away. I like to swap memories with my sister about our late grandmother. It seems healthier to enjoy the memories of a loved one than it is to dwell on longings for a future reunion.

It is important to experience the mourning and the sad feelings of missing a loved one, but we can also celebrate that person's life with all its joys and difficulties. We can share stories, look at pictures, and laugh at the quirks and unique traits of the person who is gone. Such a focus at the time of a death should give our children an appreciation for the significance and brevity of life.

Back at the doctor's office, as we returned to the car to go home, Aiden wanted to see the dead butterfly one more time. It wasn't where we had left it and Aiden insisted on finding it. I could have rushed him on or tried distracting him with another topic. But I knew that both the ideas of a butterfly and of death were important to him at this time.

Finally, we found the yellow butterfly where the wind had blown him a few feet away. We stared for a while.

Looking at death from my current paradigm, I talked to Aiden about the happy life the butterfly had. Its life was over and it was short, but it was a good one. It got to fly in the sky and look for beautiful flowers.

Aiden wanted to pick it up. I was hesitant at first to let him touch a dead insect. Then I changed my mind. This was a chance for him to examine the body of a butterfly. It was also an opportunity to look at death close up. I

162

wanted to give Aiden associations of confidence and gratitude rather than avoidance or anxiety.

I handled the butterfly by its wings and passed it to Aiden. It fascinated him. We pointed out the head, the eyes, the legs, the antennae.

It was time to go but Aiden wasn't ready to leave his specimen. Again, with hesitation, I let Aiden bring the butterfly with him in the car.

We drove to the school to pick up Trinity from kindergarten. Aiden showed her the dead butterfly. She expressed a little pity, but then said, "At least he's not sad. His brain shut off. So he's dead, but not sad."

In a discussion on my blog regarding teaching kids about death, one of my readers commented that he uses a book called *Lifetimes,* by Bryan Mellonie. He explained that the book describes the lifetimes of various living things and focuses on the life that happens in between birth and death.

He explained, "I tell my kids that they do continue, not only in the life matter and lineage cycle, but as part of the world/universe per se. 'The world produced life and us along with it. We are not separate from it. Like a drop of water taken from the ocean and returned, when we die we return to the world. There is no place else to go. Whatever we are has always been and will always be a part of it.'"

My reader then explained the results. "If you ask either of them what happens when they die, they will tell you, 'We go back to the world.'"

Another reader gave this idea. "One thing that helped with my kids was the concept of the circle of life. I asked them to think about what would happen if no one died but we kept having babies. They figured out pretty quickly that this was not a good option. Then I told them that one of the most wonderful things ever in my life was having them, and they agreed that having babies was something they wanted to do one day. The only other option, then, was to have death occur in order to make room for new babies."

I love these ideas of using positive concepts when talking about death in general.

Our children need to see us deal with death. I do not hide them from it (unless it is particularly gruesome) when they hear about someone dying. We discuss how sad it is, and then I focus the conversation on that person's life before he died.

In my opinion, death is really about life. It is the conclusion of what was hopefully a fulfilling one. Death makes life meaningful.

> " Death is really about life. It is the conclusion of what was hopefully a fulfilling one. Death makes life meaningful. "

We can talk with our children about the sadness that we feel when a person leaves us. We can talk about the love we had for that person, about the joy she gave us, the fact that she made us laugh or made us think. And we can talk about the joy our loved one had while she was here.

■ ■ ■ ■ ■ ■

Dealing with Death in the Secular Family

Rev. Dr. Kendyl Gibbons

THE HUMAN IMPULSE TO deny the reality of death is deep and ancient. It affects us all both as individuals and as a culture. Nevertheless, death confronts us all, including our children. One of the challenges of parenting is to introduce this subject and help children respond to it in developmentally appropriate ways. There is a great deal of helpful literature about how children deal with death, and both secular and religious children have much the same needs for reassurance and support when they begin to confront mortality. The particular challenge for secular families is the absence of comforting answers supplied by doctrines and images from various faith traditions. Yet by telling the truth, providing emotional comfort, and validating the child's own experiences, secular parents can give their children the tools to understand and accept death as a natural part of life and to find meaning in their grief.

> The particular challenge for secular families is the absence of comforting answers supplied by doctrines and images from various faith traditions. Yet by telling the truth, providing emotional comfort, and validating the child's own experiences, secular parents can give their children the tools to understand and accept death as a natural part of life and to find meaning in their grief.

The reality of death touches our lives in at least three distinct ways. The most obvious is when someone important to us dies. In a child's life, this will often be an older relative or beloved pet. Other more traumatic or violent losses are less common but require even more thoughtful responses. At such times, we need to help our children move through the dynamics of grieving—often while grieving ourselves. A second way in which death confronts us is at those developmental points when we realize, sometimes quite suddenly, that we ourselves must someday die, or that people we know and love will eventually die. A third way we encounter death is through fiction and the media. Whether through cartoons, action movies, or the evening news, children in our society are bombarded with images of death and need help to understand and process what they see.

Dealing with Ordinary Death

Natural death is still challenging for children, as it is for all of us. That grandparents and older relatives may die while a child is young is always a possibility, and the death of shorter lived pets is inevitable. In such situations, secular parents will want to emphasize the naturalness of such deaths and how they are part of the cycle of life. But no matter how expected such a loss may be, it still requires all of us, children and adults alike, to move through the process of grieving. Grief is a process of healing, growing, and learning that takes place over time. It is a journey without shortcuts, and if it is approached with acceptance, it leaves us wiser, more mature, and more loving than we were before.

> **One of the important gifts that parents can give their children is the knowledge that adults also grieve and that it is painful and hard work for everyone.**

One of the important gifts that parents can give their children is the knowledge that adults also grieve and that it is painful and hard work for everyone. At the same time, parents know what children do not, which is that healing and growth will come, and something precious will be gained through the process. We can help our children to grieve in a healthy way by assuring them that the process does move forward, even when it feels endless.

> We are all very sad right now, and it's okay to feel that way, but I know that after a while we will feel better again. We will be able to think about Blue and be happy while we remember him. It just takes time.

It is also important to acknowledge that grief takes many forms and is changeable. A child may experience obvious sadness and withdrawal, but at times may also exhibit manic energy, regressive behavior, anger, fear, or oblivious denial. All of these are normal feelings and coping strategies that adults may have as well. Recognizing these reactions as part of the grieving process can make them easier to deal with, for children and parents alike.

> It can be harder to go to sleep when you are thinking how much you miss Grandma. I miss her too. Would you like a nightlight or your old blankie for a while?

It is useful to remember that children are paradoxically both concrete and magical thinkers. On the one hand, they will make visible, tangible realities out of abstract concepts; on the other hand, they often think themselves responsible for events that are entirely outside their control. Thus, in dealing with death, it is important to assure a child that he or she is not responsible for a person or a pet dying, no matter how clear this is to the adults. The child may imagine that his or her momentary feeling of anger toward the deceased brought about death, or that had he or she been more loving or responsible or attentive, the death could have been prevented. Children may not speak of these apprehensions, so it is wise to offer the affirmation unasked.

> 66 It is useful to remember that children are paradoxically both concrete and magical thinkers. On the one hand, they will make visible, tangible realities out of abstract concepts; on the other hand, they often think themselves responsible for events that are entirely outside their control. 99

> Grandmother died because she was old and ill. We all took the best care of her that we could, but it just wasn't possible for her to go on living. It wasn't anybody's fault.

Both ceremony and ritual may be helpful to children—and adults are not immune to their benefits either. Ceremony is a formal act that is thoughtfully planned, even though it may only be done once. Ritual is usually something repeated that gathers meaning through being done more than once. While both of these activities can be associated with religious beliefs, they do not have to be. They can be public, or private, or personal. A formal memorial service in a church would be a public ceremony; going alone to visit your grandfather's favorite park every year on his birthday would be a personal ritual. Ceremonies help to structure the time of grieving, which can feel very amorphous and hard to define. Working with children to make a plan, so that they have something to anticipate, can give them a sense of landmarks, as well as permission to move forward in their mourning.

> Tomorrow afternoon, let's bring all of Tuffy's toys and dishes and put them in a special box to give to the animal shelter. If you want, you can choose something to keep. We can take turns saying things that we remember about him.

> Why don't you come to the store with me in the morning and pick out some flowers? We can take them to the retirement home where Uncle Gordon lived and sit on his special bench for a few minutes.

Rituals help to reassure children that the world is still dependable and that the person or pet they have lost will continue to be part of their lives through memory.

> Each year at Thanksgiving, we'll have a toast to Grandma and remember the time she dropped the turkey.

> Before you go to sleep each night this week, let's write down one thing that you liked about your teacher Mr. Gonzales.

It is important to keep in mind that once a child adopts a ritual, he or she may find comfort in it long after the adults have moved on to a different stage. Be patient with a child's attachment to whatever comforts him or her, and help children to develop personal rituals that they can maintain as long as they need to without placing unreasonable demands on the rest of the family.

Dying's part of the wheel [of life], right there next to being born. You can't pick out the pieces you like and leave the rest.
— From *Tuck Everlasting* by Natalie Babbitt

Five Affirmations in the Face of Death

There are five affirmations that everyone needs to hear when confronted with the death of a loved one. These assurances may be part of public ceremonies like a memorial service, or we may need to work through them in our own ways as a family or as individuals. Parents can help their children by making sure that each of these statements is clearly made, and some of them may need to be repeated more than once.

1. Acknowledge the reality. The first affirmation is that death has actually taken place; it is the antidote to denial. It is because of the importance of this awareness that most cultural traditions arrange for wakes, viewings, funeral services, and burials; it helps the reality of loss to sink in. Even a fairly young child can be consulted about whether he or she wishes to view the body or attend public ceremonies, if this is an option. On the one hand, children may find seeing the body of their grandparent or pet reassuring, since it may be far less terrible than their own imaginings. Being denied this opportunity, if it is something they want, may create a lack of closure. On the other hand, being pressured to do so if they do not wish to can make a difficult moment feel more traumatic. A sensitively attentive parent will listen carefully to the child's preferences and help him or her to make a choice based on the child's wishes, rather than the parent's expectations.

The wishful impulse of denial can be very powerful in a child's thinking, so that the fact of death may need to be repeated more than once over time. The idea of permanence, that something may vanish without being able to reappear, is something that develops over time in the mind, and a young child may struggle with it. Though it may be difficult for a grieving parent, the reality of a death should be calmly restated whenever the child questions it. He or she is not being silly or uncaring, but trying to understand how the world really works.

No, honey, Grandpa won't come for Christmas. He died, and dead is for always.

2. Validate sadness. The second affirmation is that loss is painful, and sadness is appropriate; it is important to acknowledge the reality of powerful feelings that we do not control. Telling anyone "Don't cry," or "Don't feel bad," is not helpful at the time of bereavement, but it is especially confusing to children, who may take this as a cue that there is something wrong with their emotional responses. In point of fact, when we have loved someone or something, our sorrow is a function and measure of that love. Loss would not be painful if there had not been a profound attachment, and in the end it is our capacity for such connections that make our lives fulfilling and meaningful.

3. Acknowledge the unknown. A third affirmation of particular importance to secular families is that death is a mystery; whatever we may think happens to a person after they die is speculation. One of the most powerful lessons parents

can teach is that adults don't know the answers to everything. This does not mean that we cannot communicate our own convictions to our children, but in this realm as in others, it is important to leave room for them to explore their own ideas. Much has been written about the significance of not telling children that death is like sleep, as this has often been observed to disrupt their sense of safety in falling asleep themselves, or allowing others to sleep. In their concrete thinking process, children may want to know where the dead person "goes." It is all but inevitable in our culture that their peers or others will talk about the idea of heaven, and perhaps even of hell. They may also have fears about the dissolution of the body, that this process will be painful for their loved one.

Secular parents will most likely want to affirm their own conviction that death is the end of all personal experience, that there are no places where the spirits of the dead "go," and that no pain or suffering is now possible for the deceased. It may be helpful to present these as "I" statements—this is what I believe—and to acknowledge that there are many other ideas, including those that the child may have been told of or be exploring in her own mind. It can be comforting even for adults, who have no actual belief in such ideas, to imagine the kind of next world or existence that would be particularly gratifying for the deceased; such pleasant fantasies may have a healing effect as long as they are acknowledged as wishes rather than realities. Such imaginings on the part of children can be treated as part of the grieving process and affirmed as feelings rather than facts.

Dog heaven is a lovely idea. I think Blue would like a place where he could run through the grass, chase sticks all day long, and never get tired. It's good to think about what we would wish for him, isn't it?

People have lots of different ideas about what might happen after someone dies, but no one knows for sure. What do you like to think Aunt Chandra might be doing?

Before you were born, you didn't exist—you didn't feel anything at all. I think that's what it's like for Gramps now; he isn't there any more, so he can't think or feel, and certainly nothing can hurt him. What do you think?

4. Celebrate individuality. The fourth affirmation declares that each individual is unique and not replaceable; this is what makes our memories precious. It is also the reason for allowing an appropriate period of mourning to pass before seeking another pet. Children need to have permission to remember their loved one in ways that are meaningful to themselves. This may involve quietly looking

at pictures or visiting a grave; it may take the form of talking about or wanting to hear stories about the deceased; it may be more active, such as drawing or writing about what they remember. Parents can affirm the child's perception of what was irreplaceable about the lost one; it is seldom helpful to argue that other people can take the dead person's place or that other pets will be equally loved. At the same time, the child may need to be reassured that his or her life will go on in a safe way; there will be change, but the change will be manageable. Children may cling to artifacts of the deceased—clothing, a stray key, a pet's bowl—for a long time, as a tangible vessel for their memories. If possible, parents should not interfere in this, but indicate that the child will know inside him- or herself when the time comes to put the object away.

> Blue did some funny things, didn't he? Remember how he always loved to lie in the sun? And how he could always hear you coming? He had the best hearing of any dog I've known.

> We can still go fishing together, but it won't be quite the same without Uncle Miguel to dig our worms for us, will it? He was really good at that.

5. Affirm the continuity of life. The final affirmation tells us that the universe remains dependable; life goes on, and what we trusted in before the loss can still be trusted—love, integrity, family and friends, the world of nature. This assurance is communicated by parents more by how they speak and behave than by most of what they say, particularly by how honestly reflective they can be about acknowledging their own feelings. To be able to say, "It's kind of scary sometimes to think about living in a world without my Mom, but then I remember all the other people who care about me, and what a brave person she was, and I think we'll all be okay," says to the child that feelings are both real in the moment as well as changeable and can be faced. The most basic affirmation of all, that the opportunity to share love is worth the pain of grief, is as important to children as it is to the rest of us.

> I'm glad we had Kitty as part of our family, even though I'm sad that she died.

Particularly Difficult Situations

It is also possible that death may touch a child's life in a more traumatic and difficult way. When someone is killed by violence or in a sudden accident, it is not a normal part of the cycle of life. When a sibling or friend near the child's own age dies, it often feels more tragic and wasteful to the adults, and bewildering to the child, because such things are not "supposed" to happen. The same is true when a pet is hit by a car or runs away and disappears. Despite the extra tragedy of such situations, children need much the same sort of reassurance, honesty, and permission to grieve as they do in more ordinary bereavement. The advice of psychological professionals can be very helpful and should be seen as an entirely ordinary resource. Just as one would consult a doctor to be sure of healing properly from a physical trauma, checking in with a knowledgeable counselor would be a routine aspect of handling such an emotional upheaval.

When confronted with a death by violence, children need to know that everything possible is being done to keep them safe and that it is very improbable that anything like this will happen to them. The specifics will depend upon the situation, but it may help to emphasize that even adults do not always understand why people make the choices they make and do what they do. Children will usually take comfort from the knowledge that the authorities are trying to catch and punish the perpetrator, because this communicates a sense of moral order in the world. Yet it is not helpful for them to displace all of their anger about death onto that individual, because in the long run this will make healing more difficult for them.

When a young person dies of a disease, it is also important to assure children that they do not have the disease themselves and are likely to live for a very long time. This is another time when it must be confessed that adults don't know everything, even though they try as hard as they can. Secular parents generally reject the explanations that god has a plan, or wanted the person in heaven, and so on. Children are able to grasp that random events sometimes happen, for no good reason, and that bodies do not always work the way they are supposed to.

When death is the result of an accident, such as a car wreck or a drowning, parents may be tempted to drive home the moral of the story with reference to the child's own potential behavior. Not only does it seem like a relevant object lesson, but assigning responsibility for carelessness is often a mechanism by which adults attempt to cope with random tragedy. However, a child may interpret such explanations as meaning that death is a punishment for something wrong that the deceased did and that sorrow is therefore unjustified. To whatever extent an accidental death may be someone's fault, it is important to emphasize that death is a disproportionately severe consequence.

Care must also be taken not to make the child unduly fearful; secular parents cannot offer their children guardian angels; instead, we want them to assess risks rationally and to respond with courage as well as good sense. The child may be sensitive to particular circumstances, such as riding in a car following a bereavement by car accident, or going in the water after someone has drowned. This kind of hesitation should be treated with gentle respect, but at the same time parents can express their confidence that fatal mishaps are very rare, assuring the child that appropriate safety precautions—seat belts, lifeguards, etc.—can minimize risks.

Confronting Mortality

It is entirely possible in twenty-first-century Western culture for an individual to be well into middle age before a loved one dies. Children may not be confronted with the process of grieving for a person or pet they care about during childhood. Nevertheless, it is an inevitable part of the developmental process that they will be exposed to the idea of death, and the dawning realization that they themselves could die, and someday will die, as well as that people they care about and depend on might die, and in fact someday will die. These realizations of mortality will occur regardless of whether a child has an intimate personal experience of loss.

The secular parent will wish to respond to this growing awareness with both realism and reassurance. The younger the child, the more important it is on every occasion to announce that neither parent nor child should expect to die for a very long time yet. It is always good to explore a little when such questions are raised and see if there is some particular incident or comment in the child's mind before embarking upon a philosophical discussion. That said, the moment will come when the child sincerely wants to know how parents have reconciled themselves to the thought of dying and how to make sense of this unwelcome news about the human condition.

It may be helpful to begin with the recognition that our evolutionary history has built into our species a very powerful instinct to want to live. People whose minds and bodies are healthy want to live and to go on living for as long as possible. This desire helps us to measure risks carefully and to do what is necessary to take care of ourselves. Knowing that other people want the same thing helps us to know how to treat them fairly and encourages us to learn as much as we can and to give as much help as we can, so that everyone can live a long and good life. It is natural to think that we would like to live forever ourselves and for those we care about to live forever.

Nevertheless, in spite of how much we would like it, that's not the way the world works. Rather, new life keeps popping up, and old life at some point dies. Nobody deliberately made it that way, that's just how evolution turned out, and how it happens to be. For a child old enough to understand the outlines of the scientific origins of life, parents can emphasize how delicate and fragile was the first coming together of chemicals that resulted in living organisms and how essentially unstable a process life is; any given individual is such a complex set of functions that it could not possibly operate correctly in all regards forever. Everything wears out eventually—even machines, even rocks.

Many people—including, presumably, most of those reading this book—believe that death is probably the final end of all personal experience and do not expect to continue their existence in some other life or other world. In this view, it is precisely the fact that our lives are limited that makes them precious. How we choose to use our time is all the more important when we know that we won't have the opportunity to do everything. The fact that we can lose the ones we love makes it urgent for us to resolve our quarrels, forgive our injuries, be as thoughtful and kind as we can, and be sure to let those we love know about it. If we were immortal, it would not matter if we chose to spend our time being bored, cranky, or spiteful; as it is, we don't have time to waste our lives with such unproductive and unpleasant attitudes.

> Many people believe that death is probably the final end of all personal experience. . . . It is precisely the fact that our lives are limited that makes them precious.

Secularism at its best can turn negative appraisals of death into affirmations of life. For a secular person, the question is not *Why did a universe designed for our benefit have to include death?* but *Isn't it amazing that we have the matter of the world arranged in such a way that we find ourselves with this incredible opportunity for consciousness?* What is surprising is not that our awareness must cease to be at some point in the unknown future, but that it has arisen now in the first place. That we are able to think and feel, to learn things and to love people, is a gift. It might just as easily not have happened. This gift of life is as arbitrary as the fact of mortality; both came about without consulting us. These are the terms on which we are here, and they are not negotiable.

There is a certain existential heroism and tragedy about living in the shadow of mortality, which teens in particular sometimes find quite romantic. This is usually a philosophical/spiritual developmental phase that in its most dramatic form eventually passes, but may be quite sincere and deeply felt at the time. A sympathetic parent can acknowledge how trivial many mundane concerns may appear in this light and still insist that they be attended to. In general, what secular parents can most helpfully do for their children is to demonstrate that a full, happy, satisfying life can be lived even in the awareness that death comes at the end—perhaps even in part because of that awareness. Paradoxically, although many popular religious cults focus on attaining an afterlife and escaping the reality of death, in their origins many of the world's highest spiritual and philosophical teachings summon people to live with a clear awareness of death. Such practices are meant to lead to maturity, serenity, and an enhanced capacity for deep happiness. I know from personal experience that it is possible to grow from a secure childhood into a well-balanced adult without ever supposing that death is anything other than the absolute end of personal consciousness. Because of this conviction, I know how urgently precious my own life and the lives of those around me are, and I find that awareness to be life-giving.

It seems reasonable that there has been evolutionary value in a fundamental fear of dying; it makes us take action when necessary and precautions when appropriate; a person with no fear of dying might be too careless or daring to survive for long. Moreover, our brains are designed to make any prolonged concentration on the inevitability of our own nonexistence extremely uncomfortable; we don't have the conceptual apparatus to do it effectively, and indeed, why should we? Thus it is normal to feel afraid when we think of dying and to be reluctant to think about it much. Hence the famous difficulty in getting people to complete their wills, even when they agree that it's a good idea. Secular parents can assure their children that all human beings have these feelings to a greater or lesser degree; they are appropriate and even useful, and we find various ways to live with them. When children express fears related to death, it is helpful to discover, if possible, something about the content of that fear. Are they afraid that those they depend on will die and leave them without protection? Are they afraid that the process of dying will be painful? Are they troubled to think of not existing any more, or are they afraid that it would hurt to be dead? The more specifically the issue is identified, the more effective a parent's reassurance can be. In the end, the child will have confidence in the parent's honesty if they calmly acknowledge that the same fears affect them.

> It's hard to talk about any of us dying, isn't it? Even for me, it can be scary. I love you so much, and I want to be around to take care of you, and watch

you grow up, and have all kinds of good times together. I know it's true that some time, a very long time from now, I will die, but I know that your love for me will still live in your heart, and I will be part of your memories always, and that helps me feel better. So let's make sure that we are as good as we can be to each other and make those memories happy ones, okay?

Death as Entertainment

It may be that the greatest challenge for a parent in twenty-first-century Western society is not to reassure children in their fears about death, but to help them come to take seriously what death really means when they are surrounded by cultural trivialization of it. As previously mentioned, the idea of permanent absence, that something or someone can disappear and not be able to come back, is a concept that requires a certain level of cognitive development for a child to grasp. For young children, the image of a cartoon character who is squashed flat and then pops back up unharmed is not fantasy; for all they know, the world may really be like that, at least in some cases. The ability to distinguish between the imaginative and the realistic develops gradually as a function of both experiential learning and increasing sophistication of the cognitive process.

There are strident arguments and competing sets of data about the extent to which exposure to violent imagery in movies, TV shows, and video games influences the behavior of children. However, there is no dissent about the power of parental influence, through both example and teaching. Secular parents who hope to raise compassionate, ethical, and life-valuing children cannot take refuge in a packaged set of religious commandments; rather, such parents must do the work of reflecting on why they themselves believe in honoring and protecting the lives of others or in what circumstances different values take precedence and killing becomes acceptable. They must then express these convictions over time to their children and engage their children's own ideas, questions, fears, and emergent beliefs. When a parent makes a decision that is an expression of conviction, this should be explained to the child, so that he or she begins to understand the connection.

While death can be accepted in the healthy mind as a convention of fiction and play, and even humor, parents must exercise some judgment about when to remind children that in the real world, dying is a serious matter with indelible consequences. As children mature enough to be able to imaginatively identify with others, parents can invite them to reconsider stories in which death is made trivial or taken for granted.

Who do you think might be sad that that character died? How do you suppose the hero's friends would have felt if he lost the fight, and got killed?

Responding to Religious Doctrines and Cultural Images

It is all but inevitable that children will encounter ideas about death and what happens to the dead that will differ from those of their secular parents. Such alternative images may be appealing, because they are more dramatic, colorful, or certain than what secular parents have offered. These may include ideas about heaven, hell, ghosts, reincarnation, and communication with the dead. It is certainly true that many people have experienced some sense of presence of loved ones who have died; a naturalistic explanation of these sensations need not deny that they can be comforting and healing, or alternatively, frightening. With older children it is possible to explore both the psychological reasons why people who are grieving might have such sensations, as well as the ways in which unscrupulous others might try to take advantage of them. In some of the same ways, the ideas of heaven and hell can be discussed as present states of mind, rather than future states of existence. With younger children, for whom the line between fantasy and reality is more permeable, it may be best to help them identify such concepts as "stories" that can be pleasant to think about, either for themselves or others. Endorsing the child's capacity for imaginative comfort does not require the parent to affirm false realities.

The kind of heaven your friend is talking about seems to me a pretty picture, though I don't see any evidence that it really exists. I know that you would like very much to think of seeing Grandma again some day; what would you like to say to her, if that could happen?

For me, hell is not meaningful as a place where bad people go after they die; once a person is dead, I don't think there is anything left to "go" anywhere. But I do think that people are sometimes in a place like hell while they are still alive, when they are stuck in their own minds, lonely and suffering.

Conclusion

Death confronts the secular family both as a challenge and an opportunity to clarify and communicate our convictions. It is part of the larger world that children encounter as they grow, a world that parents must help them understand. Ever since the origins of our kind, human beings have pondered death as one of the ultimate mysteries and sought to soften its great shadow over us. Perhaps none of us is ever fully reconciled to the loss of those we love or to the inevitability of our own demise, but we learn to live as fully as possible within the unknown limits of the time we have. Living in the secular world gives us freedom from the dogmas and superstitions of the past, but it does not eliminate the mystery and power of life's endings. When parents share those essentially human feelings with their children, they are engaged in the profound task of making meaning together, which is one of the great privileges of parenthood, or indeed of any human relationship.

Small Comforts

Yip Harburg

Before I was born, I seemed to be
Content with being non-be-able;
So after I'm gone, it seems to me
My lot should be not less agreeable.

Additional Resources
Books

• Emswiler, James, and Mary Ann. *Guiding Your Child Through Grief.* Bantam, 2000. Thorough, thoughtful, loving, well-informed. This is a powerful resource for secular parents helping a child who is dealing with loss and grief. The Emswilers confront the questions head-on and in detail, offering specific advice for dealing with holidays, helping grieving teens, even helping grieving stepchildren. The only mention of religious beliefs is an excellent one. Parents are invited to "share whatever beliefs your religious tradition holds about death and the afterlife," but are also cautioned not to say "God took Mommy because she was so good," or "God took Daddy because He wanted him to be with Him." Think about the implications of those two statements for about ten seconds and you'll see why the Emswilers label them no-nos. "Don't use God or religion as a pacifier to make grieving children feel better. It probably won't work," they note. "Do not explain death as a punishment or a reward from God." So much for the single greatest alleged advantage of the religious view of death. For secularists, there is even more to be grateful for in this terrific book: "It is also acceptable to say you're not sure what happens after death . . . it is always okay to say, 'I don't know.' "

- Arent, Ruth P., MA, MSW. *Helping Children Grieve.* Champion Press, 2005. If a loss comes suddenly, parents might not have the time or freedom to read *Guiding Your Child Through Grief.* In that case, *Helping Children Grieve* is a thoughtful, concise resource achieving much the same. Once again, the issues children face are separated by age, and once again, religious traditions are provided as potential resources but not as "answers" to the problems grief presents.

- Thomas, Pat. *I Miss You—A First Look at Death.* Barron's, 2000. Secular parents in search of ways to help the youngest children deal with death and loss can hardly do better than this lovely little book. In a scant twenty-nine pages of colorfully illustrated kid-lit format, it seems to anticipate most everything likely to go through the mind of a young one upon the death of someone special. Once again, religious ideas get a nod but are denied a pedestal: "There is a lot we don't know about death. Every culture has different beliefs about what happens after a person dies. Most cultures . . . share . . . the idea that when a person dies their soul—the part of them that made them special—takes a journey to join the souls of other people who have passed away. It's not an easy idea to understand." It's true, of course—most cultures do share some form of that belief. But instead of following this acknowledgment with a hallelujah, Thomas chooses a Taoist metaphor, one that I have always found deeply moving: "Sometimes it helps if you think of the soul as a single raindrop, joining a great big ocean." Ages 3-8.

- Bryant-Mole, Karen. *Talking About Death.* Raintree, 1999. A marvelous approach, free of religious concepts—but a tad pricy for a 32-page book. Check the library. Ages 4-8.

- Rothman, Juliet Cassuto. *A Birthday Present for Daniel: A Child's Story of Loss.* A heartbreaking and beautiful story narrated by a girl whose brother has died and whose family struggles over how to observe his approaching birthday. Prometheus, 2001. Ages 7-10.

- Trozzi, Maria, MEd. *Talking With Children About Loss.* Perigee Trade, 1999. One of the premiere references in the field of child bereavement.

- Dougy Center. *35 Ways to Help a Grieving Child.* Dougy Center, 1999. A practical, accessible resource.
- White, E. B. *Charlotte's Web.* HarperCollins, 1952, renewed 1980. In his book *The Philosophy of Childhood,* contributor Gareth Matthews calls special attention to two works of fiction for their substantive treatment of mortality: *Charlotte's Web* and *Tuck Everlasting.* Children in the terminal wards of hospitals request and read *Charlotte's Web* over and over, especially after one among them dies. Death is not avoided or sugarcoated—it is the book's pervasive theme, from Fern staying her uncle's ax from Wilbur's neck to Charlotte weaving SOME PIG to prevent him becoming the Christmas ham to Charlotte's own demise and symbolic rebirth through the springtime hatching of her egg sac. Unnatural death is something to protest, goes the message—but natural death is to be accepted with grace and courage. A stunning work of American literature, to be enjoyed repeatedly. *Special treat:* Look for the audio book of E. B. White reading *Charlotte's Web.* Considered by many, including yours truly, to be the finest children's audio book ever. If your public library does not own a copy, suggest it buys two. Ages 4 to adult.
- Babbitt, Natalie. *Tuck Everlasting.* Farrar, Straus, & Giroux, 1985. The Tuck family has happened on the secret of eternal life—much to their dismay. In the absence of death, the Tucks discover that life loses much of its meaning and preciousness. A truly original book and a worthy follow-up movie (2002). Book ages 9–12; movie for all ages.

Websites/Organizations

- The Dougy Center for Grieving Children & Families (www.dougy.org). An organization founded in 1982 to "provide support in a safe place where children, teens and their families grieving a death can share their experiences as they move through their grief process." Website includes a search function to locate grief counseling centers across the United States and around the world.
- The Good Grief Program at Boston Medical Center (www.bmc.org/pediatrics/special/GoodGrief/overview.html). One of the top childhood grief counseling and research centers in the United States, led by Maria Trozzi, MEd, author of *Talking With Children About Loss* (see above).

Wondering
and Questioning

Introduction

What we need is not the will to believe, but the will to find out.

—Bertrand Russell

One of the most astonishing experiences for a parent is watching a human mind develop before your eyes. From the moment of birth, babies are sponges, soaking in everything they can lay their senses on. Wonder is pretty obviously present from the beginning—just look at the eyes of a newborn. Light, motion, temperature, shape, noise, and a million other novelties rain down on the little brain in the first few minutes, and the eyes register a mix of dismay, confusion, and wondering.

So there's wondering. But for *questioning* we'll need words. By their first birthday, kids will often have a few usable ones; by eighteen months they are generally learning a new word or two per day. At age 4, they're up to twelve new words a day, with amazing syntax and a sense of how to generalize the rules of grammar (like plural "-s" and past tense "-ed," as evident in sentences like "We goed to the farm and seed the sheeps"). At age 6, the average child has a vocabulary in excess of 21,000 words. And we're pretty much in the dark about just exactly how that happens.[1]

Which brings us back to wonder.

Wondering and questioning are the essence of childhood. Many of us bemoan the loss of wonder and the ever-greater difficulty of finding experiences and subjects that are truly untapped enough, and still interesting enough, for our minds to feel the inrushing flood of question after question that we remember from childhood.

Children have the daunting task of changing from helpless newborns into fully functioning adults in just over 6,000 days. Think of that. A certain degree of gullibility necessarily follows. Children are believing machines, and for good reason: When we are children, the tendency to believe it when we are told that fire is dangerous, two and two are four, cliffs are not to be dangled from, and so on, helps us, in the words of Richard Dawkins, "to pack, with extraordinary rapidity, our skulls full of the wisdom of our parents and our ancestors" in order to accomplish the unthinkably complex feat of becoming adults. The immensity of the task requires children to be "suckers" for whatever it is adults tell them. It is our job as parents to be certain not to abuse this period of relative intellectual dependency and trust.

The pivotal moment, of course, is the question. How we respond to the estimated 427,050 questions a child will ask between her second and fifth birthdays[2] will surely have a greater impact on her orientation to the world outside her head than the thirteen years of school that follow. Do we always respond with an answer—or sometimes with another question? Do we say, "What a great question!"—or do we just fill in the blank? How often do we utter that fabulous phrase, "You know what . . . I don't know!" followed by "Let's look it up together" or "I'll bet Aunt Bessie would know that, let's call her"? When it comes to wondering and questioning, these are the things that make all the difference. We have 427,050 chances to get it right, or 427,050 chances to say *"Because I said so," "Because God says so," "Don't concern yourself with that stuff,"* or something similarly fatal to the child's "will to find out." This chapter, you won't be surprised to hear, opts for the former.

Though you wouldn't know it from your high school English class, Mark Twain was a passionate nonbeliever and a heartfelt critic of religious thinking. Many of his late works were devoted to skewering, needling, and puncturing religious belief by way of satire—the most unanswerable, yet underused, weapon in the progressive arsenal. *Little Bessie Would Assist Providence* (1908), one of several late skeptical works, listens in as a wildly precocious 3-year-old innocently asks her devout mother questions about the nature of God. But unlike most of us, Bessie follows inadequate answers with more and more questions, until her poor mother is forced to simply order her into silence.[3]

Child psychiatrist Robert Kay continues the thread with fifteen "Thoughts on Raising a Curious, Creative, Freethinking Child," philosopher Amy Hilden describes her childhood discovery of philosophical questions in "The Family Road Trip: Discovering the Self Behind My Eyes," and British philosopher Margaret Knight argues that the deflection of questions children so often experience around religious questions is just plain "bad intellectual training."

When children begin their inevitable Bessie-like questioning of religious claims, it's nice to know the major arguments for and against religious belief. Their number is limited, after all, and they've been bandied about for centuries, so why start from scratch? Stephen Law, a British popularizer of philosophy, follows the lead of Plato by putting all of the major arguments for and against a complex belief system in the accessible form of a good-natured dialogue among friends in "Does God Exist?" When your middle- or high-schooler expresses an interest in the questions, you can pile the collected works of religious criticism and apologetics on the dining room table or open up to this remarkably compact and engaging chapter.

Little Bessie Would Assist Providence

Mark Twain

A Nose Is a Nose Is a Nose
Yip Harburg
Mother, Mother,
Tell me please,
Did God who gave us flowers and trees,
Also provide the allergies?

LITTLE BESSIE WAS NEARLY THREE years old. She was a good child, and not shallow, not frivolous, but meditative and thoughtful, and much given to thinking out the reasons of things and trying to make them harmonize with results. One day she said:

"Mamma, why is there so much pain and sorrow and suffering? What is it all for?" It was an easy question, and mamma had no difficulty in answering it: "It is for our good, my child. In His wisdom and mercy the Lord sends us these afflictions to discipline us and make us better."

"Is it *He* that sends them?"

"Yes."

"Does He send *all* of them, mamma?"

"Yes, dear, all of them. None of them comes by accident; He alone sends them, and always out of love for us, and to make us better."

"Isn't it strange!"

"Strange? Why, no, I have never thought of it in that way. I have not heard any one call it strange before. It has always seemed natural and right to me, and wise and most kindly and merciful."

"Who first thought of it like that, mamma? Was it you?"

"Oh, no, child, I was taught it."

"Who taught you so, mamma?"

"Why, really, I don't know—I can't remember. My mother, I suppose; or the preacher. But it's a thing that everybody knows."

"Well, anyway, it does seem strange. Did He give Billy Norris the typhus?"

"Yes."

"What for?"

"Why, to discipline him and make him good."

"But he died, mamma, and so it *couldn't* make him good."

"Well, then, I suppose it was for some other reason. We know it was a *good* reason, whatever it was."

"What do you think it was, mamma?"

"Oh, you ask so many questions! I think it was to discipline his parents."

"Well, then, it wasn't fair, mamma. Why should *his* life be taken away for their sake, when he wasn't doing anything?"

"Oh, I don't know! I only know it was for a good and wise and merciful reason."

"What reason, mamma?"

"I think—I think—well, it was a judgment; it was to punish them for some sin they had committed."

"But *he* was the one that was punished, mamma. Was that right?"

"Certainly, certainly. He does nothing that isn't right and wise and merciful. You can't understand these things now, dear, but when you are grown up you will understand them, and then you will see that they are just and wise."

After a pause:

"Did He make the roof fall in on the stranger that was trying to save the crippled old woman from the fire, mamma?"

"Yes, my child. W*ait!* Don't ask me why, because I don't know. I only know it was to discipline someone, or be a judgment upon somebody, or to show His power."

"That drunken man that stuck a pitchfork into Mrs. Welch's baby when . . ."

"Never mind about it, you needn't go into particulars; it was as to discipline the child—*that* much is certain, anyway."

"Mamma, Mr. Burgess said in his sermon that billions of little creatures are sent into us to give us cholera, and typhoid, and lockjaw, and more than a thousand other sicknesses and—mamma, does He send them?"

"Oh, certainly, child, certainly. Of course."

"What for?"

"Oh, to *dis*cipline us! Haven't I told you so, over and over again?"

"It's awful cruel, mamma! And silly! and if I . . ."

"Hush, oh *hush!* do you want to bring the lightning?"

"You know the lightning *did* come last week, mamma, and struck the new church, and burnt it down. Was it to discipline the church?"

(Wearily). "Oh, I suppose so."

"But it killed a hog that wasn't doing anything. Was it to discipline the hog, mamma?"

"Dear child, don't you want to run out and play a while? If you would like to . . ."

"Mama, only think! Mr. Hollister says there isn't a bird or fish or reptile or any other animal that hasn't got an enemy that Providence has sent to bite it and chase it and pester it, and kill it, and suck its blood and discipline it and make it good and religious. Is that true, mother—because if it is true, why did Mr. Hollister laugh at it?"

"That Hollister is a scandalous person, and I don't want you to listen to anything he says."

"Why, mamma, he is very interesting, and I think he tries to be good. He says the wasps catch spiders and cram them down into their nests in the ground—*alive,* mamma!—and there they live and suffer days and days and days, and the hungry little wasps chewing their legs and gnawing into their bellies all the time, to make them good and religious and praise God for His infinite mercies. I think Mr. Hollister is just lovely, and ever so kind; for when I asked him if he would treat a spider like that, he said he hoped to be damned if he would; and then he . . ."

"My child! oh, do for goodness' sake . . ."

"And mamma, he says the spider is appointed to catch the fly, and drive her fangs into his bowels, and suck and suck and suck his blood, to discipline him and make him a Christian; and whenever the fly buzzes his wings with the pain and misery of it, you can see by the spider's grateful eye that she is thanking the Giver of All Good for—well, she's saying grace, as he says; and also, he . . ."

"Oh, aren't you ever going to get tired chattering! If you want to go out and play ..."

"Mama, he says himself that all troubles and pains and miseries and rotten diseases and horrors and villainies are sent to us in mercy and kindness to discipline us; and he says it is the duty of every father and mother to *help* Providence, every way they can; and says they can't do it by just scolding and whipping, for that won't answer, it is weak and no good—Providence's way is best, and it is every parent's duty and every *person's* duty to help discipline everybody, and cripple them and kill them, and starve them, and freeze them, and rot them with diseases, and lead them into murder and theft and dishonor and disgrace; and he says Providence's invention for disciplining us and the animals is the very brightest idea that ever was, and not even an idiot could get up anything shinier. Mamma, brother Eddie needs disciplining, right away: and I know where you can get the smallpox for him, and the itch, and the diphtheria, and bone-rot, and heart disease, and consumption, and—Dear mama, have you fainted! I will run and bring help! Now *this* comes of staying in town this hot weather."

■ ■ ■ ■ ■ ■

Thoughts on Raising a Curious, Creative, Freethinking Child

Robert E. Kay, MD

WE ARE FROM THE BEGINNING a mass of needs: for safety, comfort, pleasure, control over what happens to us, a reason for living, and good relationships with other people. Many of these needs are met by parents, with varying degrees of success. And while it's true that no more than 20 percent of us appear to have reached our full emotional and intellectual potential, it's also true that no more than 1 or 2 percent become criminals. So in one sense we're not doing too badly. In another sense, there is plenty of room for improvement.

First published in *Life Learning Magazine* as "Never Say Never," Jan./Feb. 2006. Used with permission.

In my many years of practice as a psychiatrist working with children, adolescents, and families, I have seen that a child's growth is inevitable—if parents water the plant. A great deal of the personality is inborn and will unfold spontaneously over time. Parents will do well to recognize and accept the person their child is born to be, with innate strengths, capacities, interests, and rates of development.

Like most animals, humans are fundamentally social and cooperative creatures who mature in their own sweet time when their basic needs have been met by reasonably responsive adults in a reasonably decent society where stressors are manageable.

We can, however, be damaged by any number of things: stress during pregnancy, inept parenting, abuse, neglect, poor timing, poverty, and disasters among them. And let us not forget an educational system that, while well-meaning, tends more than any other feature of childhood to bore and confuse, sacrificing creativity, curiosity, and confidence on the altars of obedience, conformity, and societal convenience.

Despite the inevitable scars, most of us make it through and end up leading a life without too much psychological pain. Parents can help maximize their children's chances for a happy, curious, creative, and freethinking life by trusting them to think, learn, and ask questions in the interests of growth. Our parental responsibilities to meet their needs, set limits, stimulate, demonstrate, model, reveal, and encourage must always be undertaken with an eye to the openness and trust that allows kids to be their own best teachers.

Keep in mind that it takes the brain twenty-five to thirty years to develop fully. We must expect a degree of immature thinking, feeling, and behavior for a long time—though hopefully with decreasing frequency as the years go by. We can help the process by remembering how responsive the brain is: No other organ in the body has the same potential to keep improving its function until the day we die if only we exercise it a bit.

So how best to encourage curiosity, creativity and free thinking in our children? A few thoughts:

1. Start from day one by ignoring experts and relatives who tell you what kids "should" be doing by a certain age or how to make it happen. In most respects your child is *the* expert on what he or she is going to learn and when. There are times, of course, when genuine expertise is needed, but not when Davy or Suzy is a day or week or month behind some oft-quoted developmental marker.

2. Never think you can "spoil" infants by feeding and cuddling them as soon as they express the need for it. They know only that they're scared or hungry;

they can't yet think ahead and know that they will be fed. Attachment studies, including Gerhardt's *Why Love Matters,*[4] have shown that the more holding and attention we give early on, the sooner children's self-confidence will allow them to strike out on their own—both physically and intellectually.

3. Never criticize them for asking questions and answer them as best you can. That doesn't mean you can't groan if the question is badly timed or inappropriate to a given situation, but do know that other adults tend to be less concerned about such things than we think.

> " The answer "I don't know" is one of the greatest gifts a parent can give to a child's intellectual development. It is an answer both honest and too seldom heard. "

4. The answer "I don't know" is one of the greatest gifts a parent can give to a child's intellectual development. It is an answer both honest and too seldom heard. Secular parents should especially embrace the opportunity to develop children's comfort with saying and hearing "I don't know," since they are under no compunction to follow that honesty with "but God knows it for us" or "the Bible has the answers" or anything of the kind. If the question is whether God exists, a perfectly fine answer might be, "We don't know for sure, but I seriously doubt it." You can also invite them to consider the possibility that the Old Testament and New Testament are

> " Active, coercive teaching cannot *make* integrated learning happen. Children often fail to listen to their parents but they seldom fail to imitate us. "

works of fiction. Most kids never receive an invitation to consider that possibility and so are derailed in their ability to think freely about religion.

5. Active, coercive teaching cannot *make* integrated learning happen. Children often fail to listen to their parents but they seldom fail to imitate us. If you want them to say "please" and "thank you," for example, say "please" and "thank you" when you talk to them. *Telling* them to say it may well be an exercise in futility, and your authority as a parent is undermined by their noncompliance. Far better in all respects to teach by example. Also remember that our cooperative instincts are far stronger than our willingness to obey. In the early years, "Please help me clean up" works far better than "Please clean up." Young, immature human beings tend to resist anything that feels like an order.

6. Be sensitive to a child's readiness to receive information. Take those rare opportunities to offer something useful. As John Holt says in *How Children Fail,* "The answers that stick are in response to the questions we ask."

7. At about the age of 10, children are ready for a greater level of active discernment in their education—an increase, if you will, in their active freethinking. Some of what we learn in school is of lasting value; some is of only passing value, necessary to learn in order to get through the educational process; and some is of no value whatsoever. A developing young mind must learn to sort these things, one from another. Suggest that they "split-brain" themselves in school: Turn half of the brain into a floppy disk on which they load all the "nonsense" the teacher will nonetheless want to hear about, while the other half becomes a hard drive on which they record everything that's actually interesting and useful, such as the ability to speak, listen, think, read, write, learn, calculate, ask questions, work, and cooperate. Reinforce the value of playing the Credential World with half the brain and the Real World with the other half. Once in a while, something that you thought was floppy material ends up interesting and potentially useful enough to download to the hard drive side. Part of being a freethinker is recognizing that and acting on it.

8. Be sure to ask if they'd like to try out one or more of the 9,800 different religions we now have on Earth. But it's okay in the process to offer your opinions on some of the more toxic ideas. It's just plain dumb to think that a mythical god can read your mind, or control what happens, or consign you to hell. These toxic ideas get in the way of their developing questions and opinions, so you are within your rights as a parent to head them off in advance by declaring them just plain dumb. If they decide otherwise on their own, so be it—but detoxifying religion at least a bit gives them that chance to think.

9. The teaching of morality follows the same rules as any other kind of teaching—*show,* don't *say.* If you want them to learn not to hurt or upset other people or the environment, show them by your actions.

> **Expose children to all sorts of ideas, *especially those with which you disagree.* Given those gifts, they will not fail to step into their role as self-teachers.**

10. Don't worry, within reason, about what they are going to need to know in the future. Expose them to reality, to people, to the world, and to all sorts of ideas, *especially those with which you disagree.* Given those gifts, they will not fail to step into their role as self-teachers.

11. Put yourself in their shoes as often as possible. See the world from their small and put-upon perspective. They will inevitably resist you from time to time in obnoxious and immature ways. You can't make another human being eat, swallow, pee, poop, think, learn, work, talk, confess, agree, or believe, so

don't even go there. Do yourself and your children the favor of trying to see through their eyes, of trying to understand the reasons behind the resistance.

12. Tell the truth as often and as straightforwardly as possible if you think they can possibly handle it.

13. The less time in front of electronic screens of all types, the better. There should ideally be no television watching before age 3 and no electronic screen of any kind in their bedroom at *any* age.

14. Tell them that their job is to have fun inside the box for a while and that someday they can make their own box. It's usually much easier to be an adult than to be a kid, largely because of the relative freedom we have to live in a box of our own creation. Tell them you know they have a harder job than you. They'll love you for recognizing that.

15. The bottom line of freethought is this: You can think whatever you want, but to live in community with other human beings, you sometimes have to control your talk and your behavior.

In summary: A child should be treated like a distinguished visitor from a foreign land who is unfamiliar with our language and our customs. Just as that visitor brings his or her own language and customs, our children come into the world with predispositions, talents, strengths, and weaknesses. We often do best by them by offering examples, sharing our own opinions, opening opportunities, then stepping aside to let them run. They will mature in their own sweet time if only we will let them.

The Family Road Trip: Discovering the Self Behind My Eyes

Amy Hilden, Ph.D.

> If we begin to think more actively, some stunning changes are possible: We can know ourselves better, we can have more options in life, we can distinguish fact from fiction and hype from hope, we can begin to think more decisively as we choose liferoads to walk down, and we can become more persuasive as we listen and talk to our fellow thinkers.
>
> —Gary R. Kirby & Jeffrey R. Goodpaster[5]

I BECAME A PHILOSOPHER in the summer of 1969 in the back seat of a Chevy. Before you jump to conclusions, let me add that I was 10 years old, riding along on the latest of many cross-country family road trips. In the days before electronic entertainment devices, before air conditioning was common in cars, before seat belt laws, I remember staring out the window, watching the telephone poles and meadows go by. There really was nothing else for me to do. I had been ordered by my parents to turn away from the sister whose all-too-sweaty body was leeching onto me and whose nasty barbs had injured me deeply for the very last time! So I just looked out there. And as I did, I began what would become a lifelong passion—wondering.

Though I have become a professional philosopher in my adult life, paid to think about thinking and wonder about wondering, it was as a child that I first became aware of that thing that makes it possible: a mind. Are there ways to nurture the development of remarkable minds in our children? What if we *welcomed* wonder? And what if we took seriously the burdens and implications of thinking hard and well about what we wonder about?

The humanistic optimist in me believes that the better we think about ourselves and the world, the better the world will be. There are choices to make, and deliberate reflection about those choices is the only way to confidently know what we are doing and why we are doing it. And since our children will also meet these challenges, it just makes sense to (1) think carefully about thinking and (2) think about how to nurture in our children the ability and desire to do it well. So how do we reflect upon ourselves as wonderers, as thinkers, as knowers in order to get a hint at the possibilities for active thinking and "stunning changes"? I have some ideas about this.

Once I started to think seriously about what it means to have a mind, to know something—anything at all—I turned to the only resource that had any chance of helping me out: my own mind and its store of ideas. But notice this: That entailed using my mind in order to know my mind—which sounds something like "a pair of pliers trying to grasp itself."[6] But while a pair of pliers cannot grasp itself, our minds can. We all have the experience of having ideas, of *thinking* about those ideas, and of *thinking about our thinking* about those ideas. And while all of this thinking usually goes on without our reflecting upon it, we still *can* reflect upon it. And reflecting upon the contents of our minds can reveal some pretty neat things about it and what it can do.

Which brings us once again to my 10-year-old self, looking out the window of a Chevy station wagon.

After a while, the looking alone no longer engaged me. I found myself wondering *about* the looking. I began to wonder about just *who* it was that was behind my eyes. I knew a little about the physical nature of the eyeball from reading the encyclopedia, but that wasn't what gripped me at that moment. I wanted to know what was *beyond* the physical eyeball. What was "*it*" that was seeing the world passing by at sixty miles per hour?

I remember thinking that "*it*" must be *me*. But what could that possibly mean? At the time I believed that each of us has a unique self, a soul that would go somewhere cool to live forever after the death of the physical body. I understood at the time that the "soul" was not the same part of me that was my body. My body would die, the worms *would* crawl in and out, and it would shrivel up and eventually turn to dust. In the long run, as hard as it was to stomach, the body wasn't important. I believed that it was my soul, that which was essential about me, that would be reunited eventually with all those I loved. This "theory of self" made childhood thoughts of death less horrific, death itself less lonely, and physical, earthly life less pointless in the face of "life everlasting."

In the road trip reflection, I transferred that belief—that "theory of self"—to the current experience of wondering who was behind the looking I was doing. It was me, myself, my I, my soul. It was certainly not my body; not my eyeballs, though they made the seeing possible. It was something beyond what was in other ways apparent. Though I've since given up the belief system and black-and-white worldview of my childhood, I haven't given up the wonder of finding myself wondering in that car.

There's no reason to think my experience was unique, nor my later reflections on it. Some might say the luxury and privilege of such free time allowed me to have this experience. And though I'm sure a lot of the content—the telephone poles, the meadows, my sister's sweat, my parents' threats, my assumptions—were unique to me and my place and time, I don't think any of that is necessary. There is just something about being human, a being with a mind that can grasp itself, that enables the art of wonder at all.

It is the human appetite for these types of questions, all of which stretch beyond the obvious, that urges us to confront something inescapable about ourselves. The great philosopher Immanuel Kant claimed that our minds can no more give up asking these kinds of questions than we could give up breathing. It is essentially human. And it's these questions, he asserted, that are more important to us than any others: *Is there a God? Will my soul live beyond my death? What is freedom?* It's part of our nature to wonder about things beyond our immediate experience. There is no shaking off its grip.

> The wondering I did on that childhood family road trip led to more wondering. It was really my first experience of taking the world seriously, of taking my life as a human being seriously.

The wondering I did on that childhood family road trip led to more wondering. It was really my first experience of taking the world seriously, of taking my life as a human being seriously, and the first step toward becoming a professional philosopher. As a philosopher, I have "permission" to keep asking and wondering about the questions that most of us set aside as young children. It was then that we were the purest we will ever be as wonderers. As we grow up, practical matters invade that purity. Our "where/when/what/why" questions—so genuinely puzzling, thrilling, and hard to answer—are met with understandable exasperation from those around us who have forgotten the delight and power of this kind of pure wonder—or who maybe just want to know what you want for lunch!

Think about a particular kind of question that small children ask: *Where was I before I was in your tummy? If I lost my arm, would I still be me? When Spot died, did he go to be with Grandma? If God made everything, who made God? Where is hell? Why do I have to share?* These are what philosophers call *metaphysical* questions—questions of personal identity, immortality, first causes, the existence of immaterial things/places, the foundations of moral obligations, and the like. Each concerns the reality of something that is partly beyond the direct experience of our senses. Our approach to this kind of question is different from our approach to a question from our child such as, *Why should I take a bath?* Metaphysical questions concern the nature of existence at a different level from mere bodily existence. They are about things we wonder and worry about, yet struggle to find answers to.

But what does it mean to "wonder" about something? When we wonder about something, we have questions about that something that are not easily answered. Getting to an even remotely satisfying answer seems to demand some real effort. In other words, we need to think about it, to search for answers which are hard to find.

> The years between 18 and 22 were not given to us to be frittered away in contemplation of future tax shelters and mortgage payments. In fact, it is almost a requirement of developmental biology that these years be spent in erotic reverie, metaphysical speculation, and schemes for universal peace and justice. Sometimes, of course, we lose sight of the heroic dreams of youth later on, as overdue bills and carburetor problems take their toll. But those who never dream at all start to lose much more—their wit, empathy, perspective, and, for lack of a more secular term, their immortal souls.
>
> –Barbara Ehrenreich, *The Worst Years of Our Lives*

But who says the answers are hard to find? When a child asks where she was before she was in Mom's tummy, why not just say, "You weren't anywhere"? Isn't that simple enough? Sure, it's a simple answer—but is it true?

Can we give such an answer with any real confidence? Can we really know that we "weren't anywhere" before the womb? We may well have beliefs about the nature of our existence and about when it begins and ends, but these beliefs are always going to be speculative, open to significant doubt. That's the nature of metaphysical questions. "I don't know, but I love thinking about it with you" is often the best answer we can come up with to certain questions. But if we were to really give ourselves and our children permission to wonder and to not require final answers, what might happen to how we think about the world? Would we be more creative? We'd surely be more open-minded, less dogmatic, wouldn't we?

In order to locate the virtue of such (potentially) bizarre wondering and thinking, perhaps it would be helpful to identify a characteristic of wondering—namely, its skepticism. If I'm wondering about something—for example, one of my favorites, whether I am the same person today as I was when I was 5—then I am skeptical about whether I'm the same person. If I weren't skeptical, if I didn't have anything to doubt or question, then I wouldn't be wondering. If I believed I *knew*, I wouldn't be wondering. *Wondering* is what we do when we don't know something and *want* to know it, but are unsure even *how* we could know it. Not knowing how to multiply fractions, for example, is a different kind of not-knowing. If I don't know how to multiply fractions, I'm not *wondering* about multiplying fractions. I just don't know how. I know what it would mean to know how to multiply fractions: I'd multiply fractions and get the correct answer.

> *Wondering* is what we do when we don't know something and *want* to know it, but are unsure even *how* we could know it.

A good dose of skepticism is healthy. If we believed everything at face value, then we wouldn't be operating at a level of our fullest human capacity to think. We might be operating on a level closer to a computer. Every bit of knowledge we hold has been downloaded onto our hard drive, and every mental or physical action is determined by the software programming that someone else fed into us. Being skeptical means wondering a bit longer, gathering evidence about whether we should accept a particular answer.

With a stalwart commitment to our mind's capacity to wonder, think critically and skeptically, and question, however, mightn't we find ourselves on the verge of insanity or ostracism if we wonder too long or question too much? How many of you have been told, "you think too much" and "you take things too seriously"? How many of you find yourselves marginalized because you push hard and critically on ideas and claims? Is it possible to think too much? Might it be that exercising the capacity that makes us unique—our capacity to think and to question things beyond the immediate—could also make us socially isolated? And isn't social isolation something we want to protect our children from? Isn't it necessary sometimes

> While the personal risks to thinking may be significant, aren't there also personal, moral, social, national, and international risks to *not* thinking? Are we a nation at war with (so many) others because we are thinking too much—or thinking too little?

to protect them by saying, "Because I said so" or "That's just the way it is—now go play"?

While the personal risks to thinking may be significant, aren't there also personal, moral, social, national, and international risks to *not* thinking? Are we a nation at war with (so many) others because we are thinking too much—or thinking too little?

The answers to these complex questions are, and ought be, elusive. At the same time, wouldn't we agree that we should aggressively pursue answers with our hard-working critical minds? It will come as no surprise that I stand in support of the risks of wondering, thinking, and questioning, even if at some personal risk. Why? I think it has something to do with what it means to *really* live a human life—first to think, and second to act on that thinking for the betterment of the world.

Facing a choice between exile, with an end to his philosophical questioning of others, or death, Socrates proclaimed that he would choose death, saying an unexamined life was not worth living for a human being. He would rather not live at all than to live without exchanging ideas about the things he wondered and worried about—things like justice, goodness, and virtue. Imagine what the world would be like if that kind of wondering were not allowed to run its open course. Is that the world we want for our children?

Yet doing this kind of critical thinking and examining of one's beliefs and the claims of others is no walk in the park. To be honest, it can be a burden, even painful. But what kinds of "stunning changes" would not have occurred if brave thinkers had been unwilling to take the risk of fully examining the implications of their thoughts and beliefs? Imagine no Buddha, Socrates, Giordano Bruno, Galileo, Sojourner Truth, Einstein, Jane Addams, Gandhi, Martin Luther King. To withstand the personal jeopardy that wondering and critical thinking can expose us to, surely the answer is to do it together *and* to work toward the creation of a society where wonder is welcomed and critical thinking is recognized as indispensable.

So take a family road trip, buckle up the kids, and turn off the electronic entertainment. Once they find the self behind their eyes, ask them where they want to go. And when they ask, "Are we there yet?", tell them, "We've just begun."

Excerpt from Morals Without Religion

Margaret Knight

If (a child) is brought up in the orthodox way, he will accept what he is told happily enough to begin with. But if he is normally intelligent, he is almost bound to get the impression that there is something odd about religious statements. If he is taken to church, for example, he hears that death is the gateway to eternal life, and should be welcomed rather than shunned; yet outside he sees death regarded as the greatest of all evils, and everything possible done to postpone it. In church he hears precepts like "resist not evil," and "Take no thought for the morrow"; but he soon realizes that these are not really meant to be practiced outside. If he asks questions, he gets embarrassed, evasive answers: "Well, dear, you're not quite old enough to understand yet, but some of these things are true in a deeper sense"; and so on. The child soon gets the idea that there are two kinds of truth—the ordinary kind, and another, rather confusing and embarrassing kind, into which it is best not to inquire too closely.

Now all this is bad intellectual training. It tends to produce a certain intellectual timidity—a distrust of reason—a feeling that it is perhaps rather bad taste to pursue an argument to its logical conclusion, or to refuse to accept a belief on inadequate evidence.

Does God Exist?

Stephen Law, D. Phil.

The Universe

I am sitting on top of a hill under a beautiful night sky.

The stars are twinkling brightly. To the east of me, the moon sits above the treetops, almost full. To the west, I can see the spires of Oxford. Above the spires there is a faint purple glow where the sun set just a few minutes ago. Between the glow and the moon are suspended two bright points of light—the planets Venus and Jupiter.

As I sit here on his hilltop, I am struck by how vast the universe is. Here we are, sitting on the cool outer crust of a huge ball of red-hot rock: planet Earth. Every now and then a little molten rock—lava—spurts out to form a volcano.

Earth turns on its axis once every twenty-four hours. That is what made the sun disappear from view a little while ago, of course: It was not the sun that moved, but Earth that turned. The moon—another big ball of rock—goes round Earth once a month. And Earth goes around the sun once a year.

Those two bright points of light over there—Venus and Jupiter—are also planets. In fact, there are nine planets[7] in our solar system, all of them rotating slowly around the sun.

Our sun is a star just like the thousands of other stars that I can see up above me. Those other stars are much further away, of course. While light from the sun takes just eight minutes to reach us, light from other stars can take tens, hundreds or even thousands of years.

The stars I see spread out above me form part of a huge whirlpool of stars called a *galaxy*. Our galaxy is called the *Milky Way*, the Milky Way being just one of the thousands of known galaxies in the universe.

Against this vast universe, planet Earth seems almost unimaginably tiny and insignificant.

From *The Philosophy Files* (titled *Philosophy Rocks!* in the United States) © 2000 by Stephen Law. Used with permission of Orion Children's Books.

Where Did the Universe Come From?

When I look out across the universe, I often ask myself: How did all this rock and dust and space come to be here? Where did it all come from? What *made* it exist? Scientists have a theory about this. They say that the universe began with a huge explosion. Scientists call this explosion the *Big Bang.* The Big Bang happened a very long time ago—between ten and twenty thousand million years ago. The Big Bang was where all the matter in the universe came from. It was the beginning of space. In fact, it was the beginning of time itself.

But when scientists tell me this, it doesn't help me very much. It doesn't re-move my feeling that something still needs explaining. Because I then want to know: *What made the Big Bang happen?* Why was there a bang, rather than no bang? That certainly is a great mystery, perhaps the greatest mystery of all.

The Meaning of Life

After a while, I stop looking up at the universe spread out above me. I look down at the grass.

I notice that, down in the shadows among the blades of grass, tiny insects are crawling about. Many of these insects are ants. They seem to be very busy. When I look even more closely, I see that the ants are pushing a leaf around.

It seems that ants are trying to push the leaf into a hole in the ground. That hole must be where the ants live. The leaf can hardly fit. The ants struggle and struggle and still they can't get it into the hole. I wonder why the leaf is so im-portant to them.

I could easily put my foot down and squash all the ants. I decide not to squash them. But I wonder what real difference it would make if I did. Look at their frantic activity, running around, trying to get that leaf into the hole. It all seems so pointless. So meaningless. What would it really matter if I did put my foot down and snuff them out?

Looked at from space, Earth must seem a bit like a huge ants' nest.

There we all are, rushing about, just like ants. We are born. We grow up. We go to the supermarket. We go to work. We watch TV. We have children. We die. Our children have children, who in turn have children. Generation after genera-tion of ceaseless activity. On and on the cycle goes. But what is the meaning be-hind our brief journey through life? What is the point of our being momentarily alive and conscious on this tiny planet amid all this vastness? Is there any point?

God

As I sit here under the stars, I have been puzzling about the existence of the universe. Why is it here? What made the Big Bang happen? Why was there a bang, rather than no bang? I have also been wondering about the meaning of life. What is the point of our being here?

Many people would answer the question about what caused the universe to exist by saying that God did: God created the universe. God made the Big Bang happen.

Many people also believe that it is God who gives meaning to our existence. They believe that there is a point to our being here. We do have a purpose, a divine purpose. That purpose involves loving and obeying God.

What Is God Like?

If God did create the universe, if He is what gives meaning to our lives, then what is He like?

God surely isn't an old man with a big beard. He doesn't *really* sit on a cloud. If you were to fly about and examine all the clouds that there are, you wouldn't find an old man sitting on any of them. Rather, this is just an image that religious people use to help them think about God.

In fact, although I talk about God as being a He, many people nowadays don't even think of God as being male.

So what is God like, then, if He isn't an old man sitting on a cloud? According to Christians, Jews, Muslims, and those of many other religious faiths, God has at least the following three characteristics:

First of all, God is *all powerful*. That means He can do absolutely anything. He created the universe. And He could destroy it again, if He so chose. God can bring the dead back to life, turn water into wine, and send you to the moon in the blink of an eye.

Second, God is supposed to be *all knowing*. God knows everything there is to know. He knows all that has happened, and all that will happen. He knows our thoughts. He knows our every secret. He even knows that it was I who sneaked downstairs last night and stole the last piece of cake from the fridge.

Absolutely nothing is hidden from God.

Third, God is supposed to be *all good*. God loves us and would certainly never do anything bad.

Why Believe in God?

Of course, many religious people have *faith* in the existence of God. They believe in God's existence without reason. They just believe.

But, as philosophers, we are interested in whether there is any *reason* to believe in the existence of God. Is there any evidence to suggest that God exists? Can we show by argument that God exists? Or is there perhaps some reason to suppose that God doesn't exist? These are the questions we are going to look at here.

Bob and Kobir Arrive

I lie back in the grass and look up at the stars. After a while I hear two voices in the distance. They seem to be getting nearer. Eventually, I recognize who it is. It's my friends Bob and Kobir, out for an evening stroll.

Bob is a soccer player. He's staying with Kobir for the weekend. The two of them have been kicking a ball around the park.

A couple of minutes later they arrive on top of the hill. We all say hello, and lie down on the grass.

I explain to Bob and Kobir that I have been thinking about God, the Big Bang, and the meaning of life.

They are pretty impressed! Bob says that he believes in God. Kobir, on the other hand, says he doesn't.

Now Bob and Kobir are good friends. But there's nothing they enjoy more than having a philosophical argument. So it isn't long before they are busy arguing about whether God exists. This is how the argument starts.

BOB: Look. You have to admit, many millions of people all over the earth believe in God. If all those millions believe, then there's got to be *something* to it, doesn't there?

KOBIR: I'm afraid that's wrong. Millions of people used to believe that the earth was flat and that the sun went around the earth. They were quite wrong about *that*, weren't they?

BOB: Well, okay. I admit they were wrong about that.

KOBIR: So you see, most people *can* be wrong. Just because many or even most people believe in God doesn't show that He exists.

BOB: Okay. I suppose it's true that most people *can* be wrong. But it's *likely* that they're right, isn't it?

KOBIR: No. Not if they don't have *reason* to believe. And of course, the explanation of why people believe things is not always that they have reason to believe. Sometimes there's another explanation.

BOB: Like what?

KOBIR: Well, any of those who believe in God are simply *brought up* to have that belief. Belief in God is often drilled into people from a very young age. That explains why they believe.

BOB: That doesn't explain why I believe in God. I was never sent to Sunday school. And neither of my parents believes in God.

KOBIR: I would also say that many people believe in God, not because they have any reason to believe that God exists, but just because they *want* to believe He exists. They believe in God simply because it is a nice, comforting thing to believe.

BOB: Why comforting?

KOBIR: Well, it's a scary thought that we are all alone in the universe, that there is no ultimate meaning or point to our existence. It's quite frightening to think that when we die, we are gone forever. It is so much *nicer* to believe that there is a loving God who watches over us and who gives some point to our lives. It is so much *nicer* to believe that when we die, we don't just cease to exist, but continue on. But just because this is a nice, comforting thing to believe doesn't give us the slightest reason to suppose that it's *true,* does it?

Is Kobir being entirely fair? Actually, in some ways believing in God can make life seem rather less comfortable. For example, some people who believe in God also believe in the Last Judgment and Heaven and Hell. They believe that after they die they will be judged by God and possibly sent to Hell as punishment for the bad things they have done.

That's hardly a very comforting thought, is it?

Still, it appears that most people who believe that God exists do also want it to be true that He exists. It seems they get quite a lot of comfort from their belief. So is Kobir right? Do most people believe in God simply because they want to believe or have been brought up to believe in God? Or is there also some reason to suppose that God exists? What do you think?

Bob's Big Bang Argument

The three of us sit up silently for a few minutes. We listen to the sound the wind makes as it hisses through the trees down at the bottom of the hill.

Suddenly, there is a whooshing sound followed by a deafening bang. It's the sound of a firework. It showers the sky to the north of us with thousands of silver flecks. We watch as they spiral downward.

BOB: Look. I certainly *don't* believe God exists just because it's a *nice* thing to believe. After all, I'd like to believe that fairies exist, but I don't. There's no *reason* to believe in them. There's no evidence that they exist. But there *is* evidence that God exists. That's why I believe in God.

KOBIR: What do you mean? What evidence is there that God exists?

BOB: Well, Stephen mentioned the Big Bang a minute ago. Don't scientists believe that the universe we see spread out up there began with a huge explosion—the Big Bang?

KOBIR: Yes.

BOB: Well then, my question is, What caused the Big Bang? Why was there a bang rather than no bang?

KOBIR: I have no idea. That is a mystery.

BOB: Yes, it's a great mystery. After all, everything has a cause, doesn't it? Things don't *just happen.* Take that firework that exploded over there a few moments ago. That explosion didn't *just happen,* did it? It had to have a cause. People had to light the fuse, didn't they?

KOBIR: I guess so.

BOB: But then the same applies to the Big Bang. The Big Bang must have had a cause, too. Now if God exists, that would solve the mystery of what caused the Big Bang. That's why it's reasonable to suppose that God exists. God explains why the Big Bang happened. God lit the fuse!

Is Bob's Big Bang Argument Any Good?

I think that often, when it seems to people that God must exist, something like Bob's Big Bang Argument is at the back of their minds. Indeed, you can find much the same sort of argument in the writings of many philosophers and religious thinkers down through the centuries.

At first sight, Bob's Big Bang Argument does seem quite convincing. But is it really any good? Does Bob's argument actually provide us with some reason to suppose that god exists?

Kobir certainly doesn't think so.

KOBIR: I'm afraid your argument is no good. You haven't given us any reason at all to assume that God exists.

BOB: Why not? Look, in a nutshell your argument is this: Everything has a cause; therefore the universe has a cause; therefore God must exist as the cause of the universe. Right?

KOBIR: Yes. I guess so.

BOB: Well then, if *everything* has a cause, then what caused God? What made Him exist?

KOBIR: Good question. That's a mystery.

BOB: So you have merely replaced one mystery with another, haven't you?

KOBIR: How do you mean?

BOB: Well, we are still stuck with a mystery aren't we? We started with a question, What caused the universe? Scientists give us the answer: the Big Bang. But then we are left with a mystery, aren't we? For then there is the mystery of what caused the Big Bang.

Now you try to get rid of *this* mystery by saying that god caused the Big Bang. But then we face the mystery of what caused God.

And so on. There's still a mystery left over.

Kobir is right. Bob suggested that it is reasonable to believe that God exists because that solves a mystery—the mystery of why the Big Bang happened. The trouble is, Bob has removed one mystery only by introducing another. Still, Bob doesn't give up that easily.

BOB: Okay. Let's suppose God doesn't have a cause. Let's suppose God isn't the sort of thing that needs a cause. If god doesn't need a cause, then there's no mystery left over.

KOBIR: But now you have contradicted yourself! You started your argument by assuming that *everything* has a cause. Now you are saying not everything has a cause—God doesn't.

BOB: But when I said everything has a cause, I didn't mean absolutely everything. I meant everything except God, obviously.

KOBIR: So you are saying there is one exception to the rule that everything has a cause: God.

BOB: Yes. God is the exception to that rule.

KOBIR: But if there has to be an exception to the rule, why not just make the universe the exception to the rule instead? What reason have you given us to add God on to the beginning of the universe as an *extra* cause? You have given us no reason. But then you have given us no reason to assume that God exists.

BOB: I guess you are right.

KOBIR: You see, Bob, I admit that there *is* a mystery about where the universe came from. I admit that it is a great mystery why there is something rather than nothing. I just deny that this mystery gives us any reason at all to suppose that God exists.

Bob's Cosmic Watchmaker Argument

Bob sits up. He starts fiddling with his watch. Bob is clearly a bit upset that his Big Bang Argument doesn't work after all. Eventually, after a few minutes, Bob takes another shot at convincing Kobir of the existence of God. He takes off his watch and tosses it on to the grass in front of Kobir.

BOB: Okay, Kobir. Here's a better argument. Take a look at this watch. Suppose that you are walking along a deserted beach on a remote island somewhere. Suddenly, you come across a watch just like this one. It's just lying there on the sand.

You ask yourself: How did the watch get here? Here are two suggestions. The first suggestion is that the watch was *designed*. It's a tool, made by an intelligent being—a watchmaker—for a specific purpose—to enable people to tell the time. The second suggestion is that the watch was made by the action of the waves, the wind, and other natural forces. They formed the watch all by themselves, without the help of any sort of designer. Which of these two suggestions is more likely to be true, do you think?

KOBIR: Well, obviously, the first suggestion is much more likely to be true.

BOB: You're right. A watch is not like a pebble, is it? Pebbles are formed without help from any intelligence. They really are formed by natural forces: the wind and the waves. But a watch is hardly likely to have been made in this way, right?

KOBIR: No.

BOB: In fact, the watch clearly has a purpose—to tell the time. So isn't it reasonable to suppose that there must be an intelligent being who designed it for that purpose? There must be a designer, a watchmaker, who made it.

KOBIR: I agree.

BOB: Now take a look at my eye. The eye is a very complicated object—far, far more complicated than a watch or anything we human beings can make. Like the watch, the eye also has a purpose—to enable the creature attached to it to see. It does this job extremely well, doesn't it?

KOBIR: Yes, it does. The eye is a marvelous piece of engineering.

BOB: Now ask yourself: How did the eye come to exist? What is more likely—that the eye came into existence by chance or that it was designed? Given that the eye has a purpose, a purpose for which it is very well suited, it, too, must have a designer. There has to be a designer—a sort of cosmic watchmaker—who designed the eye. That designer is God.

Is There a Problem with Bob's Cosmic Watchmaker Argument?

What do you think of Bob's Cosmic Watchmaker Argument? As happened to the Big Bang Argument, different versions of it have been put forward down through the centuries by philosophers and religious thinkers. But there are problems with it.

One problem with the Cosmic Watchmaker Argument is that nowadays we know all about *natural selection*. Natural selection can explain how eyes might come to exist without supposing they had any sort of a designer.

Natural Selection

Here's how natural selection works. When someone is going to build something complex like a ship, airplane, or building, they usually make a plan. This plan is called a *blueprint*. The blueprint shows exactly how the ship or whatever is to be put together.

Now, all living things also contain a sort of blueprint. They contain something called *DNA*. DNA is a long string of molecules. You will find one of these strings in every cell of a living thing's body. The string contains a blueprint for making a living thing of that sort. When plants or creatures reproduce, it is the string of DNA handed down from the parent plants or creatures that provides the blueprint for building it.

The DNA string in the new living thing is made by copying parts of the DNA string from the parent or parents. But in the process of copying, slight errors may creep in.

Because of these slight changes to the blueprint, the creature produced from it may be slightly different from its parent or parents. There will be slight changes to the creature. These changes are called *mutations*. They happen quite by chance.

Here's an example. A simple creature living in the sea may have, as a mutation, a single light-sensitive cell on its skin.

Now, this cell could be very useful to the creature. It may allow it to detect how deep it is in the sea (the deeper you go in the sea, the darker it gets). So in this environment the mutation would give the creature a slight advantage over other creatures of that sort.

Another one of these creatures may have as a mutation a brighter-colored skin. This mutation may be a big disadvantage to the creature in that environment, making it more visible to other creatures that want to eat it.

Of course, the creature with the mutation that helps it to survive is more likely to be able to mate and reproduce itself than a creature with a mutation that makes it less likely to survive. So the next generation of creatures is more likely to contain creatures with the light-sensitive cell and is less likely to contain creatures with the brightly colored skin. Those mutations which help creatures survive and reproduce in that environment are likely to be passed on and those which make survival less probable are wiped out.

As further mutations are added over thousands and thousands of generations, the creatures slowly change. They gradually *evolve.* They adapt to their environments. The process is called *natural selection.*

You have probably come across fossils—pieces of rock that have taken on the form of living creatures that lived millions of years ago. When you look at fossils, you can see the kinds of change that I have been talking about taking place. For example, it seems that the first birds to exist actually evolved from certain sorts of dinosaur.

We have even traced parts of our own evolutionary tree. We now know that human beings share a common ancestor with apes. It is no accident that we look so similar to them.

So how did the *eye* appear? It didn't just appear from anywhere. It evolved over millions and millions of years. It evolved because it helps creatures to survive and reproduce. Perhaps the process began with a single light-sensitive cell appearing in some simple organism living in the sea. Gradually, over many generations, more light-sensitive cells were added. In this way, the eye slowly began to evolve, until finally you see the sort of eye that is around today.

So one big problem with Bob's Cosmic Watchmaker Argument is this. Before we knew about natural selection, it seemed difficult to explain how eyes, and living creatures generally, could come to exist on the earth. We couldn't see how any *natural* process could have produced complex living creatures. For this reason, many people supposed that there must be a *supernatural* being—God—who made the creatures. But now that we know about evolution and natural selection, this particular reason for believing in the existence of God has disappeared.

We don't know the *whole* story of how life on earth developed, of course. I am just guessing about how the eye might have evolved. The point is that we can see that, in principle, the existence of all the different sorts of life on earth can very probably be explained in wholly natural terms without our having to talk about God at all.

What Is Reasonable to Believe?

Kobir explains natural selection to Bob. After he's explained, Bob admits that the eye does not seem to provide much evidence after all for the existence of God.

I'm now feeling pretty hungry. Bob and Kobir say that they are hungry too, so we decide to go for curry at my favorite Indian restaurant. We get up, dust ourselves off, and start off down the hill. There's a gravel path that crunches underfoot. The moon lights our way, casting long shadows out in front of us.

As we walk downhill, Kobir tells Bob that he doesn't think there are *any* good arguments for the existence of God. There is little if any evidence to suggest that God exists.

Bob tosses his soccer ball in the air a few times. Then he points out, quite correctly, that even if there is no good reason to suppose God does exist, that doesn't prove he doesn't exist. Kobir agrees that this is true.

BOB: But then shouldn't we remain *neutral* about whether or not God exists? I mean, if we can't show he does exist, but can't show he doesn't exist either, isn't remaining neutral the most reasonable view to take?

KOBIR: Actually, I don't think so. I think that if there is no reason to suppose he exists, then the reasonable thing to believe is that he *doesn't* exist.

Another firework explodes above us. We stand and watch for a moment as it sends shimmering red sparks across the sky.

BOB: But why? Look, think about the question of whether or not there is life out there in other parts of the universe. It seems that at the moment we can't show that there definitely is life out there, but neither can we show that there isn't. In which case, the most reasonable position to take is to remain neutral.

KOBIR: I agree. I think we should remain neutral on whether there is life out there. But the question of whether or not God exists is different.

BOB: Why?

KOBIR: Because while there is little if any reason to suppose God exists, there *is* some good evidence that there must be alien life-forms.

BOB: What evidence? We haven't discovered life on other planets.

KOBIR: True. But we know that life evolved here on this planet, don't we? And we also know there are countless millions of other planets in the universe, many of which are very similar to our own. In which case it seems not improbable that life will have evolved on at least one of those other planets, too. So there *is* pretty good evidence for the existence of life out there. It's just that we don't have *conclusive* evidence. On the other hand, it seems to me there is little if *any* evidence to suggest that God exists.

Bob shrugs his shoulders. He doesn't look convinced. So Kobir continues.

KOBIR: Look. Compare believing in fairies. If there's little if any reason to suppose that fairies exist, then it is probably more reasonable to believe that they *don't* exist rather than to remain neutral. Don't you agree?

BOB: I suppose so. I certainly believe that fairies don't exist. It's silly to believe in fairies.

KOBIR: Well, then. The same is true of God. If there is little or no reason to believe that God exists, then the reasonable thing to believe is that he doesn't exist. Isn't it as silly to believe in God as it is to believe in fairies?

Bob feels quite insulted by Kobir's comparing belief in God to belief in fairies. And perhaps Kobir is being a bit unfair. After all, plenty of very intelligent people believe in God. And believing in God is certainly not silly in the sense that it is frivolous or trivial: Believing in God can have huge, life-changing consequences.

Still, the question remains: Is there any more reason to believe in God than there is to believe in fairies? If Kobir is right, there isn't. But then isn't it more reasonable to believe that God *doesn't* exist, rather than to remain neutral on whether or not he exists? What do you think?

The Problem of Suffering

As we near the bottom of the hill, a large shadowy shape starts to loom up in front of us. It's the local hospital. Many of the windows are lit. Through some of the windows we can see figures moving around. At one window quite near to us, we notice a woman. She looks sad, as if she has been crying.

As we walk past the hospital, Kobir starts to explain why he thinks that, actually, there is very good evidence to suggest that God *doesn't* exist.

KOBIR: I think you should agree, Bob, that if there's no reason to suppose God does exist, then the reasonable view to take is that he doesn't. But in any case, we have all been overlooking something. You keep suggesting that there is no reason to suppose that God doesn't exist. But, actually, there is.

BOB: What do you mean? What evidence is there that God *doesn't* exist?

Kobir stops and points at the hospital.

KOBIR: *There's* my evidence. God is supposed to have at least three characteristics, isn't he? Isn't he supposed to be all powerful, all knowing, and all good?

BOB: That's right.

KOBIR: Well now, there is a great deal of pain and suffering in the world, isn't there? People get horrible diseases. Many of the people in that hospital right now are suffering from terrible, painful diseases. There are also wars. Famines. Earthquakes. You have to admit that in many ways the world is not a very nice place to be. It seems it could definitely be nicer.

BOB: That's true. It could be nicer.

KOBIR: The problem is, if God has these three characteristics—if he really is all-powerful, all-knowing and all-good—then *why* is there pain and suffering in the world? Why isn't the world nicer?

BOB: I don't really see the problem.

KOBIR: Well, if God is all-powerful—if he can do anything—then he can stop the pain and suffering, can't he?

BOB: Yes. I guess he could.

KOBIR: In fact, he could have made the world so that it contained no pain and suffering in the first place, couldn't he? He could have made it so that we couldn't feel the sensation of pain, for example. He could have made a world free of disease. He could have made a much more pleasant world for us. In fact, he could have made the earth like Heaven is supposed to be. But he didn't. So *why* didn't he?

BOB: I don't know. Maybe he didn't realize how things would turn out.

KOBIR: But he *must* have realized. God is supposed to be all-knowing. He knows everything, including how things will turn out. In which case it seems that God makes us suffer *on purpose!*

BOB: But God would never do that! God is good. He would never make us suffer on purpose.

KOBIR: There's the problem. Either God isn't all-powerful, or God isn't all-knowing, or God isn't all-good. But God, if he exists, has all three of these characteristics. Therefore God doesn't exist!

This is a very old, very famous, and very serious problem facing those who believe in God. Religious thinkers have been struggling with the problem for a very long time. Let's call it the *Problem of Suffering.* Can the problem be solved?

The Free-Will Answer

The three of us think about the Problem of Suffering as we continue to walk. Some people who believe in God have tried to deal with the Problem of Suffering by arguing that responsibility for the pain and suffering in the world lies not with God but with us. And in fact this is precisely what Bob now suggests.

BOB: You are forgetting something. God gave us *free will.*

KOBIR: How do you mean?

BOB: God gave us the ability to *choose for ourselves* how we will act. Without free will, we would be just like machines or robots. We'd simply be made to act in the way we do. We couldn't do otherwise. For example, we chose to walk up this hill this evening. But we could just as easily have chosen to go to the movies instead.

KOBIR: How does free will help you solve the problem of suffering?

BOB: Well, unfortunately we often choose to do things that result in pain and suffering. We start wars, for example. Now God can't be held responsible for a war, can he? The suffering caused by our wars is *our* fault, not his.

KOBIR: But wouldn't it have been better if God hadn't given us free will? Wouldn't it have been better if he had just *made us* so we always do the right thing? Then there wouldn't be any pain and suffering. There wouldn't be any wars.

BOB: No, because then we would be mere puppets, mere robots, wouldn't we? It is much better that we have free will, despite the fact that we do sometimes end up causing suffering.

A Problem with the Free-Will Answer

Let's call Bob's answer to the Problem of Suffering the *Free-Will answer*. The Free-Will answer is quite ingenious.

However, there are big problems with it. As Kobir points out, one of the most obvious problems with the Free-Will Answer is that it seems much of the pain and suffering in the world isn't caused by us.

KOBIR: The trouble with your argument is that not all of the suffering in the world is our fault. Okay, we cause wars. But what about a horrible disease like cancer, which kills millions of people every year in a very unpleasant way? How is that disease *our* fault? Or take a flood that drowns thousands of people. How can that be *our* fault? It seems it can't be. But then there can be no God.

Bob throws his soccer ball in the air a few times while he thinks for a moment.

BOB: Maybe the disease and the flood *are* caused by us and we just don't *realize* that we caused them.

KOBIR: How do you mean?

BOB: Well, for example, maybe the flood was indirectly caused by our cutting down the rain forests, causing the weather to change a lot. That caused a heavy rain to fall, which in turn caused the flood.

KOBIR: Maybe. But it's very hard to believe that *all* of the pain and suffering in the world is caused by us, isn't it? How do we make earthquakes happen, for example? it's certainly very hard to believe that if only *we* were to act in certain ways, there would be no pain or suffering at all!

BOB: I guess you are right. I guess God, if he exists, must be responsible for at least *some* of our suffering.

Is Suffering God's Punishment?

Bob has one last stab at dealing with the Problem of Suffering.

BOB: Maybe the suffering that God causes is intended as a *punishment*.

KOBIR: A punishment for what?

BOB: For our sins. For the wrongs we have done. God is good. He loves us. But just as good and loving parents must sometimes punish their children when they do something wrong, so too must God sometimes punish us.

Bob's suggestion makes Kobir rather angry.

KOBIR: Honestly, that really is a terrible suggestion!

BOB: Why is it terrible?

KOBIR: Look. Many of the disasters that occur happen to people who can't be blamed for anything at all. Very young babies, for example. Even if *we* have done something wrong, they haven't done anything wrong, have they?

BOB: I guess not.

KOBIR: So why is it fair to punish *them?* Suppose our law courts were to punish the babies of adults who had committed crimes? That would hardly be fair, right? In fact, that would be a pretty *horrible* thing to do, wouldn't it?

BOB: I guess so.

KOBIR: Right. So why is it any less horrible if God punishes the babies of adults who have done wrong? A good God would never do such a cruel and despicable thing.

Bob and Kobir have been talking about the *Problem of Suffering.* The problem is, if God is all good, all knowing, and all powerful, then why is there so much suffering in the world? As you can see, this is a very serious problem for those who believe in God. Bob hasn't really managed to solve the problem. Can you think of a better solution?

Faith

The three of us finally arrive at the restaurant and go inside. I'm now very hungry, so I order a huge plate of poppadoms[8] for us to nibble on while we make up our minds about what curry to order. In between nibbling on his poppadom, Bob makes a very interesting point about believing in God.

BOB: Okay. Suppose I accept that there's little if any evidence that God exists. Suppose I accept there's even some evidence to suggest that God doesn't exist. Still, this is all irrelevant when it comes to my belief in God.

KOBIR: Why?

BOB: Because when it comes to believing in God, it's not a question of believing for a *reason*. *Reason* has nothing to do with it. Belief in God is a matter of *faith*. You must *just believe*. Many people have faith in the existence of God. And faith is a very positive thing to have, don't you agree?

Is Bob right? Is faith in God's existence a good thing to have?

It is worth remembering that faith can sometimes be a dangerous thing. For example, faith can be used to control people. Once people have let go of reason, once they "just believe," then they are easily controlled. An unscrupulous leader of a religion can take advantage of a simple, trusting faith and use it to his or her own advantage.

Faith, taken to an extreme, also makes it difficult to communicate with people. One can no longer reason or argue with them. If people with an extreme faith get it into their heads that they should do some terrible thing (perhaps kill those with religious beliefs different from their own), it may be impossible to make them see that what they are doing is wrong. They won't listen to reason.

On the other hand, there is no doubt that faith in the existence of God can have a positive effect. It can and does help many people. If you trust in the existence of a good God, that may help you to deal with some of the bad things that happen to you in life.

It is also true that faith in the existence of God has transformed some people's lives for the better. Rather than being selfish and cruel, they have become generous and noble.

Religious faith has even led some people to lay down their lives to save others—though we should remember that it is not only those who believe in God that do such noble and unselfish things. So there are good things about having faith in the existence of God.

What Does It All Mean?

For those who have religious faith, life does have meaning. We are here for a purpose: God's purpose. Many believe that this purpose is to love and obey God. But what if you don't have faith? What if you don't believe there is a God? What is one to say about the meaning of life then? If there is no God, is life meaningless?

If there is no God, then perhaps it is up to us to give life its meaning. The purpose our lives have is the purpose that we give to them. If that is true, then we each have a big responsibility. You can choose to live a meaningless life or a meaningful one. What sort of life you live is up to you.

Chapter Seven Endnotes

1. William O'Grady, *How Children Learn Language* (Cambridge, UK: Cambridge University Press).
2. An unscientific estimate of my own, based on the 78 questions I once counted from my daughter in a two-hour period, times 5 (for a 10-hour day), times 365 days, times 3 years. Told you it was unscientific.
3. This excerpt is only a single chapter of Twain's hilarious satire. Though unpublished during Twain's lifetime, *Little Bessie* is available in an early biography of Twain by Albert Bigelow Paine, as well as the compilation *Fables of Man,* edited by John S. Tuckey (University of California Press, 1972).
4. Sue Gerhardt, *Why Love Matters: How Affection Shapes a Baby's Brain* (London: Brunner-Routledge, 2004).
5. Gary R. Kirby & Jeffery R. Goodpaster, *Thinking: An Interdisciplinary Approach to Critical and Creative Thought,* 4th ed. (Upper Saddle River, NJ: Pearson/ Prentice Hall, 2007), p. xiii.
6. Ibid, p. xiv.
7. Alas, with the recent demotion of Pluto, this should now read "eight planets." A fine example of self-correcting science in action!
8. An Indian crispy bread popular in the UK.

215

Additional Resources
Books

- Clayton, John C. *Alexander Fox and the Amazing Mind Reader.* Prometheus, 1998. A con man calling himself Mr. Mystikos has come to town, telling fortunes, reading minds, knowing things he couldn't *possibly* know about the people of the town—and parting the gullible townsfolk from their cash. Young Alexander Fox is plenty impressed at first—until he starts thinking carefully. A terrific illustration of the power of skepticism. For years after reading it, your kids will turn to you every time they see a faith healer or other huckster on TV, saying, "It's Mr. Mystikos!" Ages 6–10.

- Stock, Gregory. *The Kids' Book of Questions: Revised for the New Century.* Workman, 2004. A kids' version of the now-classic *Book of Questions* for adults, this is a collection of 268 open-ended questions to get kids to articulate their own values and preferences: "If you could change one thing about your parents, what would it be?" "If you knew you wouldn't get caught, would you cheat by copying answers on a test?" Several are great conversation-starters for religious questioning: "Of all the things you've heard about God and religion, what do you think is true and what do you think is just a story?" "Do you believe in God? If not, why do you think so many people do?" Ages 6–12.

- Law, Stephen. *The Philosophy Gym: 25 Short Adventures in Thinking.* Thomas Dunne, 2003. An introduction to philosophy for adults, written in the same accessible dialogic style as his essay in the current book.

- Law, Stephen. *Philosophy Rocks!* Volo, 2002. The book from which our essay "Does God Exist?" is excerpted. Law presents several other philosophical questions in the same engaging dialogic form. An excellent introduction to philosophical questions.

- Law, Stephen. *The War for Children's Minds.* Routledge, 2006. In a powerful new book that has been called "a defense of the philosophically liberal life," Stephen Law calls for a rejection both of right-wing demands for a return to authoritarian religious morality and postmodern relativism. He advocates instead that children be educated in ethics based in the philosophy of the enlightenment. For adults.

CHAPTER 8

Jaw-Dropping, Mind-Buzzing Science

Introduction

If a child is to keep alive his inborn sense of wonder, he needs the companionship of at least one adult who can share it, rediscovering with him the joy, excitement, and mystery of the world we live in.
— Rachel Carson, *The Sense of Wonder*

Science, as a way of engaging the world, is the new kid in town. There's evidence of religious belief and practice in Neanderthal burials over 40,000 years ago, but science and the scientific method as we understand them today didn't truly take hold until the sixteenth century—the last *one percent* of the known history of religion. Yet in that blip of time, the infant called science has doubled the human life span, conquered countless diseases, taken us up off the planet and down into the microscopic world, measured the age and size of cosmos, discovered the laws of nature—and yes, made possible weapons of mass destruction, CFCs, and many other environmental and human catastrophes.

Imagine what the toddler years have in store.

Science—from Latin *scientia*, "to know"—is a tool, a method, a process, and can be used for good or ill. But one thing remains indisputable: It is our very best means of gaining actual knowledge. This chapter is a celebration of the ability of science to reveal reality, but even more so of its ability to amaze and inspire us as it does so.

Childhood is the natural home of wonder. At no other time in our lives are we as open to the experience of wonder. If religion were the only available means to it, I would be religious—wonder means that much to me, and I want wonder and inspiration in my children's lives just that much. Fortunately, no such compromise is needed. The essay "Teaching Kids to Yawn at Counterfeit Wonder" argues that scientific wonder leaves the religious variety far behind—and that all a parent really needs to do is point it out. If that. Amanda Chesworth, director of CSICOP's[1] Inquiring Minds program for kids, suggests that one of the great joys of parenthood should be offering "brain food" to the ravenous young mind, and Yip Harburg chimes in with a poem about a confused ape in "We've Come a Long Way, Buddy."

Over half of the chapter is devoted to Kristan Lawson's "The Idea That Changed the World," a thorough but accessible explanation of the theory of evolution. This is one of the most important pieces in this book, for more than any other idea in human history, Darwin's description of evolution by natural selection remade our understanding of the world and our place in it. Copernicus took us out of the center of the universe, but Darwin's "decentering" was far more personal. It was also more beautiful, taking us from a cold pedestal above our fellow creatures to a deep kinship with them. And, as philosopher Daniel Dennett notes, it made disbelief in God "intellectually respectable" by explaining at last the immense complexity of life on Earth and the astonishing illusion of design that had seemed, for so many centuries before, to necessitate a designer.

Yet poll results consistently show only about a third of Americans accepting evolution as true, and most of these still put God at the helm of the process—an idea that can only be sustained by completely misunderstanding what natural selection *means*. That percentage is the lowest in the developed world. Even among the third who do accept it are very few who have made the effort to understand it, to really understand it. You'd think it was impossibly technical, hopelessly inaccessible. *It isn't,* and Lawson proves that. Neither is it a piece of cake—some concentrated attention is required—but an above-average middle schooler will be up to the task.

Having no theological implications to fret over gives secular families an enormous advantage. We can walk right into the awe-inspiring space opened up by Darwin's insights and revel in every implication without fear of having pet dogmas dethroned. *That* is why Lawson's essay is included: so that when at last a child expresses an interest in knowing where we came from and how we fit into the puzzle of life—regardless of whether their local school boards or legislatures have watered down or pushed out evolution—parents will have the right resource at hand. At the end of a mere twenty pages of text and great activities, the child (or the parent, for that matter!) will have joined the very select group of people who have known, *really known,* who we are—by learning about the most world-shaking idea anybody ever had.

Teaching Kids to Yawn at Counterfeit Wonder

Dale McGowan, Ph.D.

A LOT OF PEOPLE BELIEVE that you can't experience wonder without religious faith. The life of a person without supernatural beliefs is thought to be cold, sterile, and lifeless.

If that were the case, this book would have to sound the alarm. Childhood, after all, is our first and best chance to revel in wonder. If parenting without religion meant parenting without wonder, I might just say to heck with reality.

Funny, though, how often I've experienced something that seemed an awful lot like wonder. It couldn't have been actual *wonder*, I'm told, since real wonder comes only from contemplation of God and a knowledge that he created all that is.

Call me Ishmael, but that never did much for me. I always found the biblical version of wonder rather flat and hollow, even as a kid. It never moved me even as metaphor, rendered pale by its own vague hyperbole.

Now try these on for size:

1. If you condense the history of the universe to a single year, humans would appear on December 31st at 10:30 PM—99.98 percent of the history of the universe happened before humans even existed.
2. Look at a gold ring. As the core collapsed in a dying star, a gravity wave collapsed inward with it. As it did so, it slammed into the thundering sound wave heading out of the collapse. In that moment, as a star died, the gold in that ring was formed.
3. We are star material that knows it exists.
4. Our planet is spinning at 900 miles an hour beneath our feet while coursing through space at 68,400 miles per hour.

5. The continents are moving under our feet at 3 to 6 inches a year. But a snail's pace for a million millennia has been enough to remake the face of the world several times over, build the Himalayas, and create the oceans.

6. Through the wonder of DNA, you are literally half your mom and half your dad.

7. A complete blueprint to build you exists in each and every cell of your body.

8. The faster you go, the slower time moves.

9. Your memories, your knowledge, even your identity and sense of self exist entirely in the form of a constantly recomposed electrochemical symphony playing in your head.

10. All life on Earth is directly related by descent. You are a cousin not just of apes, but of the sequoia and the amoeba, of mosses and butterflies and blue whales.

Now *that,* my friends, is *wonder.*

I was first introduced to genuine, jaw-dropping, mind-buzzing wonder as a teenager by Carl Sagan. Carl was a master of making conceivable the otherwise inconceivable realities of the universe, usually by brilliant analogy, taking me step by step into a true appreciation of honest-to-goodness wonder. I was aware, for example, that humans were relative newcomers on the planet, but it wasn't until I came across Sagan's astonishing calendar analogy at the age of 13—the one above that puts our arrival at 10:30 PM on New Year's Eve—that I actually *got* it, and swooned with wonder.

A little precision can make all the difference in the experience of wonder. Merely knowing that the universe is really really really really big is one thing, but that only rated a two on the wow-meter for me as a child, as it does for my son and daughters. A few more specifics, though, can snap it into focus, and up goes the meter.

Put a soccer ball in the middle of an open field to represent the sun. Walk twenty-six paces from the ball and drop a pea. That's Earth. An inch away from Earth, drop a good-sized breadcrumb for the Moon, remembering that this inch is the furthest humans have been so far. Jupiter is a golf ball 110 paces further out, and Pluto's a tiny BB about a half mile from the soccer ball.

So how far would you have to walk before you can put down another soccer ball for Proxima Centauri, the very nearest star to our Sun? Bring your good shoes—it's over 4,000 miles away at this scale, New York to Berlin. That's the *nearest star.* And there are about a trillion such stars in the Milky Way galaxy alone, and roughly a

> " We inhabit a universe made of a curved fabric woven of space and time in which hydrogen, given the proper conditions, eventually evolves into Yo Yo Ma. "

> ❝ Two hundred years ago it was possible, even reasonable, to believe that we were the central concern of the Creator of it all—and therefore reasonable to teach our children the same. ❞

hundred billion such galaxies, arrayed through 12 billion of those light years in every direction, a universe made of a curved fabric woven of space and time in which hydrogen, given the proper conditions, eventually evolves into Yo Yo Ma.

Two hundred years ago it was possible, even reasonable, to believe that we were the central concern of the Creator of it all—and therefore reasonable to teach our children the same. But anyone who was engaged for the whole process above will still be blank-eyed and buzzing at all

> ❝ Religious wonder—the wonder we're said to be missing out on—is counterfeit wonder. As each complex and awe-inspiring explanation of reality takes the place of "God did it," the flush of real awe quickly overwhelms the memory of whatever it was we considered so wondrous in religious mythology. ❞

we have learned about ourselves and our context in the past two centuries. Just as infants mature into adults by gradually recognizing that they are not the center of the universe, so science has given humanity the means to its own maturity, challenging us not only to endure our newly realized smallness, but to find the incredible wonder in that reality.

Religious wonder—the wonder we're said to be missing out on—is counterfeit wonder. As each complex and awe-inspiring explanation of reality takes the place of "God did it," the flush of real awe quickly overwhelms the memory of whatever it was we considered so wondrous in religious mythology. Most of the truly wonder-inducing aspects of our existence—the true size and age of the universe, the relatedness of all life, microscopic worlds, and more—are not, to paraphrase Hamlet, even dreamt of in our religions. Our new maturity brings with it some real challenges, of course, but it also brings astonishing wonder beyond the imaginings of our infancy.

There is no surer way to strip religion of its ability to entice our children into fantasy than to show them the way, step by step, into the far more intoxicating wonders of the real world. And the key to those wonders is precisely the skill that is so often miscast as the death of wonder: skepticism.

Nothing wrinkles noses faster than a skeptical attitude—"Why do you have to be so negative, why do you have to tear everything down?"—yet there is nothing as essential to experiencing true wonder in its greatest depth. Skepticism is the filter that screens out the fool's gold, leaving nothing behind but precious nuggets of the real thing. Tell me something amazing, and I'll doubt it until it's proven. Why? Because fantasies, while charming, are a dime a dozen. I can tell you my dreams of purple unicorns all day, spinning wilder and wilder variations for your amusement. You'll enjoy it, perhaps even be moved by it, but you won't *believe*—until I show you one, take you for a ride on its back, prove it's more than just a product of my imagination. Your skepticism up to that point will have served you well; it fended off counterfeit wonder so you could feel the depth of the real thing.

> After sleeping through a hundred million centuries, we have finally opened our eyes on a sumptuous planet, sparkling with colour, bountiful with life. Within decades we must close our eyes again. Isn't it a noble, an enlightened way of spending our brief time in the sun, to work at understanding the universe and how we have come to wake up in it? This is how I answer when I am asked—as I am surprisingly often—why I bother to get up in the mornings.
>
> —Richard Dawkins, *Unweaving the Rainbow*

We must teach our kids to doubt and doubt and doubt *not* to "tear everything down" but to pull cheap façades away so they can see and delight in those things that are legitimately wonderful. How will they recognize them? It's easy—they're the ones left standing after the hail of critical thinking has flattened everything else. Magnificent, those standing stones.

Supporters of the scientific worldview are sometimes accused of having "faith" in ideas such as evolution and therefore practicing a sort of religion. The less you know, the more reasonable that assertion is. Evolution by natural selection was positively barraged with skepticism throughout the end of the nineteenth century and well into the twentieth. Darwin and Huxley spent the remainder of their lives answering doubts about the theory. And, when the dust cleared, the theory remained, intact, beautiful in its inevitability, awe-inspiring not because it drew no fire but because it *drew* the fire and survived spectacularly. That is what is known as the truth, or our best approximation of that elusive concept. It is so precious to get a glimpse of real knowledge, so breathtaking, that no lesser standard than trial by skepticism will do. It leaves behind only those things wonderful enough to make us weep at the pure beauty of their reality and at the equally awesome idea that we could find our way to them at all.

A theologian friend of mine once suggested to me that the metaphors of religion are beautiful "responses to mystery." If, each time a mystery is dispelled by real understanding, the metaphor stepped aside, ceding the ground of wonder to its successor, there would be no problem with such metaphors. The problem—as illustrated by the creation/evolution "controversy"—is that we fall so deeply in love with our metaphors that we are often unable and unwilling to let go when the time comes and mystery is replaced with knowledge. "If you are awash in lost continents and channeling and UFOs and all the long litany of claims," Carl Sagan said, "you may not have intellectual room for the findings of science. You're sated with wonder." It's this all-too-human tendency that presents a challenge for parents wishing to raise independent thinkers: the magnetic power of the lovely metaphor, standing in the doorway, impeding progress toward real answers.

> **We fall so deeply in love with our metaphors that we are often unable and unwilling to let go when the time comes and mystery is replaced with knowledge.**

The most compelling cases of preferring fact to fiction are the most practical. All the prayer, animal sacrifice, and chanting in the world couldn't cure polio—the Salk vaccine did. And how did we find it? Through rigorous, skeptical, critical thinking and testing and doubting of every proposed solution to the problem of polio until only one solution was left standing. Let others find uncritical acceptance of pretty notions a wonderful thing. I'm more awestruck by the idea of ending polio because someone cared enough to find more wonder in testable reality than in wishful fantasy.

Some would protest, rightly, that science stops at the measurable, that those things that cannot be quantified and calculated are beyond its scope. That's entirely true. But the foundation of reality that science gives us becomes a springboard to the contemplation of those unmeasurables, a starting point from which we dive into the mystery *behind* that reality. Our reality has astonishing implications and yields incredible mystery, questions upon questions, many of them forever unanswerable. But is it not infinitely better to bathe in what we might call the *genuine* mystery behind our *actual* reality, instead of contemplating the "mystery" behind a mythic filial sacrifice, or transubstantiation, or angels dancing on the head of a pin?

It's easy to get a child addicted to real wonders if you start early enough. Simply point them out—they are all around us—and include a few references to what was once thought to be true. Take thunder. Explain that a bolt of lightning rips through the air, zapping trillions of air molecules with energy hotter than the Sun. Those superheated molecules explode out of the way with a *crack!* Then the bolt is gone, and all those molecules smash into each other again as they fill in the emptiness it leaves behind. That's the long rumble—waves of air swirling and colliding like surf at the beach.

Forgive me if I find that completely wonder-full.

Then explain that people once thought is was a sound made by an angry god in the sky, and enjoy your child's face as she registers how much less interesting that is.

Repeat steps one and two until college.

■ ■ ■ ■ ■ ■

Natural Wonders

Amanda Chesworth

NOT SO LONG AGO, FEAR was believed to be an indispensable tool in educating the young. Consider the picture painted by James Joyce in *Portrait of the Artist as a Young Man.* Stephen Dedalus was in class when

> The door opened quietly and closed. A quick whisper ran through the
> class: the prefect of studies. There was an instant of dead silence, and then
> the loud crack of a pandybat on the last desk. Stephen's heart leapt up in
> fear. "Any boys want flogging here, Father Arnall?" cried the prefect of stud-
> ies. "Any lazy, idle loafers that want flogging in this class?"

Fear has been used throughout history as a weapon to control the masses. The institution of religion has been especially successful in using fear to make people conform and yield to its power. Fear is the destroyer of inquiring minds. The wonder and curiosity inherent in a child are at risk of being annihilated through faith-based education. "There is another form of temptation even more fraught with danger," warned Saint Augustine. "This is the disease of curiosity. It is this which drives us on to try to discover the secrets of nature, those secrets which are beyond our understanding, which can avail us nothing, and which men should not wish to learn."[2]

Fortunately we live in a more enlightened age. "The great human adventure," says humanist philosopher Paul Kurtz, "is to live creatively and exuberantly. . . . Courage is still the first humanistic virtue; it is out of this fearless posture and because of it that men and women were able to leave the caves of primitive existence and to build civilizations. It is the continuing human adventure that captivates and enthralls us. . . . If the human species is to survive and embark upon exciting new voyages of wonder and discovery, it will be only because it can still marshal the determination to take responsibility for its own destiny and the courage to fulfill its unique ideals and values, whatever they may be. It will always need *the courage to become.*"[3]

There will always be those, however, who hanker after the "good" old days. On one telecast of *The 700 Club,* Pat Robertson suggested that "It is absolutely impossible to have genuine education without the holy scriptures." I contend that a humane, pragmatic, and ever-evolving approach is the only one justified if our ultimate goal is to nurture the wonder in children, giving them the chance to grow into decent human beings with a passion for life and learning. Not many theories of education that came out of the hothouse of social science qualify as theories, or even as hypotheses. They have not been repeatedly tested, no rigorous attempts are made to falsify them (indeed, some may be unfalsifiable and therefore completely unscientific). On the whole I suspect that they would be better classified as cultural myths, alongside the tenets of dogmatic religion.

Raising a child according to fixed notions, using fear and reward as incentives and encouraging students to memorize the information provided, are teaching strategies utterly devoid of life and ultimately useless, if not damaging, to our future. They run contrary to our evolutionary heritage, where wonder and curiosity play an integral role in our survival.

Attorney Clarence Darrow noted that "The origin of what we call civilization is not due to religion but to skepticism. The modern world is the child of doubt and inquiry, as the ancient world was the child of fear and faith."[4]

> " Every child stands at the morning of the world; every day is a voyage of discovery in which your sons and daughters are as intrepid as Magellan. Yours is the immense privilege of providing these bright, awakening minds with brain food. "

In a spirit of simple pragmatism, let's consider what you have to work with as a parent. What is it that makes it relatively easy to teach a child? Perhaps the most helpful and wonderful thing about childhood in this regard is the newness of everything. Every child stands at the morning of the world; every day is a voyage of discovery in which your sons and daughters are as intrepid as Magellan. Yours is the immense privilege of providing these bright, awakening minds with brain food.

Science and wonder are natural companions, notes Oxford biologist Richard Dawkins:

> We have an appetite for wonder, a poetic appetite, which real science ought to be feeding but which is being hijacked, often for monetary gain, by purveyors of superstition, the paranormal and astrology. . . . Since the appetite for wonder is fed so much more satisfyingly by science, it ought to be a simple matter of education to combat superstition.[5]

There are many kinds of brain food available. What you choose will depend on a variety of personal factors including your own interests and environment. My own inclination is toward the concrete, leaving the abstract to develop once the child has a good grasp of the real world outside his or her head. Our beginning explorer sees a world uncluttered by theory and paradigms, a world that is tangible, colored, wet or dry, sweet- or foul-smelling—and above all, immediate. It attracts or frightens, assaulting the senses from all directions. It is the source of wonder: *A colorful bird flying above my head, a purple stone beneath my feet, a train rumbling down the tracks before its sound is drowned out by a jet plane soaring through the skies, snow falling gently onto the tip of my tongue, stars twinkling and forming patterns in my mind. There is an infinite supply of wonder around me, with new amazements arriving daily. As my understanding grows, my world becomes brighter, my life more fulfilled. I walk hand in hand with science.*

Mystery is a very necessary ingredient in our lives. Mystery creates wonder and wonder is the basis for man's desire to understand. Who knows what mysteries will be solved in our lifetime, and what new riddles will become the challenge of the new generation? Science has not mastered prophecy.

–Neil Armstrong, in a 1969 speech to Congress

As a child you learn the magic word "why" and drive your parents and teachers nuts with it. If they don't give you a concrete answer that you can understand, you continue with a string of "whys" until they do.

There are many ways of answering the word "why." Kipling's *Just So Stories* illustrate one technique—and a valuable one for stimulating the imagination. The story "explains" how the camel got its hump: When the genie told him not to be so lazy, the camel said "Humpf!"—and the genie punished him by putting the humpf on his back. Not a very convincing explanation, even in the unlikely event that humpf was the original spelling of hump, but a fun and satisfying "child's play" version of inquiry and learning, of asking why and finding out.

The *Just So Stories* of science are even more stimulating because they are based on our long experience of the real world outside our heads, the very world to which the child is awakening. It's a world where you can't get something out of nothing, a concept a child can easily grasp—and, with growing maturity, may learn to call the conservation of matter. Think of the story of Humpty Dumpty and the fact that all the king's horses and all the king's men couldn't put him together again. It's the second law of thermodynamics in nursery rhyme form. A famous thermodynamicist named Myron Tribus once said to a class that all actions are reversible. Okay, said one student—how do you unscramble an egg? Feed it to a chicken, he replied. Maybe that's what all the king's horses and all the king's men should have done. (It doesn't lead to true reversibility, or course—you wouldn't get Humpty Dumpty . . . just another egg!)

> Think of Humpty Dumpty and the fact that all the king's horses and all the king's men couldn't put him together again. It's the second law of thermodynamics in nursery rhyme form.

Curiosity has its own reason for existence. One cannot help but be in awe when one contemplates the mysteries of eternity, of life, of the marvelous structure of reality. It is enough if one tries merely to comprehend a little of this mystery each day.

–Albert Einstein

Many of the important default positions of science, outlined by Garrett Hardin in *Learning to Live within Limits*, can be grasped in rudimentary form by a child. Gradually, and with appropriate guidance, their explorations lead them to an appreciation of reliable default positions. They learn that we live on a finite planet and share a biosphere with countless other species and that the implacable competition that takes place there, the process we call natural selection, has shaped us and other species into the organisms that we are.

What you want your child to have is an acquaintance with those default positions that allow him or her to discriminate between reliable knowledge and unreasonable speculation. That, ultimately, is the true wonder of science—the ability to spot the reasonable "just so stories."

The importance of reaching this state was expressed well by the fine scientific journalist Judith Stone in *Discover* magazine:

> We can't all be Einstein . . . At the very best, we need a sort of street-smart science: the ability to recognize evidence, gather it, assess it and act on it. As voters, we're de facto scientific advisors. . . . If we don't get it right, things could go very wrong.[6]

Street-smart science begins with our young Magellans asking "why" as they set off to explore our magnificent universe. With any luck the voyage will lead to a lifetime of intellectual excitement. And when finally they are ready "to sail beyond the sunset, and the baths of all the western stars," as Tennyson put it, they will consider their lives well spent.

■ ■ ■ ■ ■ ■ ■

Celebrating the wonder of science is the focus of Inquiring Minds, a program sponsored by the Center for Inquiry (CFI) and the Committee for the Scientific Investigation of Claims Of the Paranormal (CSICOP). It serves as a resource for educators, parents, and children and works to complement both formal and informal science education within our communities. A primary goal of Inquiring Minds is to prepare children to use their magnificent brains to navigate effectively through the minefield and make choices that are reasonable and safe. They are provided with the tools to reach their own conclusions. Ultimately the skepticism and independent thinking promoted within our organization may help children to lead fuller, happier lives, based on their realization that they have developed the intellectual backbone to resist the outrageous claims and messages that, 200 years after the "Age of Enlightenment," we are still prey to.

The young are the future of civilization. We need to nurture the wonder inherent within us and encourage young people to flourish. We share Carl Sagan's belief that science is our candle in the dark, a candle to light our children's future. Visit www.inquiringminds.org.

We've Come a Long Way, Buddy

Yip Harburg

An ape, who from the zoo broke free,
Was cornered in the library
With Darwin tucked beneath one arm,
The Bible 'neath the other.
"I can't make up my mind," said he,
"Just who on earth I seem to be—
Am I my brother's keeper
Or am I my keeper's brother?"

■ ■ ■ ■ ■ ■

The Idea That Changed the World

(Chapter 6 from *Darwin and Evolution for Kids*)

Kristan Lawson

Darwin's Theory of Evolution

EVEN THOUGH THE WORDS "Darwin" and "evolution" are familiar to almost everyone, very few people understand how Darwin's theory of evolution actually works. This chapter will explain it in terms that anyone can comprehend. Before you can fully grasp it, however, you'll need to be familiar with a few key concepts.

Variation

No two creatures are exactly the same. If you have brothers and sisters, look at them and compare them to yourself. Are all the children in your family the

---

First appeared in *Darwin and Evolution for Kids,* © 2003. Used with permission of Chicago Review Press.

same height? Do they all have the same shoe size? Same shape of nose? Are some smarter than others? Can some run faster? Are some braver, shyer, or nicer than others? The more you look, the more differences you'll find. Yet you and your siblings have the same parents. Doesn't that mean you should be exactly alike? The answer is no. Every individual person or animal is a unique combination of genes inherited from his or her parents. Like snowflakes, no two individuals can be precisely the same as each other. Even small animals that all look alike—such as mice or goldfish—are, when inspected closely, different from each other in one way or another. These differences between similar creatures are called *variations*.

The biological reasons for variation were not discovered until the twentieth century, long after Darwin's lifetime. But, like Darwin, we don't need to be experts in genetics to know that variation occurs all the time. It's easy enough to observe variations with your own two eyes.

Heritability

Did you ever notice that children tend to look like their parents? No one is ever an exact copy of his or her mother or father, but parents and kids are always somewhat similar. Does your mother have two arms, two legs, two eyes, a head, ten fingers, a mouth, and a brain? Then you do as well. If your parents have big noses, odds are you'll have a big nose too. If your parents have brown skin, you will have brown skin. If your parents are short, you'll probably be short. This is true in every family.

And it's not just true in human families. A Siamese cat will always give birth to Siamese kittens—it will never give birth to a puppy, an alligator, or even a different breed of cat. This may seem obvious, but it's an important aspect of evolution. Even the smallest features can be passed on from parent to offspring. The word for this is *heritability*. As with variation, the exact biological cause for heritability was not discovered until after Darwin had died. Even so, farmers, animal breeders, and parents all over the world know that heritability is one of the basic features of all species.

Overpopulation

In the natural world, all animals and plants produce many more offspring than can ever survive. For example, think about a pair of adult rabbits. The average female rabbit gives birth to a litter of four baby rabbits, five times a year. (Many types of rabbits can have more offspring than this per year; this is just an average.) After one year, that first pair of rabbits will have made 20 baby rabbits

(4 babies × 5 times a year). Half of these (10) will be female rabbits. Each of these 10 young female rabbits will grow up; after about six months they can start having babies of their own. After another year, all of the 10 female rabbits will themselves each have given birth to 20 or more rabbits—10 females and 10 males. Now you'll have at least 200 rabbits (10 mothers × 20 babies). The next year those 100 female rabbits will produce 1,000 more females. Then 10,000, then 100,000, and so on. After only twelve years you'll have over a trillion rabbits! Soon enough, the entire world would be completely covered in rabbits.

Now imagine this: The same tendency to overpopulate is true for almost every species. Frogs and goats and bees and fish and pigeons and a million other kinds of animals. The name for this tendency of organisms to produce more offspring than they need is *superfecundity*. If every baby animal survived, there would be uncountable numbers of every kind of animal filling every square inch of the planet, with millions more appearing every day, without end.

But this obviously isn't the case. So, where do they all go?

The Age of the Earth

In Darwin's time, no one really knew how old the Earth was. Some people thought it was only 6,000 years old. Others thought perhaps 30,000 years, or 100,000. But discoveries in geology and paleontology throughout the nineteenth century indicated that the planet was much older than that—millions of years old, at least. Darwin knew that evolution took a long time to happen, so he was very concerned with proving that the Earth had been around for a long time.

He need not have worried. It was not until the twentieth century that scientists were first able to accurately measure the Earth's age, using very sophisticated techniques. We now know that the Earth is about 4.5 *billion* years old! That's hundreds of times older than anyone in Darwin's era even imagined. And it's more than enough time for evolution.

Activity: Make Your Own Geological Strata

Early geologists proved that the Earth was at least many millions of years old by inspecting geological strata visible in exposed cliffs. This proof of the planet's age was an important factor in the acceptance of the theory of evolution, because animals need a long time to evolve. It's not always easy to find a place near your home where real strata are visible, but you can make your own strata with material you find in your backyard and kitchen.

What you need

a tall glass jar with a lid, preferably with the label removed

several plastic or paper cups

Choose five to eight of the following:

dark soil

light soil

sand

crushed dry leaves

dark gravel

light gravel

small pebbles

dry or crushed cement powder

plaster of Paris powder

salt

flour

small macaroni or crushed noodles

instant coffee

sugar

dried beans or lentils

hot chocolate powder

unpopped popcorn

crushed cereal

Put each ingredient into a separate cup and divide the cups into two categories, light and dark. (Put the flour, the light soil, the popcorn, and the sand on one side, for example, and all the dark ingredients on the other side.) Make sure the jar's label has been removed (and the glue that was attaching the label as well), and that it is dry. The taller the jar, the more strata will be visible.

One by one, gently pour about a quarter-cup of each ingredient into the jar, alternating between light and dark. Do not tilt or shake the jar while you are filling it up. Make each layer between half an inch (12 mm) and an inch (25 mm) thick. If the top of the layer is irregular when you first pour it in, gently tap the side of the jar or smooth down the top with a finger or spoon. The layers need not be perfectly even. Try to use each ingredient at least once before starting over with a second layer of the first ingredient. Remember to alternate light, dark, light, dark.

When you are almost finished, fill up the jar to the very top with the last layer, so there is no empty space in the jar at all. Tightly screw on the jar lid. Now you have your own personal jar of strata. Inspect the different layers and imagine them full of fossils, crystals, and mysteries from the Earth's past.

If there were fossils in your strata, where would the oldest fossils be found? Why? If a paleontologist compared fossils found on two different layers, what would the paleontologist be able to say about the fossil found on the lower layer?

Changing Environments

In most cities and states the weather is usually the same from one year to the next. In Phoenix, it is very hot every summer. In Minnesota, it snows every winter. Weather patterns pretty much stay the same. At least they seem to during the space of a single lifetime.

Over long periods of time, however, the Earth's climate and environment have gone through many, many changes. Long ago, the Sahara Desert used to be covered with plants. Hawaii wasn't even an island—it was under water. During the Ice Ages, much of Europe and North America were buried in ice. Throughout Earth's history, its climate has shifted back and forth many times in many different ways. It's even happening right now; the whole planet is getting warmer and warmer every year. Meteorologists predict that in a hundred years, the weather around the United States (and elsewhere) will be quite different than it is today.

Darwin knew that changing environments were an important element in his theory. Every time an environment shifts, the organisms in that environment must adapt to survive.

Evolution Through Natural Selection: Darwin's Theory Explained

Darwin spent years thinking about variation, heritability, overpopulation, the age of the Earth, and changing environments. He was trying to understand the origin of animal species. One day, the final piece of the puzzle clicked into place.

This was his brilliant insight: Every type of animal produces far more offspring than can survive. Most baby animals die before growing up. If not, the world would long ago have become overrun with animals. How do they die? Some are eaten by predators. Others starve to death. Others die of disease. Some grow to adulthood but can't find a mate and never have any offspring. Only a few actually succeed in growing up and reproducing.

But why do some die and others survive? What's so special about the survivors? Are they just the lucky ones? The answer, Darwin realized, lay in the variation among members of the species. Not all animals in any species are exactly the same. Those animals with some features that helped them avoid predators, get food, or find mates more successfully tended to survive longer than their brothers and sisters who lacked those features. Only the animals best adapted to their environment would survive long enough to grow up. Those animals that were weak or slow or foolish would tend to be the first ones to die. Darwin called this *natural selection*, but people often like to call it *survival of the fittest*.

The few surviving animals would reach maturity and have offspring. Because of heritability, their offspring would tend to resemble the well-adapted parents. Since the parents were generally the ones with the most useful features, they would pass those features on to their offspring. This way, all the harmful variations would die out, but the useful variations would be passed down and spread. Darwin's term for this was *descent with modification*.

But what if the animals' environment changed? The features that helped survival wouldn't necessarily remain the same. As generations passed, animals with new and different variations would be the ones surviving and passing their traits on to their children. The more the environment changed, the more the species would have to change to survive in it.

Darwin realized that with enough time, an animal species could accumulate so many changes that it would no longer resemble the original species from which it descended. He called this process *transmutation through natural selection*. All that was needed to turn one species into another was time—countless generations of animals changing little by little as they adapted to their shifting environments. And his own investigations had shown him that the Earth was indeed old enough for evolution to explain the existence of every single living thing Darwin felt that all people, all animals, and even all plants were related to each other. At some point in the distant past a microscopic living organism first appeared, and all life forms on Earth were descended from that one tiny creature.

So here's Darwin's theory of evolution in a nutshell:

1. Any group or population of organisms contains variations; not all members of the group are identical.
2. Variations are passed along from parents to offspring through heredity.
3. The natural overabundance of offspring leads to a constant struggle for survival in any population.
4. Individual organisms with variations that help them survive and reproduce tend to live longer and have more offspring than organisms with less useful features.
5. The offspring of the survivors inherit the useful variations, and the same process happens with every new generation until the variations become common features.
6. As environments change, the organisms within the environments will adapt and change to the new living conditions.
7. Over long periods of time, each species of organism can accumulate so many changes that it becomes a new species, similar to but distinctly different from the original species.
8. All species on Earth have arisen this way and are thus all related.

Is That Everything I Need to Know About Evolution?

There's more to evolution than what's been discussed so far; biologists happily spend their whole lives studying it. Often, the more people learn about evolution, the more questions they have. To get you started, here are answers to some of the most common questions about evolutionary theory.

- *Does evolution really make animals change shape? Can I see it happen?*
  That would be exciting, but unfortunately the answer is no. Evolution is not like a science-fiction film with special effects showing an alien creature growing a new head. Given enough time, evolution can make a *species* change shape, but not an individual animal. Every plant, animal, and person remains the same throughout its whole life. *Groups* evolve, not individuals. You'll never be able to see a fish grow legs and start to walk; evolution doesn't work that way. What evolution does is control what percentage of a group's individuals possess a certain trait or feature.
- *Does evolution* always *happen to every species? Or do some animals never change?*
  You might think from the description of evolution that natural selection is always working to bring about changes in species. But in reality most of the time natural selection *prevents* evolution from happening. Most of the variations and new features that might arise in organisms are not helpful at all, because evolution has al-

ready been going on or a very long time. Every species has already adapted to its environment as best as it can. Just about any change to a species would end up hurting it. Natural selection is continuously "weeding out" those variations that make an organism less adapted to its environment. Natural selection usually leads to evolutionary changes only if a species' environment and living conditions are shifting. In many cases, animals and plants that live in a stable environment hardly evolve at all. Horseshoe crabs are a famous example. They're fairly common on beaches around the world today. But archaeologists have found fossils of horseshoe crabs that look exactly like modern horseshoe crabs—except that the fossils are over 200 million years old. Horseshoe crabs have not evolved one bit in all that time because their environment—shorelines and beaches—hasn't changed much either.

- *Is evolution the same thing as "progress"?*

Not necessarily. During the Industrial Revolution and the Victorian era, people thought that history was always progressing forward, that life got better and more advanced every day. So they naturally assumed that evolution worked the same way. It seemed that life on Earth had started as a tiny organism and had *progressed upward* through evolutionary changes to become the complex and superior creatures known as human beings. Yet Darwin showed that evolution does not always imply advancing toward more complicated or larger forms. Many animal species a hundred thousand years ago were larger than they are today; changes in climate made them evolve *downward* to become smaller. Other species, such as the peppered moth, evolve *sideways* (by changing color) but do not become any more or less advanced. Species merely adapt to their current environments. But that doesn't mean they're getting "better."

EVOLUTION IN ACTION: The Peppered Moth

People used to think that the transmutation of species took such a long time that it could never be directly observed. But sometimes we can actually see natural selection happen in nature over the span of just a few years. Darwin did not know it at the time, but an example of rapid evolution was happening in England during his lifetime. He would have been overjoyed if he had been able to observe it himself.

In northern England lives a type of insect called the peppered moth, whose wings are speckled with white and black spots. These moths prefer to rest on trees that have light-colored bark and whitish lichen growing on them. The local birds love the taste of these moths and eat them whenever they can. But the moths' wings serve as camouflage; the speckled white-and-black coloration blends in with the bark and lichen, making them hard to notice.

At the beginning of the nineteenth century most of these moths had lighter colored wings with more white speckles than dark speckles. A small percentage liked to rest on darker trees and so had darker wings. But as the Industrial Revolution progressed, the factories of northern England spewed so much coal smoke into the air that the pollution not only killed the lichen but also covered the trees in soot. The moths' environment changed. Now, when the lighter winged moths landed on the darkened trees, the birds could easily see and eat them. Only the darker winged moths remained camouflaged. They avoided being eaten by the birds and survived to have offspring that inherited their darker wings. Little by little, the number of moths with darker wings started to grow. Naturalists carefully studied peppered moths for years, and by 1900 they counted that 98 percent of the moths had dark-speckled wings! Most of the light-winged moths had been eaten and had not reproduced more of their kind. Transmutation through natural selection had been directly observed just a few miles from where Darwin was born.

The story of the moths is not over. Starting in the 1950s, England passed strong new air-pollution laws that limited the amount of exhaust coming from factories. By the 1990s most of the pollution had been eliminated. As a result, lichen grew back on the trees and the light-colored bark was again visible. Now the situation was reversed. The dark moths were plainly visible against the light background, and the birds ate them. But the few remaining light moths blended into the background, and they survived. Accordingly, the moths have evolved back to the way they were before—now most of them are light-colored again!

- *Are animals and plants really "perfect" in their design?*
  William Paley's Divine Watchmaker argument relied on a basic assumption that all animals were "perfect," intentionally designed like a watch to have all the right parts in all the right places. But Darwin and other naturalists discovered this was far from true. Animals often have weaknesses and deficiencies that could easily

have been improved upon or eliminated if someone had designed them from scratch. Many animals have *vestigial organs*, body parts that don't work and for which the animal has no use. Various kinds of snakes, for example, have leg bones. Why would God give snakes leg bones if they have no legs? Evolutionists will tell you that snakes evolved from earlier reptiles that *did* have legs—legs that slowly disappeared as the species changed. The *external* legs disappeared, that is; the useless leg bones continued to exist inside the snakes' bodies. And if every species was "perfect," then why don't all animals have the best possible features: flawless vision and hearing, strong and fast legs, big brains, sharp teeth, and so on? Most don't, because each species is just a hodge-podge of adaptations. Animals aren't "designed" to be any way at all; they're just an accumulation of evolutionary changes, some of which no longer serve any purpose.

Where Are the Missing Links?

Ever since Darwin's day, critics of evolution have pointed out the absence of what have become known as "missing links." (Scientists prefer to call them "transformational forms.") If, as the zoologists claim, bats evolved from mouselike rodents, then where are the fossils of the creatures that were halfway in-between—a mouse with partial bat wings? None has ever been found. If there's no evidence of transitional forms between two species, then how can we be so sure that evolution really happened?

Here are *five* good answers to that question.

1. Missing links *do* exist. Difficult as it may be to visualize, all modern birds are the descendants of prehistoric dinosaurs. Scientists have uncovered several fossils of the missing link between dinosaurs and birds, a transitional form called Archaeopteryx that looked like a flying lizard with feathers. They've also found many bones and fossils of transitional forms between ancient primates and modern apes and humans, both of which are descended from the same ancestors. Many other transitional forms in the evolution of horses and reptiles have also been found.

2. At least 99.99 percent of all the fossils in the world have not yet been discovered. They're not easy to find! But paleontologists are searching for them every day, all over the world. So we haven't found all the missing links . . . *yet*.

3. Only in the rarest of circumstances do animal remains become fossilized to begin with. True, scientists have not found the fossils of most transitional forms, but neither have they found the fossils of most "stable forms" either. The fossils may never have been created in the first place. Unless the conditions are just right for creating fossils, animal remains and bones will quickly disintegrate and disappear. Since transitional forms probably occurred under changing environmental conditions, it's unlikely that their skeletons would be preserved undisturbed for millions of years.

4. Evolution does not happen at a consistent rate all the time. Most plants and animals will remain in the same environment for extremely long periods—millions of years, in some cases. As long as their environment stays the same, the animals won't evolve very much, if at all. But when organisms are forced into a new environment, they must adapt quickly to survive. In a relatively short span of time (perhaps as little as 100,000 or even 10,000 years, which is like the blink of an eye in geological terms) a species could radically evolve, passing through many transitional forms. When it reaches a form that is best adapted to its new environment, that species will remain stable and essentially stop evolving for a long time again. This stop-and-start aspect of evolution is called *punctuated equilibrium*, because stable, perfectly balanced ecosystems (equilibrium) are occasionally interrupted (punctuated) by rapid change. As a result, almost all fossils are laid down during times when species aren't changing, which is why transitional forms are rarely found.

5. Many top scientists answer the question in a completely different way: Every fossil ever found is a transitional form! *All* organisms, living or dead, are transitional forms from one species to another. It just depends on how you look at it. The animals of today could be considered transitional forms between their ancient ancestors and the unknown creatures into which their descendants will evolve far in the future. Maybe human beings will one day be thought of as the missing link!

• *What is a "hopeful monster"?*
Darwin was careful to point out that evolution does not happen in sudden jumps from one generation to the next, but rather in small steps. It's extremely unlikely, for example, that some long-ago horse just happened to be born with black-and-white stripes, and that all modern zebras are descended from this one freakish

striped horse. These freaks of nature were later called *hopeful monsters*. (Deformed and freakish animals *are* born every now and then, but their deformities almost always hurt rather than help their chances for survival.) Many people in Darwin's era mistakenly thought that evolution required these "hopeful monsters" to work, an idea which was ridiculed as being impossible. As a result, Darwin worked hard to show that evolutionary changes happen very gradually and that his theory did not depend on the existence of freaks.

Natural Selection: A Closer View

Natural selection happens in many different ways. Animals have evolved countless strategies to find food, avoid being eaten by predators, attract mates, and survive all kinds of dangerous situations. Any trait that allows an animal to survive and reproduce is "chosen" by natural selection because the animals with that trait will pass it on to their offspring. These are just some of the fascinating adaptations that various animals have developed through natural selection.

Camouflage

Camouflage—markings that help an animal blend into the background—is one of the most common adaptations in nature. It's the easiest way to avoid being seen by predators. (Remember the peppered moth?) Green tree frogs are barely noticed when they're sitting on green leaves. Some animals change their colors according to the seasonal changes in their habitat. Jackrabbits are brown in the summer, making them hard to see against brown leaves and soil; in winter, their fur changes to pure white so that they're camouflaged against the snow. Chameleons don't have to wait for a new season. These lizards can change their skin color in seconds to match any color of their surroundings.

Predators also use camouflage to keep a low profile while hunting. The golden brown color of a lion's fur is the same color of the dry grass where it hides while stalking prey. A bright pink lion would have a lot of trouble sneaking up on its victims!

Activity: Camouflage Egg Hunt

In the natural world, predators are always looking for something to eat. The easiest way to escape them is to blend into the background so they don't notice you. Animals that are *camouflaged* have the same color and patterns as the environment around them. A predator will generally notice, catch, and eat only the most easily captured prey; after its belly is full, there is no need to keep hunting. This activity will demonstrate how the principle of camouflage can help organisms survive.

What you need

1 dozen eggs
stove and pot
a set of colored felt pens, or crayons
a friend (or relative)
pencil and paper

Ask an adult to hard boil a dozen eggs for you. Once the eggs have boiled for seven or eight minutes, cool them down by running cold water over them in the sink or placing them in the refrigerator.

Put all twelve eggs back in the carton and bring them, along with a friend, outside to a natural area with grass, dirt, bushes, and other plants. Your backyard or front yard is the best place for this activity but a park is fine too. Bring a set of colored felt pens—make sure to have a selection of greens and browns—or crayons (pens work better on eggs) and a pencil and paper.

Sit down in a comfortable spot. Look at the surrounding environment and choose pens that match the colors of the plants and other features around you. You and your friend should then take three eggs each and, one by one, draw camouflage designs on them. Use different colored pens to match the shadows and stripes and other patterns you see. Think about where you might be placing these eggs when deciding how to camouflage them. If you are going to place them in the grass, use a variety of greens. If you are going to place them in a bed of dried leaves, use browns and grays. Remember to leave six eggs plain white, completely uncamouflaged.

Once you're done coloring, ask your friend to close his or her eyes while you place all twelve eggs around the yard or park. For the experiment to work properly, the white and colored eggs should be placed in similar locations—you shouldn't hide all the camouflaged eggs in the most difficult spots while leaving the uncamouflaged eggs out in the open. For every white egg you place in the grass, place a camouflaged egg in the grass. After the eggs have been hidden, ask you friend to look around and pick up the *first* six eggs he or she finds. After six, have your friend stop looking and bring all six back to you.

On one half of your paper write "Camouflaged," and on the other half write "Uncamouflaged." Make a mark under each heading for each egg found.

If the color of an egg's shell didn't make any difference to your friend, the "predator," he or she should find, on average, just as many camouflaged eggs as white eggs: three each. But how many of each kind did your friend *actually* find?

Retrieve the remaining six eggs, then repeat the experiment, but this time have your friend hide the eggs while you close your eyes and then search. Write down the data from the new trial. Repeat the experiment several more times until you begin to see a pattern in the totals. Did the coloring on the eggs help or hurt their chances of being detected by a predator?

Mimicry

Some animals use *mimicry*—imitating or pretending to be something else—to help them survive. Certain butterflies and moths have spots on their wings that look like scary eyes; from a distance they look like the eyes of a large predator, so birds are afraid to eat these butterflies. The "walking stick" is an insect that looks so much like a twig that you can scarcely tell it apart from the real thing, even up close.

Speed

This one's obvious: The faster an animal can run, the better it can escape from whatever's chasing it. Most animals have evolved to run as fast as they possibly can, considering their size, body shape, and environment. Predators have to go fast too, or they'll never catch their prey. A cheetah chasing a gazelle is a sight to behold!

Deception

Animals that are slow and easy to catch sometimes develop ways of tricking their enemies into going away. Opossums and certain kinds of snakes will occasionally pretend to be dead, hoping that whatever is fighting them will lose interest and leave them alone.

Deterrence

One way to avoid being eaten is to be hard to eat. Armadillos have tough, bony plates covering their bodies; when they curl up into a ball, there's no way for a predator like a wolf to get inside. Porcupines and hedgehogs are protected by hundreds of dangerous, sharp spines.

Toxicity

If something's poisonous (toxic) or tastes bad, then predators will quickly learn that it's not good to eat. This strategy is most common among plants, insects, and fish.

Acute Perception

This too is one of the most common adaptations in nature. The better any animal can hear, see, or smell, the better it can hunt for prey or detect predators before they get too close. Some animals have developed all kinds of amazing perception systems that we humans don't have. Dolphins and bats use sonar (bouncing ultrasonic waves off prey) to hunt. Scorpions and elephants can detect vibrations in the ground. Owls and ocelots have acute night vision and can see in almost total darkness. Even dogs can hear sounds that humans can't hear.

Dietary Diversity

Animals have acquired all kinds of adaptations that allow them to eat a wide variety of foods. Giraffes, of course, have evolved long necks to reach leaves on the tops of tall trees. Cows have four stomachs that allow them to eat and digest grass, which most animals cannot digest. Some animals have developed an immunity to poison, which allows them to eat other animals that have evolved to be toxic!

Even plants have evolved unique strategies for getting food. Venus flytraps catch insects in their leaves and dissolve them with special digestive fluids. A sundew snares bugs on its sticky hairs; the plant then swallows up its prey and digests it. Darwin was so fascinated by these carnivorous plants that he spent years researching them.

Choosing Partners

If camouflage is so important for survival, then why are some animals brightly colored? How can natural selection explain something as flamboyant, beautiful, and seemingly useless as a peacock's tail? Peacocks with smaller, duller tails would be less visible to predators, so it seems that they would be more likely to survive and that colorful tails should never have evolved. Yet they have. Why?

The answer is a form of natural selection called *sexual selection*. While it is not as important as other aspects of natural selection, it does account for many of the features that otherwise seem to have no evolutionary explanation.

Darwin's theory of sexual selection states that an animal must do more than merely stay alive to pass its traits on to later generations—it must also have offspring. And the only way to have offspring is to mate with a partner. So evolution will tend to favor those animals that are best at attracting mates. Unattractive animals will tend to have fewer offspring, and their features will die out.

But what determines "attractive"? This is a mystery no one has yet figured out. Whatever the reason, we do know that many animals regard certain features as especially appealing. Peahens (female peacocks) think that the peacocks with the flashiest tails are especially handsome. As a result, the most colorful peacocks have the most success finding partners, have the most offspring, and pass on the flashy-tail genes to the next generation. Over the years, the peacock species thus evolved to have colorful feathers. Dull peacocks may have had more success avoiding predators, but they left fewer offspring.

Activity: The Benefits of Beauty

According to the theory of sexual selection, being attractive is sometimes more important than being strong or clever. Birds with big flashy tails attract more mates—but they also can attract more predators. Is it really worthwhile to have an attractive feature if it only makes you more likely to be eaten? This activity shows how visually striking traits can become common in a species even if they seem to hurt chances for survival.

What you need

8 nickels (or any other small, plain objects, such as buttons, erasers, macaroni noodles, checkers, etc.)

40 pennies (or any other small, pretty objects, such as marbles, candies, plastic toys, hair ornaments, etc.)

This activity is a simple version of a life-simulation game that scientists use to model how evolution works. The game will show how certain features can spread throughout a population over several generations.

In this game, the objects all represent male members of the same species—a plain-looking kind of bird we'll call the Dum-Dum Bird. The nickels are the standard form of the species—bland and unremarkable, having evolved to avoid predators by blending into the background. But a new variation in the Dum-Dum Bird population has arisen—a few of the males now have some bright red feathers. This new variation is represented by the pennies.

The female Dum-Dum Birds are attracted to the males with red feathers. But the color also draws the attention of the foxes—the predators that like to eat Dum-Dum Birds whenever they can.

The rules

At the start, 80 percent of the birds are plain (nickels), and 20 percent have red feathers (pennies). With each passing generation, only one-fourth of the plain birds get eaten by foxes; but *half* of the red birds get eaten. On the other hand, each plain bird will be lucky to find one partner willing ever to accept him, so he will leave just one male offspring over his entire lifespan. The red birds, however, are so popular with the female birds that each will leave on average four male offspring over his entire lifespan. In both cases, the offspring will inherit the same coloration of their fathers.

How to play

Place 10 coins in a row: 8 nickels and 2 pennies. This is your first generation of 80 percent plain birds and 20 percent red birds. Now, apply the rules described above to this generation (and all later generations). One-fourth of the plain birds will be eaten by foxes, so remove one-fourth of the nickels: 2 nickels. Half of the red birds will be eaten, so remove half of the pennies: 1 penny. You're left with 6 plain birds and 1 red bird.

Now it's time to make the next generation. Each plain bird will leave only one plain male descendant, so slide all 6 nickels down a few inches.

But each red bird will leave 4 red male offspring, so place 4 pennies adjacent to the nickels in the new row.

You're now on the second generation. Notice how the population has changed: Even though a greater percentage of red birds was eaten before they could leave offspring, their mating success has paid off. In the second generation the plain birds are down to 60 percent of the population, and the red birds are up to 40 percent.

Repeat the process for three more generations. Round all numbers up: One-fourth of 6 will be 1.5, which you should round up to 2. What happens to the population of the Dum-Dum Birds? At the end of the game, what percentage of the birds will be plain (nickels), and what percentage will have red feathers (pennies)?

This is how sexual selection works: Species can evolve to acquire appealing but harmful adaptations too, because reproductive success is just as important as survival. Beauty has its benefits!

The same principle holds true with many other animals and features. The females of some bird species show a preference for male birds that do a mating dance. Male frigate birds and hummingbirds flap and fly and chirp in amazing displays that can last for hours. Sexual selection has preserved these seemingly strange behaviors.

Other behaviors related to sexual selection are not about impressing the females: They're about intimidating rival males. Bull elephant seals become extremely aggressive and violent around mating season. The bossiest males get more partners not because the females like them any better but because they've scared away all the other males.

More Than Just an Idea

It's not hard to imagine why it took Darwin twenty years to write the *Origin of Species*, his book about evolution. The basic idea was clear to him, but there were so many details to work out, so many questions that had to be answered. In fact, he never felt that he had properly explained his theory. To Darwin, *Origin* was just a brief *summary* of the arguments for evolution. Before events forced him to describe his theory as quickly as possible, he had been planning to write a book about evolution that was ten times as long!

He also wanted to make sure his idea stood up to any possible criticism. He spent years accumulating evidence and facts to back up his theory. Often, he made the investigations and confirmed the facts himself. It was essential that his theory was *scientifically rigorous*, or confirmed by scientific observations. This was a new way of doing things in natural history. The earlier evolutionary thinkers were just that—only thinkers. Their theories had just been speculations. No one really knew whether or not their guesses were correct. Darwin, on the other hand, wanted to make sure that evolution was the only possible explanation for all the factual evidence he had collected from geology, anatomy, paleontology, and biology.

Those aren't the only reasons Darwin was reluctant to go public with his theory. He knew from the beginning how controversial his idea would be. Few people had ever before dared to imply that humans were related to apes. But he hated controversy. He never argued with anyone, and the thought of speaking in public frightened him. Like any proper Victorian gentleman, he wanted to avoid scandal at all costs.

Yet he was a scientist, with a duty to reveal the truth as he knew it. He was caught in a terrible dilemma. In the end, he felt he had no choice; he published his theory, no matter what. It was a brave thing to do.

Sure enough, the response to *Origin* was immediate and explosive. Speakers insulted him. Preachers condemned him in their sermons. All of society was scandalized. "How dare this man question the unique and lofty status of the human race," they demanded. "Is he suggesting that we are descended from monkeys? How dare he say we are not created in God's image! This book is an insult to the Bible," they said.

Fearing just these kinds of attacks, Darwin purposely never mentioned in the *Origin of Species* that human beings were the result of evolution as well. But it didn't matter. Everyone jumped to that conclusion. Philosophers began to ask questions that Darwin could not answer. If, as everyone agrees, each human being has a soul, then when did we as a species acquire our souls? As far as anyone knew, animals didn't have souls, but if evolution is true, then long ago we were animals just like any other. Was there some moment in history when an intelligent monkey first acquired a soul and became a human being?

Darwin did not realize it at the time, but he changed forever the way the human race sees itself and the world. And he changed how scientists search for the truth.

Chapter Eight Endnotes

1. CSICOP: The Committee for the Scientific Investigation of Claims Of the Paranormal.
2. Quoted in *Dragons of Eden* by Carl Sagan (New York: Random House, 1977).
3. Paul Kurtz, *The Courage to Become* (Westport, CT: Praeger/Greenwood, 1997).
4. Quoted in *Summer for the Gods* by Edward J. Larson (Boston: Harvard University Press, 1998).
5. Richard Dawkins, *Unweaving the Rainbow* (New York: Houghton Mifflin, 1998).
6. Judith Stone, "Light Elements," *Discover* (July 1989).

Additional Resources

Books

- McNulty, Faith. *How Whales Walked into the Sea.* Scholastic Press, 1999. Traces the evolution of whales from wolflike land mammals over the course of twenty million years. The fossil intermediaries that filled in the blanks in whale evolution are brand-spanking new discoveries from the 1990s, so this fascinating book has the distinction of being well ahead of many high school and college textbooks. Each two-page spread takes a single, easy-to-follow evolutionary step, providing hypotheses for how natural selection may have spurred the development of each new form. A book likely to send parents' voices trailing off in wonder as they are reminded just how lovely and compelling the evolutionary process is. Ages 6–12.
- McCutcheon, Marc. *The Beast in You!—Activities & Questions to Explore Evolution.* Williamson, 1999. A marvelous, colorful, engaging look at our animal nature and ancestry, filled with activities and illustrations to introduce basic evolutionary concepts. A one-page nod to the question of faith vs. science, essentially embracing Steve Gould's idea of two mutually exclusive magesteria ("The Bible isn't a scientific textbook—it was never meant to be"). Ages 8–12.
- Lawson, Kristan. *Darwin and Evolution for Kids—His Life and Ideas with 21 Activities.* Chicago Review Press, 2003. This is the book for kids who are finally ready to learn how evolution works and the amazing story of its development over centuries, its unlikely nineteenth century expositor, and the sixty-year torrent of outrage, critique, and discovery that followed the 1859 publication of the *Origin.* At the end, your 12-year-old will know evolution in greater depth and detail than most adults. Ages 12 and up. [N.B. The essay "The Idea That

Changed the World" in the current book is reprinted from *Darwin and Evolution for Kids*.]

- Peters, Lisa Westerberg. *Our Family Tree: An Evolution Story*, Harcourt Children's, 2003. Ages 4–9.
- Gamlin, Linda. *Eyewitness: Evolution,* DK Children, 2000. Ages 10–14.
- Pfeffer, Wendy. *A Log's Life*, Simon and Schuster Children's, 1997. Winner of the Giverny Award for Best Children's Science Picture Book, this description of the life cycle of a tree is just one in a long line of outstanding children's science books by Wendy Pfeffer. Ages 4–8.
- Couper, Heather, with Nigel Henbest. *Big Bang—The Story of the Universe.* Dorling Kindersley, 1997. A gorgeously illustrated explanation of the "Big Bang" theory of the origin of the universe. May be a bit challenging, depending on a child's prior exposure to science vocabulary and ideas, but worth the effort. Ages 12–18.
- Bailey, Jacqui. *The Birth of the Earth* from The Cartoon History of the Earth series, Kids Can Press, 2001. An inventive comic-book style presentation of good science. Ages 9–12.

Videos

- *Cellular Visions: The Inner Life of a Cell.* A captivating, award-winning animated short created by XVIVO Scientific Animation to show the incredible complexity and beauty of life at the cellular level. A three-minute version of the animation is available on many websites—search for "Cellular Visions" or "The Inner Life of a Cell." Ages 6 and up.
- *Wonders of the Universe* Video Series (Ambrose Video, 1996). Thirteen half-hour segments exploring different aspects of the cosmos. Animation quality somewhat dated and varies in pace and engagement—but when it's good, it's very, very good. Ages 10 and up.
- *Walking with Cavemen.* BBC, 2003. A fascinating attempt to condense human evolution into a graspable storyline with actors in epic layers of latex makeup portraying the various species along the way. An impressive stab at a subject that is devilishly hard to depict. Ages 8 and up, though clearly pitched to adult viewers.
- *Walking with Dinosaurs.* BBC, 1999. This time the medium is the cutting edge of computer animation. The result is the most realistic depiction ever of life in the age of dinosaurs. An astonishing technical and artistic feat. Ages 10 and up, due mostly to some graphic scenes of dino-on-dino gore. Kids as young as 6 can watch and divert their eyes when the music says.

- *Intimate Universe: The Human Body.* BBC Warner, 1998. Easily among the most compelling science documentaries ever made, this four-volume set explores all phases of human development from conception through birth, puberty, pregnancy, aging, and death, using a combination of endoscopic camera work and cutting-edge animation to take the viewer places that—believe you me—you *never* thought you'd go. Entirely wonder-inducing and conversation-starting. Ages 6 and up.
- *Evolution,* PBS series produced by WGBH Boston and Clear Blue Sky Productions, 2001. Outstanding, high-quality documentary series available in VHS and DVD. Should be in every public library.

Websites

- Inquiring Minds (www.inquiringminds.org). The educational wing of CSICOP (The Committee for the Scientific Investigation Of Claims *(*deep inhale*)* of the Paranormal. A relatively young venture, still building its offerings, but off to a grand start with classroom curricula, activities, and links.
- National Geographic Xpeditions (www.nationalgeographic.com/xpeditions). An extraordinary collection of activities for home or classroom related to seasons, ocean geography, astronomy, natural disasters, biodiversity, migration, and much more.

Seeking Community

Introduction

Two are better than one, because they have a good reward for their toil. For if they fall, one will lift up the other; but woe to one who is alone when he falls and does not have another to help.

– Ecclesiastes 4:9–10

Is there a more fatalistic bit of reading material on Earth than Ecclesiastes? "For every thing there is a season," that's very nice — but as for the rest: *All is vanity, the end is the same no matter how you've lived, great works and upright living mean nothing, no one and nothing will be remembered, death is better than birth and mourning better than feasting* . . . You can see why the OT writers were longing for a messiah.[1] There's one passage in particular to make free-thinkers howl: *For in much wisdom is much grief: and those who increase knowledge increase sorrow.*

Hoo, boy.

But when the authors of Ecclesiastes said two are better than one, I'll have to admit they were onto something. After three chapters bemoaning God's fixed plan for humanity—"it is an unhappy business that God has given to human beings to be busy with—all is vanity and a chasing after wind"— they offer this glimpse of nothing less than *humanist community*. Toil all you want under God's blind eye, they say, but if you expect support when you fall, you have only each other to turn to.

We need each other. Prolonged isolation is, for most of us, one of the most difficult ordeals to endure. Not for nothing is solitary confinement sometimes considered cruel and unusual. Occasional solitude can be a precious gift—but if it goes on too long, it can begin to erode our sense of ourselves, since much of that ongoing definition takes place relative to our fellow human beings.

One of the great advantages of membership in a religious community is in that second word, *community:* the ability to surround one's self with an extended family, others who care for, support, nurture, and encourage one's own way through the world, who lift each other up when they fall. This chapter focuses on the many ways in which such community can be achieved without compromising what we hold to be true.

Among the more interesting developments in this area is nontheistic religion. You read that right—religious organizations without gods. Theology is only one part of the religious impulse, as you've known now for 200 pages or so. There's the predefined set of values, the common lexicon and symbology, rites of passage, a means of engendering wonder, comforting answers to the big questions, and consoling explanations to ease experiences of hardship and loss—and an established community in which to experience these benefits. Most Christians attend church not to worship, but to enjoy these benefits. "God" is simply the frame in which these concepts are hung. Remove the frame, and the beautiful picture—which is the point of it all, of course— remains.

We've mentioned Unitarian Universalism in passing more than once, a denomination that grew out of two separate heresies: Unitarianism (the idea that God is one thing, not three) and Universalism (the notion that everyone is loved equally by God and that all receive salvation). They merged in the 1960s as one of the most liberal Christian denominations, opening their doors to all people regardless of belief, but by the 1990s had become majority nontheistic. The specific character varies tremendously from one UU fellowship to another, but having visited more than a dozen, I can make the following observations: UUs tend to be wonderfully warm, welcoming, and relaxed people; though creedless, they are powerful social activists, opposing violence and supporting civil rights for all; and most fellowships give no special place to Christian teaching or symbols—some even avoiding them entirely. Religious literacy is an important part of the UU fellowship (see Chapter 2, "On Being Religiously Literate")—not indoctrination, but study and appreciation, the kind of approach that makes religion downright interesting rather than threatening. Again: By recognizing the validity of many expressions of humanness, you deny any one of them the high ground.

Another example of nontheistic religion is Secular Humanistic Judaism, a fully secular expression of Jewish culture founded forty years ago by Rabbi Sherwin Wine. Most readers will be familiar with the idea of "cultural Jewishness." Humanistic Judaism provides a unifying community for this expression—again, the beautiful picture without the obsolete frame.

There has been a strong revival of interest in a third (essentially) nontheistic religion: Liberal Quakers. And the reason is wonderful. Millions of people have taken the Belief-O-Matic quiz (at www.beliefnet.com), only to discover that their beliefs identify them *not* with the Methodist, Baptist, Episcopal, Catholic, or Lutheran churches to which their families and offerings go, but with the Liberal Quakers. Quaker organizations have reported as much as an eight-fold increase in inquiries since the Belief-O-Matic went online. And that's good news, since Liberal Quakers believe that one's beliefs cannot be dictated by another person—that one's relationship with whatever reality there is, is one's own, and cannot be mediated. In other words, no indoctrination, no evangelism, no dogmatic nonsense—just another community devoted to nonviolence, positive social action, building community, and alleviating suffering. While Southern Baptists were forming their denomination around the biblical support of slavery, Quakers were among the most prominent abolitionists. While Catholics in the United States represented the single largest organized opposition to women's voting rights, Quakers were in the streets getting arrested in defense of those rights. Quakers have been in the forefront of every anti-war movement. Funny what the absence of dogma will do.

Many Quaker schools have been established around the United States, and freethinkers should feel entirely comfortable if they choose to enroll their children there. They will be exposed to models of positive moral action, not indoctrination.

Siddhartha Gautama—the historical Buddha—has been called the earliest significant nontheist. As happens in every major spiritual movement, Buddha's followers quickly heaped layers of superstition on top of what had been perfectly naturalistic teachings. But many modern expressions of Buddhism are utterly nontheistic. If, upon learning a bit about Buddhist philosophy you find it attractive, look into your local Buddhist communities. You'll find many ways to be Buddhist without gods.

Finally there is the Ethical Culture movement, "a humanistic religious and educational movement inspired by the ideal that the supreme aim of human life is working to create a more humane society."[2] Like UUs, Ethical Culture societies focus on service to the community, encouraging the knowledge, practice, and love of ethical behavior, and deepening the collective sense of the spiritual — again, without supernatural overtones.

If every church in the United States began its service this week with the announcement that the congregation would continue meeting every Sunday, continue singing songs and sharing hopes and offering solace and acceptance and the occasional chance to do good works and to be a part of something larger than one's self, but that these tokens of love and joy and togetherness would henceforth be directed to each other rather than to the idea of a god—after the initial shock and rending of garments, I honestly doubt it would take long to adjust. Most people attend church first and foremost for those humanistic reasons, after all, not to worship an abstraction. And if that's the part of religion we *really* need, a nontheistic religion might not be such an oxymoron after all. "A passionate and committed atheism can be more religious than a weary or inadequate theism," says religious historian Karen Armstrong, who further quotes Albert Camus' deeply humanistic assertion that "people should reject God defiantly in order to pour out all their loving solicitude upon mankind."[3] It is to that passionate, committed vision of loving human community that this chapter is devoted.

■ ■ ■ ■ ■ ■

There are uncountable ways to define and achieve community. Pete Wernick returns to tell of his long and impressive attempts to build secular community infrastructures so that nontheistic individuals and families can call upon the same resources as theists. It's slow going, and there's much work to do, as Pete's honest and thoughtful piece attests. Amanda Metskas and August Brunsman team up to describe one of the great secular community success stories, Camp Quest, a summer camp where children can explore the natural world and ask questions without the religious context of "Vacation Bible School" camps. Unlike the "Kids on Fire" evangelical camp profiled in the chilling documentary *Jesus Camp*,[4] Camp Quest neither promotes nor encourages disrespect or hatred for people of differing views.

In our final piece, longtime atheist activist Bobbie Kirkhart outlines the many available freethought organizations, complete with strengths, weaknesses, and their reasons for being.

Religious community builds on millennia of tradition, rooted in the age when humanity believed a supernatural intelligence was running the show. By comparison, the effort to create secular community—to come together as a loving, compassionate human family in the light of our new understanding of reality — is in its infancy. More than anything, this chapter can serve as an invitation for you to join courageous people like Pete Wernick, Bobbie Kirkhart, Unitarian Universalists, Humanistic Judaism, Nontheistic Friends, and all the rest who are working not to displace religion, but to provide secular alternatives for the growing numbers who have set religion aside. How might we achieve Russell's vision of the good life, inspired by love and guided by genuine knowledge, while addressing our genuine human needs?

Building the Secular Community—
However Slowly

Pete Wernick, Ph.D.

SECULAR FAMILIES HAVE SCARCELY any of the resources that Christian, Moslem, Jewish, and other theistic families in this country have in abundance. Religious communities have attractive places for families to gather every week to be spiritually uplifted and share community, youth groups built around their family's beliefs and values, and trained personnel to guide them in their spiritual lives and help them work through problems in ways consistent with their beliefs. They have libraries of inspiring reading and songs handed down by a variety of music traditions, with spiritual messages seasoned over many years.

As one half of a "mixed" religious/secular couple,[5] I would have benefited greatly from access to such an infrastructure when raising our son. My wife had access to the fully developed Catholic infrastructure, while I had very little that could compare. She had beautiful churches, both at home and anywhere we traveled, whereas humanist and atheist organizations own scarcely any buildings anywhere in the world. She had a network of trained professionals to minister to their flock and educate the children, right up to the Vatican in Rome!

Compared to the volume of Christian literature and music that fills libraries and concert halls worldwide, we secular types have very little that is specifically identified with our worldview. They have the world's bestselling book, the Bible, with translations in all languages, and spinoffs like attractively illustrated Bible stories for kids.

> They have the world's bestselling book, the Bible, with translations in all languages. And what do we have to compare with "Ave Maria," "Silent Night," Mozart's "Requiem," Mahalia Jackson, or bluegrass gospel harmony by the Stanley Brothers?

Then there's the music. What do we have to compare with "Ave Maria," "Silent Night," Mozart's "Requiem," Mahalia Jackson, or bluegrass gospel harmony by the Stanley Brothers? As a musician, I'm especially disappointed by the virtual lack of secular inspirational music (*not* an oxymoron, as I'll show later).

And how many couples do we all know who, after espousing secular viewpoints for years, have sent their kids to religious education they didn't believe in ". . . because we wanted the kids to have something. . . ."

It's very regrettable, this enormous gap. What to do? Well . . . get busy, I decided.

Though quite daunted by the enormity of the task, I produced a number of essays on the theme of "creating a nontheistic religion." I imagined places where secular folks could gather in community on a weekend morning to celebrate the glory and wonders of our world, inspire greater fulfilling of human potential, as well as steadfastly and sensitively address our ever-present human frailties and the challenges of trying to live harmoniously.

There would be books of clear and poetic affirmations of beliefs, collections of wisdom to help people live better lives, and as a centerpiece, a *single book*—comparable to the Bible, but a lot better. It would include beautifully written, fact-based accounts of how the earth and living things came to be and how humans learned to live together, develop civilizations and cultures, and create meaning and harmony in their lives. It would distill the best of human wisdom (no doubt including excerpts from various "holy books") into sayings, essays, and stories that would show humans at their best. It would teach and inspire and along the way give good reason to suspect and reject supernatural thinking. In short, it would be a secular alternative to the Bible, with the powerful advantages of being factual *and* sensible *and* reader-friendly. Something we'd be proud to leave a copy of in a motel room drawer, head-to-head with the Gideon Bible.

It comforted me to think that even in a relatively religious country like the United States, estimates of "secular" people (atheists and agnostics) range from 8 to 14 percent, or 22 to 40 million people. But with all the secularists in the United States, where are the *communities?*

When I first began my search for secular infrastructure, I'd heard of "Ethical Culture" nonbeliever communities, but they existed mostly in the Northeast, as does Jewish Reconstructionism. There were two Unitarian congregations here in Boulder, Colorado. I found that Unitarian Universalists had evolved quite a bit from their "liberal Christianity" roots, including quite a variety of believers and lifestyles within their large umbrella. One of the congregations had a fair number of pagans, GLBT folks, new age types, and general "seekers." In examining the seven UU principles (www.uua.org/principles.html), adopted by the UUA in the 1970s, I found a lot to agree with, especially the principles of "a free and responsible search for truth and meaning" and "encouragement to spiritual growth in our congregations."

> When at a [Unitarian] meeting I heard someone talk of her joy at having successfully channeled a past life, I was more startled than joyful for her. Trying to connect to our society's druid and animist roots or adapt some Native American sacred practices for a Sunday service left me feeling more adrift than rooted.

Religion is more than a set of beliefs; it's also a set of practices, styles, and attitudes. The UU style I was exposed to was sort of "feel-good" and noncritical. When at a meeting I heard someone talk of her joy at having successfully channeled a past life, I was more startled than joyful for her. Trying to connect to our society's druid and animist roots or adapt Native American sacred practices for a Sunday service left me feeling more adrift than rooted. I realized I would feel most at home in a congregation where my own beliefs were clearly and proudly stated as a consensus of the group. On some occasions this would happen at the Unitarian Church, but as usual, it's hard to mix "I don't believe in the supernatural" into a group that includes believers in any number of supernatural beliefs and where acceptance is the norm.

It sounds selfish, doesn't it? I want the congregation to be open-minded in accepting my beliefs, but highly skeptical of things I don't believe.

The UUs at least had tolerance to offer, wherein my beliefs were given honor and acceptance. But I would have felt more welcome and included in a context where I could hear *my own actual beliefs* concerning religion spoken from a pulpit, sung about, and celebrated in art and music.

I subscribed to a number of atheist publications, and investigated whether anyone was already working on developing a "nontheistic religion." I couldn't find anyone, save a kook or two who mostly gave me the willies. Secular folks' efforts seemed mainly concerned with pointing out the absurdities and injustices of religion and occasionally battling with public officials over transgressions of religion into state matters.

Somewhere along the way, someone I told of my search suggested I look into "humanism." The word sounded familiar but I'd never known it was akin to atheism. I read up on humanism, and indeed, there was the emphasis on the positive, right there with open nontheism. I became involved with humanist groups both nationally and locally. While some of what I saw was promising, I was and remain quite disappointed at the generally malnourished and malnourishing humanist infrastructure. The national organizations' memberships combined were and still are well under 100,000, in a country where surveyed percentages of nonbelievers indicate two to four *hundred* times that many. The publications were usually dull, dry, and academic, without illustrations or photos. Where was the *joie de vivre,* the spark, the excitement of positive beliefs flourishing?

I was amazed at first that though I was a secularist since age 15, in an academic environment with many thinking people, many of them secularists, it had taken me thirty years to discover humanism. The more I investigated, the more I understood why it had been so invisible to me: I saw an inward-turned community that scarcely ever reached out and tried to grow itself. Virtually nothing for kids and families, no pictures, no humor, no fun. *Yuck!*

These people needed a dose of PR thinking. Having some skills in that area, I thought hard about how to attract like-minded people, especially younger folks. I checked out billboard pricing, designed a nice-looking leaflet, and talked at local meetings about doing outreach. But staring me in the face was a tough puzzle: How do you organize around *the denial of an attractive abstraction?*

Right from the start, there is a major challenge to organizing secular folks. It is relatively easy to organize for a particular *goal* (e.g., "Pass Referendum X") or a *person* ("Vote for Bill," or "Believe Cynthia's message"), but less magnetizing to organize around an *abstraction* (nontheism), which is in fact the *denial* of an abstraction—and a rather attractive, beloved one at that. Talk about having the deck stacked against you!

Humanism harnesses a strong desire among nontheists for a positive set of beliefs, not just "what we're against." In the 1930s a concrete statement of affirmations, the first Humanist Manifesto, was published with the signatures of many respected thinkers of the time. Rather than focusing on denying gods and theism, it emphasized what humanism stands *for,* such as fairness and freedom and dependence on science and reason rather than on supernatural authority.

We are not just non-supernaturalists, it says in essence. *We have positive beliefs and our nontheism is a consistent part of this, our larger philosophy.* Nontheism is the natural outgrowth of a *devotion to truth and reason,* so the core value is "devotion to truth and reason."

Yes, it's a major challenge to organize people around "devotion to truth and reason." One might as well start a university! And it turned out: Devotion to truth and reason, good as it sounds, is not what people are really after when they become active secularists. What actually motivates nontheists to stand up and be counted is a feeling more like, "Religion, off my back!" So we want to come across positively, but we are driven by feelings of defensiveness and negativity.

Virtually every person I met who was doing hard work on behalf of humanism and atheism had, like me, experienced the challenge and even threat of organized religion too close for comfort — that is, in their own homes or extended families, or perhaps in their kids' schools. Most of these compadres have siblings, parents, an ex-spouse, and/or kids who are strongly religious. They become activists first and foremost to bolster their own stance in regard to their relatives — just like me.

So many secularists, so little activism around that banner. The jokes come easy: "A flag with nothing on it . . ." "All praise to . . . nobody." "Let's all get together behind . . . nothing!"

When a humanist friend and I, both with 9-year-old sons, staged a protest against war toys at a mall toy store around Christmas time, we made it known that we were from Humanists of Colorado offering nice leaflets with a contact address and even managed to get in the newspaper — but without much result. This is the kind of thing that needs to be sustained for a time before bearing real fruit.

Some secularists see no need for secularist promotion and solidarity. Some will say, "I don't need to go to a church Sunday morning. I can feel spiritual hiking in the woods or listening to a great symphony," or "My gods are science and reason, and whenever science is conducted, my beliefs are being upheld." Or "Think of all the great music and art and thought that doesn't mention God. Isn't that enough for you?"

That last comment points to a key to the puzzle. Inspirational writing, art, and music free of supernaturalism are all around us. Yet it's not been gathered together in a specifically secularist framework. I decided to work on that.

I took a shot at running a monthly "service equivalent" called Living Humanist Values. I did it for five years, with a typical attendance of about a dozen out of a total "congregation" of maybe two dozen. I researched and assembled the best and wisest inspirational writings I could. I decorated a rented room at the Crossroads Mall with scenes of beautiful landscapes, and pithy sayings such as Thomas Paine's "The world is my country, and to do good is my religion." Sermon on the Mall, my wife and I jokingly called it.

I'd go down early to set up the coffee pots and cookies and put up posters, and when the folks arrived I would offer readings and songs and facilitate discussions on a variety of topics concerning living the good and secular life. We talked about role models, holidays, how to deal with transgressions ("sins" is a simpler but loaded word), resolving conflicts peacefully, and dealing with our secular identities in a theistic culture.

I found it quite enriching to hunt and gather this kind of nontheistic written material. I incorporated the prose of Robert Ingersoll and Kenneth Patton especially, both great wordsmiths able to state things clearly and inspiringly at the same time. Humanist publishers also offer various tracts such as suggestions for humanist weddings and funerals.[6]

After five years, I reflected on all my amateur efforts and found them feeble compared to what trained professional spiritual leaders could do. Abetted by the trappings of dress and context, and backed by a lot of volunteers and a national organization professional, clergy earn the trust that attracts people, to be taken inward and upward. I decided to settle for a half-hearted association with the Unitarian Universalists. I swallowed my differences with the UUs and became an occasional UU churchgoer, though not a member.

There are national networks of "humanist counselors" who earn certification from either of the two major American humanist organizations, The American Humanist Association and Council for Secular Humanism. These folks, numbering a few hundred nationwide, perform weddings and funerals and are available for individual counseling, but apparently do not conduct regular "services."

My next project was a redesign and reissue of a booklet by Family of Humanists called *Humanism for Kids*. I felt good that one little part of a secular infrastructure for kids was now available. Our little group ran a few ads in UU and secularist publications, and the modest 40-page book sold well over 1,000 copies, with multiple orders flowing in steadily for years. But the organization, in all-too-typical low-energy fashion, does not have the inclination to weigh in and "go national" with it. *Sigh.* Maybe someday!

A few other glimmers of growth on the national scene have occurred in the last ten years or so. The Council for Secular Humanism now has a publication called *Family Matters,* and Camp Quest, founded in 1996, provides a basic summer camp experience for secular kids.[7]

But what about secular communities? Probably hundreds of small groups across the United States meet monthly, but as of 2006 only one I know of meets as often as weekly, The Humanist Community in Palo Alto (http://www.humanists.org), while the North Texas Church of Freethought (http://www.churchoffreethought.org), which meets monthly at a Holiday Inn near Dallas, reports regular attendance of over 100 and is saving up for a building of its own. These two most-robust groups have one employee between the two of them, still a wee bit short of the scale of our Christian friends.

Art and music are not typically sorted into a "secular" category. After all, most music and art is not specifically theistic, thus is secular by default. Yet it is not immediately obvious what pieces of art and music are the best for secular audiences seeking a spiritual lift. I am aware of no published collections for this purpose.

As a musician, I felt compelled to look for some good choices. The music of the 1960s and 1970s had a lot to offer: "Imagine," "Get Together," "Teach Your Children Well," and many others. A humanist group in New Jersey even sponsored a contest for original music of this stripe. But no published collections are in general circulation. A number of individual "freethought" performers have released albums of songs with songbooks, but the songs tend to be more in the mode of religious critique than uplifting.

As a songwriter myself, I've had some success in the world of bluegrass music with a song called "Just Like You." It reached number one on the Bluegrass Radio Play Chart when first released and has had enduring popularity, having been recorded by perhaps a dozen groups.

The song has an interesting history: Driving home from a bluegrass festival in North Carolina back in 1975, having just attended the typical Sunday Gospel Show, I found myself wishing I could write a gospel song while staying true to my beliefs. I thought of a bass singer chiming in, "Let me tell you my friend," going into the chorus and wondered what I would want to "tell my friend." I spun out some stories about old people who were lonely, and after each verse, the refrain goes, "Let me tell you my friend, he's just like you." "Just Like You" has a clear gospel feel, but its message is empathy for people who need it, without supernatural overtones. Many people say they consider it a special song, and in interviews I've sometimes been asked how the song came to be written.

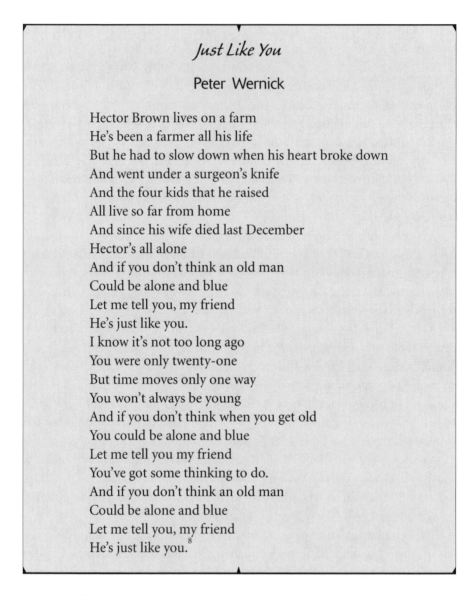

Just Like You

Peter Wernick

Hector Brown lives on a farm
He's been a farmer all his life
But he had to slow down when his heart broke down
And went under a surgeon's knife
And the four kids that he raised
All live so far from home
And since his wife died last December
Hector's all alone
And if you don't think an old man
Could be alone and blue
Let me tell you, my friend
He's just like you.
I know it's not too long ago
You were only twenty-one
But time moves only one way
You won't always be young
And if you don't think when you get old
You could be alone and blue
Let me tell you my friend
You've got some thinking to do.
And if you don't think an old man
Could be alone and blue
Let me tell you, my friend
He's just like you. [8]

With all the great secular inspirational music, writing, and art out there, there is ample material to distill into user-friendly collections that can serve humanist families trying to raise good and god-free children. In time, humanist communities may become widespread and provide the living infrastructure so many of us need. The job of distilling and building remains before us, and I intend to be in there working on it as long as I can.

Summer Camp Beyond Belief

Amanda K. Metskas and August E. Brunsman IV

SUMMER CAMP. AHH, IT BRINGS back memories—swimming in the lake, toasting marshmallows, riding horses, meeting new friends, singing songs around the campfire. Many of us recall fondly our summer camp experiences as kids. For most of us those camps probably had some religious component, as minor as prayers before meals and kum-ba-yah around the campfire, or as involved as daily chapel and Bible study. If only parents could give their kids all of the positive benefits of summer camp—and there are many—without the accompanying religious messages. While in some parts of the country, particularly the Northeast and West Coast, parents may find comprehensive summer camps that fit this bill, in many other parts of the country options like this may be practically nonexistent. It was with this in mind that Camp Quest, the first residential summer camp in the United States for children from nonreligious families, was founded in 1996 by Edwin and Helen Kagin.[9]

Sending kids off to summer camp is an American tradition stretching back over 140 years.[10] According to a study commissioned by the American Camping Association and conducted by Philliber Research Associates, the camp experience makes kids more comfortable trying new things, increases their ability to make new friends, allows them to develop independence and maturity, and increases their self-esteem.[11] "For many children, sleep-away camp is the first time they have been away from home for any appreciable amount of time. The weeks at camp become a chance to grow up—at least a little," reports Dr. Marie Hartwell-Walker.[12]

Despite these benefits, the nature of summer camp in America is changing, with an increasing number of specialty camps devoted to helping kids develop skills in an activity they are already interested in, such as soccer or horseback-riding. As one *Washington Post* columnist complained, "Whatever happened to camp camp?"[13] Summer camps are also dealing with increased pressure from parents to be in touch with their kids while they are at camp, including parents who hide cell phones in their camper's suitcases, hoping counselors won't find the banned electronic devices.[14] Both of these developments potentially threaten the benefits that a traditional comprehensive summer camp provides kids—independence, self-esteem, and a chance to try new things.

At Camp Quest, children experience all sorts of activities common to traditional summer camps—horseback riding, swimming, arts and crafts, canoeing, ropes courses, singing songs by the campfire, et cetera, all in an environment free from the pervasive religious messages in the rest of U.S. society. But Camp Quest isn't just a traditional summer minus God. In addition to typical camp activities, Camp Quest campers learn about "famous freethinkers" from around the world. These include people they may have heard of, like Thomas Jefferson and James Madison, the deist authors of the U.S. Constitution, and people they may be less familiar with, like A. Philip Randolph, an African American civil rights leader who organized the March on Washington at which Martin Luther King Jr. gave his famous "I Have a Dream" speech. Kids learn that there are many people like their families, people who are skeptical of religious belief and have done great things. It gives them people to look up to and lets them know that they and their families are not alone.

Camp Quest also focuses on critical thinking, scientific reasoning, and ethics. Campers are given "challenges" where they work together as a cabin to design and perform a skit that answers a question given to them on the opening night. Some past questions include "Did some being design our planet and us? Wouldn't it take an intelligence of some sort or other to put together something as complicated as living things? Many say there are no other possible good explanations for how we got here. Is that true? What do you think, and why?" and "Let's say that you could start everything all over again. Imagine that you suddenly have no rules or laws of any kind. Imagine that you have no countries and no religions—but that you do have many different races and many different languages. Please make up ten (10) rules that everyone on the planet Earth would have to obey at all times. These must be rules everyone will agree with, and they must be rules that will make life better for everyone all the time." While the questions may be serious and lead to serious discussion in the cabins, the skits that result are often hilarious, and entertain the entire camp at the closing campfire.

Other Camp Quest programs involve discussions with campers about what they tell their friends about their beliefs and how they handle situations like saying the Pledge of Allegiance at school. Counselors leading these discussions serve only as moderators, giving the kids a chance to talk about things they have experienced and strategies they have used. Following on the motto used at Camp Quest Classic in Ohio this year, "Reason and Compassion in Action," campers worked on ways that they could get involved in improving their communities.

Camp Quest is very careful not to indoctrinate campers, letting them come to their own conclusions in a supportive environment. In answer to a question about what she learned at Camp Quest on her camp evaluation form, one camper wrote, "I learned that it is okay not to believe in god." Note that she didn't say that she learned that there is no god, she learned that it is *okay not to believe.* That is probably the most important thing that Camp Quest offers—an environment where kids can be kids and have fun without compromising their beliefs and without controversy. They build lasting friendships with fellow campers from all over the country.

> ❝ In answer to a question about what she learned at Camp Quest on her camp evaluation form, one camper wrote, "I learned that it is okay not to believe in god." Note that she didn't say that she learned that there is no god, she learned that it is *okay not to believe.* ❞

When they go back home, they are a little more comfortable with who they are, a little more confident in their abilities, and a little more willing to branch out.

Since 1996, Camp Quest has expanded substantially in the number of campers it serves and in the variety of sessions offered. Camp Quest has grown from one location serving 20 campers in 1996 to approximately 120 kids who attended six different Camp Quest sessions in California, Michigan, Minnesota, Ohio, Ontario, and Tennessee in the summer of 2006. Each of the camps is independently operated, but all follow the same mission. All offer some of the same activities, but each also has its own feel and flavor.

Camp Quest is run entirely by volunteers who devote a week of their time to be on camp staff and devote time throughout the year developing programs and performing administrative and support roles. The organization also strives to be affordable for every child by raising money to provide full or partial camperships so that no camper is turned down for financial reasons. Camp Quest is open to any child from the age of 8 to 17. For more information, please go to www.camp-quest.org. Links to all of the Camp Quests are available there.

Let's Get Organized

Bobbie Kirkhart

MY DAUGHTER WAS 10 WHEN she found out that I was attending meetings at our local atheist group. "You mean we're atheists?" She ran to the phone to call her friends, exclaiming, "I'm so tired of being nothing!"

Humans are social animals, and our children seek a tribe to identify with. It requires as much faith as any religion to believe we can meet this need by chanting, "The world is my country" or saying we must let them decide for themselves. They will decide for themselves, of course, and they will grow beyond the boundaries of the little groups they depend on in childhood, but our eagerness for this to happen does not alleviate our responsibility to provide them with a community.

For activist and political reasons, I encourage all nonbelievers to join at least one freethought organization, but for parents, I think it is a must for two reasons. First, whether your child is quiet or confrontational, you can't guarantee that she won't be subject to harassment or worse. In that case, you and he will need a group to fall back on, and you both will be much more comforted if it is a group she knows. And then there's the tribe thing. Your child *will* identify with a tribe, and both he and you will be happier if it is *your* tribe.

All national organizations will put you in touch with your local affiliate organization. Not as accurate, but worth a try, is the Freethought Directory, online at www.atheistalliance.org, also available on CD from the Atheist Alliance. If you don't find a local group, start one. The national associations will offer help in this area, and both you and your child need to know that you are not alone.

Once you locate a freethought community, you may discover that it is virtually childless, with mostly older people and no programs or institution for children. Your instinct may be to cut and run, but unless there is another freethought group in your area, your job is to make a place for your child in such a population. It won't be as hard as it looks. Even those groups that appear unfriendly to families almost certainly lament the lack of youth in their organization.

268

I suggest that parents first go to the group alone and size up the situation. If there is a children's program, check it out, but don't demand perfection. It will almost certainly be acceptable and will often be excellent.

If there is none, which is more likely, look for resources: other kids, a side room, a safe outdoor play area, even extra space in the back of the room. Talk to the leaders, share with them your desire to make a place for your child in their community, and elicit their help. Identify resources you have noted and ask to be put in touch with other parents. Talk about encouraging teens and young adults to become leaders for children's groups. "Youth leader" looks great on a résumé.

Although groups may be open to the general idea of becoming more family-friendly, you may encounter resistance to concrete suggestions for change. The fact is that we atheists-humanists-rationalists-skeptics-brights really like to listen to lectures and debate philosophy. Surprisingly, some of us have not noticed that our children believe the word "lecture" has the same root as "torture" and that a debate is nothing more than an argument. They don't enjoy it, and our idea that they should doesn't change their feelings.

Sometimes the best you can do is plan an occasional activity outside the group with a few friends and their grandchildren, but be sure your child is aware of your community in other ways. If you can't afford to send your child to Camp Quest, ask your association for a scholarship. If you can afford Camp Quest, brazenly suggest to the group that they send your child off with a small gift, like a book to read on the plane. Be shameless in informing your organization of your child's accomplishments—grade school graduation, any honors she wins. Cards from a few of the members will let your child know that he has a community of support.

Older children and teens still are unlikely to want to listen to lectures, but they may be willing, even eager, to participate in other group activities. I was proud, she was proud, and I think most of the membership was proud when my 16-year-old daughter won Atheist United's annual speech contest. At any age, your child will enjoy outdoor events, especially if she takes a friend and isn't asked to sit quietly for the program.

If all this sounds like too much trouble — it is. Freethought groups should conscientiously and effectively welcome families, and many do. Find your group, and if it is welcoming of your child, consider yourself lucky.

Below are descriptions of the major national membership organizations and their child- and family-centered activities. Some exist for reasons of advocacy, some for socializing, some to provide professional services, and some as a combination of all three. Though all are god-free, some even speak of themselves as "nontheistic religious communities" — so there should be something here for every secular stripe.

American Atheists (AA)
P.O. Box 5733
Parsippany, NJ 07054-6733
Phone: 908-276-7300
www.atheists.org
www.atheists.org/family

American Atheists works for the civil rights of Atheists and for state/church separation and is probably the most militant of all the freethought groups. The organization runs a Youth and Family website where anyone can get advice on raising atheist children—nonprofessional but often good—and gain support from the Atheist community. This site includes advice on starting local, grade school, or high school Atheist groups. They assist with legal advice and start-up kits when necessary.

American Atheists awards $3,000 per year in scholarships for Atheist activism.

American Ethical Union (AEU) aka Ethical Culture
2 West 64th Street
New York, NY 10023
Phone: (212) 873 6500
www.aeu.org

Ethical Culture is a humanistic religious and educational movement inspired by the ideal that the supreme aim of human life is working to create a more humane society. It is arguable whether Ethical Culture is a freethought organization, but it is godless and has the most extensive resources for children.

The AEU provides curriculum, activities, and support for those societies that have a religious education program. Most larger societies have a Director of Religious Education (DRE) who works with the children's programming. Samples of their extensive curricula can be found on their website.

American Humanist Association (AHA)
1777 T Street, NW
Washington, DC 20009-7125
Phone: 800-837-3792
www.americanhumanist.org

The American Humanist Association works to raise the profile and public acceptance of Humanism. AHA is an excellent organization, though its membership tends to be older and so focuses less on family issues than some other groups.

The Humanist Society provides resources on humanist education and certifies celebrants, who officiate at everything from baby-naming ceremonies to memorial services.

Atheist Alliance International (AAI)
P.O. Box 26867
Los Angeles, CA 90026
Phone: 1-866-HERETIC
www.atheistalliance.org

The Atheist Alliance is the only fully democratic national freethought organization in the United States. This is a loose alliance of independent atheist groups, so local groups vary greatly. AAI provides children's programs at its national convention on Easter weekend. Sponsors "Young Atheists and Freethinkers' Discussion List," an e-group that provides young doubters a forum to air their doubts about religion and their questions about atheism. It is strictly moderated to keep out proselytizers, so that kids may feel comfortable expressing their doubts. Gives cash "Future of Freethought" awards for outstanding freethought work for students elementary through college age.

Council for Secular Humanism (CSH)
P.O. Box 664
Amherst, NY 14226-0664
Phone: 716-636-7571
www.secularhumanism.org
www.inquiringminds.org/education

The Council for Secular Humanism is an educational organization dedicated to fostering the growth of democracy and secular humanism and the principles of free inquiry in contemporary society. A professional organization, CSH offers the Inquiring Minds program of educational resources for school and family activities through the Secular Family Network, runs Camp Inquiry, a one-week camp for children 7 through 16 with emphasis on science education, and publishes *Family Matters,* an online newsletter for families.

Freedom from Religion Foundation (FFRF)
P.O. Box 750
Madison, WI 53701
Phone: 608-256-8900
www.ffrf.org

The Freedom From Religion Foundation has been working to keep state and church separate and to educate the public about the views of nontheists. FFRF publishes *Just Pretend, Maybe Yes Maybe No,* and *Maybe Right Maybe Wrong,* all freethought books for children by Dan Barker.

The Foundation sponsors an essay contest for high school and college students. One chapter, the Alabama Freethought Association, sponsors a Fourth of July celebration that is the only national family freethought event in the country at Lake Hypatia, near Munford, Alabama. There are speeches and such, but also many outdoor activities at this child and family-friendly event. Campsites are available on the adjoining grounds.

Secular Student Alliance (SSA)
P.O. Box 3246
Columbus, OH 43210
Phone: 1-877-842-9474
http://www.secularstudents.org/

The Secular Student Alliance is an independent international umbrella organization for high school and college freethought groups. This is a great organization. When your child reaches high school age, buy him or her a membership!

The Skeptics Society
P.O. Box 338
Altadena, CA 91001
Phone: 626-794-3119
www.skeptic.com

The Skeptics Society is a scientific and educational organization of scholars, scientists, historians, magicians, professors and teachers, and anyone curious about controversial ideas, extraordinary claims, revolutionary ideas, and the promotion of science. This is a professionally run organization, providing more service than socialization to members.

Junior Skeptic runs in the back of *The Skeptic,* the organization's magazine. The Society also publishes the Baloney Detection Kit, a resource booklet for parents and educators.

Society for Humanistic Judaism (SHJ)
28611 W. 12 Mile Rd.
Farmington Hills, MI 48334
Phone: 248-478-7610
http://www.shj.org/

Humanistic Judaism embraces a human-centered philosophy that combines the celebration of Jewish culture and identity with an adherence to humanistic values and ideas, giving the family secular alternatives to Jewish religious rites. SHJ sponsors Camp Keshet, a two-week camp for children 8 to 17 years old, and an annual conclave for teens and young adults.

Chapter Nine Endnotes

1. Never take my word, of course—read Ecclesiastes yourself. It's a quickie, about six pages in most versions.
2. www.aeu.org.
3. Both quotes from Karen Armstrong's *A History of God.* See Chapter 3 for full citation.
4. See www.jesuscampthemovie.com. Fortunately, this troubling camp is representative neither of most Christians nor most Christian summer camps.
5. See "Parenting in a Secular/Religious Marriage" in Chapter 2.
6. See in particular the Additional Resources sections of Chapters 3 and 9.
7. See Metskas and Brunsman, "Summer Camps Beyond Belief," in this chapter.
8. © 1975 by Peter Wernick. For complete lyrics, go to www.DrBanjo.com.
9. Camp Quest website: www.camp-quest.org
10. Douglas Belkin, "Cutting Ties that Digitally Bind," *The Boston Globe* (August 18, 2006).
11. "Directions: Youth Development Outcomes of the Camp Experience," 2005. www.acacamps.org/research/directions.pdf.
12. Marie Hartwell-Walker, Ed.D., "What's So Great About Summer Camp?" http://psychcentral.com/library/id211.html. 7/13/00.

13. Ruth Marcus, "Camping Alone; Ready for S'More Networking Billy?" *The Washington Post* (July 19, 2006).

14. Douglas Belkin, "Cutting Ties that Digitally Bind," *The Boston Globe* (August 18, 2006).

Additional Resources
Books

- Morain, Lloyd and Mary. *Humanism as the Next Step,* Humanist Press, 1998. Considered by many to be the ideal first introduction to humanism. Presents humanism as a "joyous view" and connects it admirably to other worldviews, beginning with the "Golden Rule" thread: "Throughout the ages, religions of many kinds have contained a common spirit."
Introductions to nontheistic religious organizations:
- Kogel, Renee, ed. *Judaism in a Secular Age: An Anthology of Secular Humanistic Jewish Thought.* Ktav, 1995.
- Seid, Judith. *God-Optional Judaism: Alternatives for Cultural Jews Who Love Their History, Heritage, and Community.* Citadel, 2001. An excellent introduction to secular Judaism for those who wish to remain connected to traditions and history of Judaism but do not believe in God.
- Dant, Jennifer. *Unitarian Universalism Is a Really Long Name.* Skinner House, 2006. Introduction to the UU denomination for ages 5 through 9, including answers to questions like "Do We Pray?" and "What Do We Believe?"
- Boulton, David, ed. *Godless for God's Sake: Nontheism in Contemporary Quakerism.* Dale's Historical Monographs, 2006. An anthology of writings by twenty-seven nontheistic Quakers in four countries.
- Radest, Howard. *Toward Common Ground: The Story of the Ethical Societies in the United States.* Ungar, 1969. Hard to find, but a good historical introduction to the Ethical Culture movement.
- Freethought Directory. Best comprehensive list of freethought organizations around the world. Go to www.atheistalliance.org, click on Freethought Directory.

Glossary

AGNOSTIC: One who withholds judgment on the existence or nonexistence of supernatural entities on the grounds that it cannot be known with any certainty. Coined by nineteenth-century biologist Thomas Huxley.

ATHEIST: Someone who does not believe in the existence of a god or gods.

BRIGHTS: A recent attempt at a positive term for those whose worldview is naturalistic, without supernatural or mystical elements. Philosopher Daniel Dennett has suggested SUPERS as the corresponding name for those who believe in the supernatural.

CREATIONISM: The belief that the universe was created by a supernatural entity. See also INTELLIGENT DESIGN.

DOGMA (pl. DOGMATA): A belief or conviction that is held to be unquestionable. Not all religious systems are dogmatic, and not all dogmas are religious; it is the act of disallowing challenge in any form that makes an idea dogmatic.

ETHICS: Systematic frameworks for morality, or the study of moral questions. Whereas morality refers to individual actions and motivations, ethics deals with the creation of rules and systems to encourage moral understanding and behavior. See also MORALITY.

EVANGELICAL: General description of any Christian denomination that is fundamentalist and literal in its orientation to the Bible. Includes the belief that one has a duty to spread one's own belief system as widely as possible.

EXISTENTIAL: Relating to questions of individual human existence. Questions about individual existence, mortality, life, death, freedom, and choice are all existential questions.

FAITH: Belief based on intuition or the desire to believe rather than reason or evidence. The nonrational acceptance of a claim or belief.

FREETHINKER: Someone who does not passively accept views or teachings, especially on religion, preferring to form opinions as a result of independent inquiry.

HERETIC: Someone whose beliefs do not conform to the dominant belief system or who challenges conventional beliefs.

HUMANISM: A concern with the well-being and interests of humanity as opposed to supernatural beings and ideas. Humanism most often includes the rejection of all supernatural beliefs, including belief in God. Sometimes the prefix "secular" is added to make it clear that this more precise meaning is intended.

INTELLIGENT DESIGN: The belief that the existence and nature of the universe is best explained as the intentionally designed work of an intelligent entity rather than the result of natural processes. See also CREATIONISM.

MORALITY: The discernment between right and wrong actions or motivations. See also ETHICS.

PHILOSOPHY: Literally "the love of wisdom," philosophy is the act of asking questions in order to build an understanding of reality.

PROSELYTIZE: To actively attempt to convert another person to one's own religious beliefs.

SCIENCE: The systematic critical study of the physical world by means of observation and experiment.

SKEPTIC: A person who requires sufficient evidence before accepting a conclusion.

UNITARIAN UNIVERSALISM: A religious denomination that attempts to capture many of the best features of religious communities without demanding a single belief or creed of its members. UU churches are "creedless" and nondogmatic. Most members and attenders are nontheistic.

UTILITARIANISM: The principle that the most morally correct action is that which confers the greatest happiness/good upon the greatest number.

Additional Resources—
General

Books

- *Humanism for Kids.* Family of Humanists, 1997. A short, simple, charming booklet for kids. Straightforwardly addressed questions like "How did we get here?", everyday ethics, and human potential, giving no credence to supernatural explanations. Sample quote: "Some religions teach that a powerful, invisible, father-like being ('God') made the earth and started it turning, and then made the first of each kind of plant and animal. These religions started a long time ago before scientists learned about nature. As we understand nature better, we often see that the old explanations were only guesses." Order through Family of Humanists at www.familyofhumanists.org.
- Knight, Margaret, and James Herrick, eds. *The Humanist Anthology.* Prometheus, 1995. A powerful and readable collection of short excerpts from humanist and freethinkers of the past 3,000 years. One of the most important and thought-provoking anthologies in the freethought literature, now in its second incarnation.
- Stone, Anne. *Living in the Light: Freeing Your Child from the Dark Ages.* American Atheist Press, 2000. The closest predecessor to the current book (along with the Willson title *Parenting Without God*—see Chapter 1), *Living in the Light* adopts a different tone, more on the order of "raising atheist children." Stone is fully cognizant of *why* religion persists, but unapologetic in her assessment of it.

On her website, Stone describes the book as "an anti-religious book for parents who want to teach children spiritual values without teaching them religion." Much that is worthwhile and well-presented.

Websites

- Parents' Corner on the Secular Web: http://www.infidels.org/families/parents/
- America Online chat and message boards for atheist parents: Keyword Atheism, follow links
- Yahoo's Atheist Parenting group: http://groups.yahoo.com/group/atheistparenting/
- iVillage Atheist/Agnostic Parenting message board: http://messageboards.ivillage.com/iv-ppatheist
- Atheist Parents: www.atheistparents.org
  Despite the promising title (and as confessed by the site's founder), Atheist Parents has drifted from its original parent-focused intention into a general atheist site, with essays, reviews, and links. Some parenting info is in the mix. Worth a look.
- Family of Humanists: www.familyofhumanists.org
- Ethical Atheist: www.ethicalatheist.org
  Includes discussion boards for atheist parenting, resources, articles. An interesting split choice: Visit the main website, which presents nontheism resources and information, or click on The Dark Side, which takes you to the more confrontational, anti-religious side.
- Atheist Alliance Family Issues: www.atheistalliance.org – click on Family Issues
  A fine, fine collection of articles, essays, and interviews—but not updated for a while, since the editor went on leave to (ahem) write this book.
- Humanist Network News—Sweet Reason: www.humanistnetworknews.org
  An excellent e-zine for humanists, including "Sweet Reason" columnist Molleen Matsumura who frequently addresses secular parenting issues.
- American Atheists Youth and Family page: www.atheists.org/family/
  Articles, reviews, and links. Look in particular for the good work of Dave Silverman.
- Agnostic Mom: www.agnosticmom.com
  The website of agnostic columnist and former Mormon mom Noell Hyman.
- The Atheist Mama: www.theatheistmama.com
  A good blog by an articulate activist mom. Many fine links and features.
- Club Mom: www.clubmom.com
  Search for columns by agnostic contributor Noell Hyman by typing "Hyman" into the search field.

About the Authors

NORM R. ALLEN, JR. is the executive director of African Americans for Humanism (AAH) and the co-director of the Center for Inquiry's transnational programs. He is editor of the *AAH Examiner,* the international newsletter of AAH, and deputy editor of *Free Inquiry* magazine. Allen has edited two books: *African American Humanism – An Anthology* and *The Black Humanist Experience: An Alternative to Religion.* His writings have appeared in several books, including *Voices for Evolution* and *Varieties of African American Religious Experience.* He has lectured at such institutions as Harvard, SUNY Buffalo, the University of Pittsburgh, and the University of Ibadan in Nigeria.

DONALD B. ARDELL, Ph.D., publishes the *Ardell Wellness Report (AWR),* a quarterly newsletter in continuous circulation since 1984, as well as the weekly electronic AWR, with 350 editions in circulation. He is director of the largest wellness website, www. SeekWellness.com. His first book in 1977, *High Level Wellness: An Alternative to Doctors, Drugs and Disease* is credited with starting the wellness movement. A freethinker whose work promoting healthy lifestyles focuses on critical thinking, humor, and meaning and purpose as well as all the usual suspects (fitness, responsibility, etc.), Don is also a national and world champion age group triathlete named Grandmaster of the Year in 2005 by USA Triathlon.

DAN BARKER is the author of *Losing Faith in Faith: From Preacher to Atheist.* He is married to Annie Laurie Gaylor, with whom he is co-president of the Freedom From Religion Foundation in Madison, Wisconsin (www.ffrf.org), an organization working to keep state and church separate and to promote freethought. Dan has five children and has written three books for children: *Just Pretend: A Freethought Book for Children, Maybe Yes, Maybe No: A Guide for Young Freethinkers,* and *Maybe Right, Maybe Wrong: A Guide for Young Skeptics.* He is also a professional jazz pianist and has composed more than 200 published songs, many for children.

AUGUST E. BRUNSMAN IV has been the Executive Director of the Secular Student Alliance since 2001. In 1997 he founded Students for Freethought at The Ohio State University. He graduated Phi Beta Kappa from OSU in 2001 with a major in psychology and minors in mathematics and cognitive science. August is also the Director of Camp Quest Classic where he has volunteered since 1999. August and Amanda Metskas married in 2005 and live together in Columbus, Ohio, with their two cats, Shiva and Vishnu.

ED BUCKNER, Ph.D., has been a professor, a school administrator, and executive director of the Council for Secular Humanism. He and his wife Lois Bright have edited several books and published Oliver Halle's *Taking the Harder Right* (2006). He wrote the concluding chapter of Kimberly Blaker's *Fundamentals of Extremism* (2003) and co-edited, with his son, *Quotations that Support the Separation of State and Church* (second edition, 1995). Buckner has debated and spoken across the United States, often about the Treaty of Tripoli and "This Is a Free Country, Not a Christian Nation." He serves on several national advisory boards and committees.

MATTHEW CHERRY has spent more than fifteen years as a professional leader in the humanist movement in three different countries. In 2000 he became executive director of the Institute for Humanist Studies, which serves as a resource for and about the freethought movement. He is the author of *Introduction to Humanism: A Primer on the History, Philosophy, and Goals of Humanism* for www.HumanistEducation.com. In 2004, and again in 2006, he was elected president of the NGO Committee on Freedom of Religion or Belief at the United Nations in New York. He's the first nonreligious representative to serve in this role.

SHANNON CHERRY, APR, MA, is the president of Cherry Communications and its subsidiary Be Heard Solutions. Working with small businesses, she helps entrepreneurs to find their voice, tell their story, and be heard. Shannon publishes the highly recommended e-zine, *Be Heard!* and is the co-author of *Become Your Own Great and Powerful: A Woman's Guide to Living Your Real Big Life.* She also is the creative mind behind www.mommy-inc.com, the only blog about being an entrepreneur mom with twins. She lives in Albany, NY, with her partner, Matt, daughters Sophia and Lyra, and a menagerie of animals that keeps her smiling.

AMANDA CHESWORTH is Educational Director for the Committee for the Scientific Investigations Of the Paranormal (CSICOP) and holds a Bachelor's in Interdisciplinary Sciences and a Master's in Science Education. Amanda produces inquiry-based programs and materials for educators, families, and young people. Her work includes the Inquiring Minds Program, Camp Inquiry, and Imaginary Worlds, and serving as editor of *Darwin Day Collection One.*

Oxford ethologist RICHARD DAWKINS is among the most accomplished and celebrated living contributors to science and its popular understanding. His first book, *The Selfish Gene* (1976), became an immediate international bestseller, followed by the seminal classic *The Blind Watchmaker.* His other bestsellers include *River Out of Eden, Climbing Mount Improbable,* and *Unweaving the Rainbow.* At this writing, his book *The God Delusion* is nearing release. In 2005, a *Prospect Magazine* poll named Dawkins the third most influential public intellectual in the world. Dawkins is a Fellow of both the Royal Society and the Royal Society of Literature. Since 1996 he has served as Vice President of the British Humanist Association. He is married to actress Lalla Ward and has one daughter, Juliet.

MARGARET DOWNEY is the founder of the Freethought Society of Greater Philadelphia and editor of *The Greater Philadelphia Story,* a newsletter written by and for the Atheist community. Margaret has represented nontheists at several UN conferences dealing with Freedom of Religion or Belief. A past board member of the American Humanist Association, the Humanist Institute, and the Thomas Paine National Historical Association, Margaret is currently on the boards of the Freedom From Religion Foundation, the Godless Americans Political Action Committee, Scouting For All, and the Robert Green Ingersoll Museum. She is also a Secular Humanist Celebrant and current president of the Atheist Alliance International.

TOM FLYNN is editor of *Free Inquiry,* the world's largest circulation English-language secular humanist magazine, a cofounder of the newsletter *Secular Humanist Bulletin,* and director of the Robert Green Ingersoll Birthplace Museum, the only U.S. freethought museum. An outspoken secular humanist activist, Flynn decided that Christmas was not the birthday of anyone he knew and abandoned observance of the holiday in 1984. He has been "Yule free" ever since. Flynn's books include *The Trouble with Christmas* (1993), the novels *Galactic Rapture* (2000) and *Nothing Sacred* (2004), and the forthcoming *New Encyclopedia of Unbelief,* which he edited.

ANNE NICOL GAYLOR is a founder and president emerita of the Freedom From Religion Foundation. She served as executive director from 1978 to 2005 and is now a consultant to the Foundation. Born in rural Wisconsin, she graduated from the University of Wisconsin in Madison. She owned and managed successful small businesses and was co-owner and editor of an award-winning suburban weekly newspaper. A feminist author, she has done substantial volunteer work for women's rights, including serving as volunteer director of the Women's Medical Fund. Under her leadership, the Freedom From Religion Foundation has grown from three members to a national group with representation in every state and Canada.

ANNIE LAURIE GAYLOR co-founded the Freedom From Religion Foundation with her mother, Anne Nicol Gaylor, in 1976. With Dan Barker, she is co-president of the Foundation (www.ffrf.org). She graduated from the University of Wisconsin-Madison in 1980 with a journalism degree. She edited a feminist newspaper from 1980 to 1984 and became editor of FFRF's newspaper, *Freethought Today,* in 1980. Her books include *Woe to the Women: The Bible Tells Me So* (1981, revised 2004), *Betrayal of Trust: Clergy Abuse of Children* (1988, online-only now), and *Women Without Superstition: No Gods—No Masters,* an anthology of women freethinkers (1997). She and Dan have one daughter, Sabrina, born in 1989.

REV. DR. KENDYL GIBBONS is the senior minister of the First Unitarian Society of Minneapolis. She is a graduate of the College of William and Mary and holds a Master's degree from the University of Chicago Divinity School as well as a Doctorate of Ministry from Meadville/Lombard Theological School. She is co-dean of The Humanist Institute and is active in the interfaith clergy community of Minneapolis. She serves as an adjunct faculty member of Meadville/Lombard in Chicago and the United Theological Seminary in the Twin Cities, where she teaches in the areas of worship and liturgy and dynamics of professional leadership.

EDGAR YIPSEL "YIP" HARBURG, among the greatest and most beloved lyricists of the twentieth century, was also a nonbeliever and a secular parent. Author of such classics as "Somewhere Over the Rainbow," "Brother, Can You Spare a Dime?", "April in Paris," and "Paper Moon," Yip created lyrics and poems that were brilliant and unbearably clever. He often addressed serious social issues, such as war, intolerance, and injustice, with incisive and devastating wit. The seven poems appearing in this book are excerpted from *Rhymes for the Irreverent,* a recent collaboration between the Harburg Foundation and the Freedom From Religion Foundation, and are reprinted with their kind permission.

JAMES HERRICK has worked for thirty years in the humanist movement in the UK. He is former editor of the *New Humanist* and *International Humanist.* His writings include "Vision and Realism: A hundred years of *The Freethinker,*" *Against the Faith: Some Deists, Skeptics and Atheists,* and *Humanism: An Introduction.* He is a co-founder of the Gay and Lesbian Humanist Association and has written theatre reviews regularly for various journals. Now in retirement, Jim writes, gardens, and plays the oboe.

AMY HILDEN, Ph.D., received her PhD in Philosophy, with a supporting program in Feminist Studies, from the University of Minnesota, Twin Cities. Her current scholarly interests include developing arguments in support of reclaiming the Enlightenment values of free and independent thinking, rationality, and a humanistic understanding of progress, as well as arguments for reparations for U.S. slavery and genocide. She lives with her husband and two teenage children in Minneapolis and teaches in the Philosophy Department at the College of St. Catherine in St. Paul. Her children have had numerous long car trips, with some obligatory "unplugged" time.

Better known as "Agnostic Mom" online, NOELL HYMAN contributes monthly columns to the Humanist Network News, the weekly e-zine for the Institute for Humanist Studies, and is an expert writer for the website ClubMom. An energetic mother of three young children, Noell and husband Israel are currently involved with numerous podcasting and blogging ventures. Relatively new to the secular landscape, Noell declared herself a humanist in 2002 after leaving the Mormon Church. Noell's aim is to reach other nonreligious parents who find themselves isolated in the struggle to raise a healthy family without religion.

PENN JILLETTE is the Emmy Award–winning illusionist/entertainer/debunker of the duo Penn & Teller. Author of several books, star and producer of such films as *The Aristocrats* and *Penn & Teller Get Killed,* he and his partner have also served as visiting lecturers at MIT and Oxford. Jillette's current efforts are split between a live national talk show, the Showtime series *Bullshit!* (which debunks such frauds as alien abduction, magnetic cures, and talking to the dead), and a daily live show in Las Vegas. Penn is married to producer Emily Zolten Jillette, with whom he has two young children, Moxie (born in 2005) and Zolten (born in 2006).

ROBERT E. KAY, MD, is a retired psychiatrist who graduated from Tufts University Medical School and did his residency at Walter Reed General Hospital. After serving in the Army, he settled in Philadelphia where he has treated both adults and children in many different inpatient and outpatient settings. Publications include articles on raising children, teaching reading, the problem of school, ADHD versus the TV set, and the difficulties inherent in a becoming a good psychiatrist without objective verifiable data in terms of etiology, diagnosis, treatment, or results.

BOBBIE KIRKHART is a former Sunday school teacher whose first national publication was in *Christianity Today.* She is currently vice president of the Secular Coalition for America and has served as co-president of Atheists United and as president of the Atheist

Alliance International. In addition to her regular President's Messages in *The Rational Alternative* and *Secular Nation,* her work has been printed in *Free Inquiry* and *American Atheist* magazines. She is a contributing author of *The Fundamentals of Extremism: The Christian Right in America,* published by New Boston Books.

DAVID KOEPSELL, JD, Ph.D., is a philosopher and lawyer specializing in research ethics, meta-ethics, and society and politics. As executive director of the Council for Secular Humanism, he lectures and speaks to the media on issues of secularism, freedom of conscience, and civil rights. Koepsell holds a Ph.D. in philosophy and JD from State University of New York at Buffalo, where he has taught law, critical thinking, writing, research ethics, and ontology. He is a Research Fellow in the Department of Philosophy at SUNY Buffalo and the author of numerous articles and reviews.

STEPHEN LAW, D. Phil., is lecturer in philosophy at Heythrop College, Univeristy of London, and editor of THINK, the Royal Institute of Philosophy's new popular journal. After beginning his career as a postman in Cambridge, Law studied philosophy at Trinity College and Queen's College, Oxford, where he obtained his doctorate. He is the author of several popular introductions to philosophy, including an illustrated children's introduction to philosophy titled *The Philosophy Files* – sold in the United States as (*sigh*) *Philosophy Rocks!* The book was *The Guardian*'s number two best-selling British title for the year 2000 and has been translated into nine languages. Law's latest, *The War for Children's Minds,* is included in the Additional Resources.

KRISTAN LAWSON is a writer and entrepreneur. Founder and publisher of Jolly Roger Press in the 1990s, Kristan is also a renowned travel expert, authoring several major travel guides for California and Europe, including *California Babylon* (St. Martin's Press), *Weird Europe* (St. Martin's Press), *America Off The Wall: The West Coast* (Wiley, 1989), and *Europe Off The Wall* (Wiley, 1988). He is a 1981 graduate of the University of California, Berkeley.

GARETH B. MATTHEWS, Ph.D., is Professor of Philosophy (emeritus) at the University of Massachusetts at Amherst. He taught previously at the University of Virginia and the University of Minnesota. He is the author of many articles and three books on ancient, medieval, and early modern philosophy: *Thought's Ego in Augustine and Descartes* (Cornell, 1992), *Socratic Perplexity and the Nature of Philosophy* (Oxford, 1999), and *Augustine* (Blackwell, 2005). He is also the author many articles and three books on philosophy and childhood: *Philosophy and the Young Child* (Harvard, 1980), *Dialogues with Children(* Harvard, 1984), and *The Philosophy of Childhood* (Harvard, 1994). These books have been translated into a dozen languages. Gary has three children and six grandchildren.

DALE McGOWAN, Ph.D., is a writer, editor, and critical thinking educator in Minneapolis. His satirical novel *Calling Bernadette's Bluff* has been called "an undoubted triumph of satire" and "wicked funny." He recently completed *Northing at Midlife,* a humorous narrative of a midlife crisis encountered on the trails of Britain. McGowan is editor of *Rumors of Peace,* the international newsletter of Nonviolent Peaceforce, is on the board of the Critical Thinking Club, Inc., and has taught critical thinking skills in the college classroom, the corporate boardroom, and public venues. He is a father of three and husband of one.

JEAN MERCER, Ph.D., is a developmental psychologist with a Ph.D. from Brandeis University and is Professor Emerita at Richard Stockton College in New Jersey. She has been a board member and officer of the New Jersey Association for Infant Mental Health for many years and is on the faculty of Youth Consultation Service in East Orange, NJ. The author of a number of books and articles about early development, she has for the last five years been seriously engaged in the fight against "Attachment Therapy," a cult-like belief system that encourages intrusive and harmful physical practices in the guise of child psychotherapy.

AMANDA K. METSKAS received her M.A. in political science from The Ohio State University in 2005. She graduated Magna Cum Laude from Brown University in 2002 with Honors in International Relations. Amanda is currently a Ph.D. candidate in the department of political science at Ohio State. She has been involved with Camp Quest Classic (Ohio) since 2003 and is currently serving as the President of the Camp Quest Classic Board of Directors. Amanda and August Brunsman married in 2005 and live together in Columbus, Ohio, with their two cats, Shiva and Vishnu.

THE REV. DR. ROBERTA M. NELSON is Emeritus Minister of Religious Education at the Cedar Lane Unitarian Universalist Church in Bethesda, Maryland. She has also served congregations in Needham, Massachusetts, and in Oakton, Virginia. She has served as president of the Liberal Religious Educators Association and as vice-president of the UU Ministers Association. She is a member of the Meadville/Lombard Theological School Board of Trustees. She has also served as a board member of the Religious Education Association. She is coauthor of the curricula *Parents as Resident Theologians, Parents as Social Justice Educators,* and *Parents as Spiritual Guides.*

EMILY ROSA grew up in Colorado. In 1998, the appearance of her study on Therapeutic Touch in the *Journal of the American Medical Association* created a media sensation and put her in the *Guinness Book of World Records* as the youngest person to publish serious medical research, conducted two years earlier at age 9. She later experimented with "healing magnets" and in the eighth grade won first place in her division at the Colorado State Science Fair for measuring the circumference of the world with homemade instruments and unique units of measurement. She just finished two years of university at CU-Boulder. Her academic interest is in forensic psychology.

Grammy Award–winning comedian JULIA SWEENEY is also an actor, playwright, and monologist. Perhaps best known for her androgynous character Pat on *Saturday Night Live* and her critically acclaimed one-woman monologue *God Said, Ha!,* Sweeney has also appeared in films, including *Pulp Fiction* and *Stuart Little.* Her monologue *Letting Go of God,* which chronicles her journey from faith to philosophical naturalism, was Critics' Choice for the *Los Angeles Times* and Pick of the Week for the LA *Weekly.* She is the author of *My Beautiful Loss of Faith Story* and was the 2006 recipient of the Richard Dawkins Award for raising public awareness of the nontheistic life stance. She is the adoptive mother of a 7-year-old girl named Mulan.

STU TANQUIST is a national speaker, seminar leader, and published author with over twenty years of experience in the learning and development industry. He facilitates learning on variety of topics including critical thinking. His employment ranges from working as an emergency paramedic to serving as a strategic-level director for training and development for a large urban medical center. Stu holds three degrees including an MS in Management. In his free time, he coordinates the South Metro Chapter of the Critical Thinking Club of Minnesota.

Bronx-born Coloradoan PETE WERNICK earned a Ph.D. in Sociology from Columbia University while developing a career in music on the side. His bestselling instruction book *Bluegrass Banjo* allowed "Dr. Banjo" to leave his sociology research job at Cornell to form Hot Rize, a classic bluegrass band that traveled worldwide. Pete served as president of the International Bluegrass Music Association for fifteen years. Pete, his wife, and son survived the disastrous Sioux City plane crash in 1989. A *Life Magazine* article following the crash identified Pete as a humanist and noted that he didn't see a supernatural factor in his survival. An atheist since age 15, Pete was president of the Family of Humanists from 1997 to 2006. Today he continues to perform, run music camps nationwide, and produce instructional videos for banjo and bluegrass.

A lifelong agnostic, JANE WYNNE WILLSON became involved in the Humanist movement in the UK when her oldest child met religion head-on at a state primary school. Since then she has been active at local, national, and international levels, serving as president of the London-based International Humanist and Ethical Union and Vice-President of the British Humanist Association, and author of *Parenting Without God, New Arrivals, Sharing the Future,* and *Funerals Without God.* A retired special needs teacher with four children and ten grandchildren, Jane has a deep interest in bringing up children happily with a strong basis for morality but no religion.

Index